The Sales Rep
Survival Guide

The Sales Rep Survival Guide

The Complete Sales Manual

Mike Swedenberg
JMDS1951@Hotmail.com

Writer's Showcase
San Jose New York Lincoln Shanghai

The Sales Rep Survival Guide
The Complete Sales Manual

Writer's Showcase
an imprint of iUniverse.com, Inc.

For information address:
iUniverse.com, Inc.
5220 S 16th, Ste. 200
Lincoln, NE 68512
www.iuniverse.com

The characters portrayed in this book are fictitious.
Any similarity to actual persons living or deceased is merely coincidental.

ISBN: 0-595-17943-6

Printed in the United States of America

List of Contributors

My Special thanks to those who helped make this book possible.

Steve Bregman, my editor
Director, Bellmore Memorial Library, former Assistant Director, Nassau Library System

Sam Chinkis, my mentor from the early days
Sound Advertising, Massapequa, New York

Cover Photograph: Franklin Square Photographers, Franklin Square, N.Y. Rush Limbaugh, Dittos. "Well, if Rush can do it, so can I." Listening to you talk about writing your books, *The Way Things Ought to Be, and See, I Told You So*, motivated me to write my own.

Bill Gates, Founder of Microsoft. I never would have attempted this book without Windows and MS Word. You opened a whole new world to millions and changed the course of history.

Boopa, thank you for the love and support.
Tracy, Kimberly and Alison, never ever give up, no matter what!

Epigraph

The secret to success is to get up one more time than you fall down.
- Unknown

Contents

Foreword

An open letter to Mr. Negative.

Dear Mr. Negative,

You are the greatest salesman in the world, you can overcome any objection and fulfill any opportunity. And whenever I forget that, you quickly remind me.

You claim were in the field selling before I was born and that you have forgotten more about sales than I will ever learn. While I was sitting in front of the TV with my milk and cookies watching Howdy Doody, you were pounding the pavement barefoot, through an Alaskan blizzard, selling snow cone machines to Eskimos who had no electricity.

Nothing anyone can do can help you sell better. I showed you the rough draft of this book, to get your opinion. You glanced through the table of contents, handed it back, and said, "I could have written that." I asked, "So why didn't you?" You shrugged, then lumbered off to demoralize someone else.

Mr. Negative, I've worked with too many people like you. You are totally resistant to change. You believe what worked for you in 1960 is just fine for today. You regard any sales technique like Consultant Sales or Persuasive Selling as so much psycho-babble. Your only sales tool is to shoot from the hip. In some cases, you act as though you are doing your customers a favor just by calling on them. When a struggling retailer once gave you a small order, you angrily asked him, "Is that all you are buying from me?"

A manufacturer hired you fresh out of high school. You had the ten-minute tour of the factory, picked up a few brochures and went out to write business. They offered no formal training and relied on the old adage; "A salesman is born, not made." Through trial and error, you taught yourself a way to sell. After twenty-five years, you truly believe you know it all. When new tools were developed; you were completely resistant to them. When you were forced to sit in a sales training class, you would spend the time doodling on a pad. You shot down every new idea without even trying to understand. I've attended some of those classes with you. There were very capable instructors, who captivated the audience. They opened our minds to new techniques of communication and practical application of psychology, proven to bring in more business. I've seen these people psych up a group, only to have you, Mr. Negative, undermine everything they did. During the break, you would pull aside the young reps and tell them, "Ignore all of that bull. Here is what you really do..." They walked away confused. The company was spending thousands on effective selling seminars and you, the elder salesman, the one they looked up to, would tell them the complete opposite. The fact is, Mr. Negative, you are no longer number one. Those who tried and accepted the new tools surpassed you.

You wear your computer illiteracy as a badge of honor. Management placed a laptop in front of you and said you must use it to place orders, manage your database and communicate. They demonstrated how it would make your job easier and offered to work patiently with you until you fully understood. You smiled politely and closed the cover. That computer still sits in your office unused. Instead of electronically posting your orders, you insist on mailing them in as you have always done. This delays your business as it travels through the mail and Order Processing tries to interpret your chicken scratch.

Don't dismiss this book just yet. Hide it in your brief case so no one else can see. Flip through a few Chapters, just for laughs of course. Amazingly as it may seem, I can still help you sell more just by improving your productivity through territory and time management. I can get you in front of more people every day so you can use your superior sales ability to write more orders. I will stand back in awe and watch you do your magic.

I don't want to belabor the point Mr. Negative, you probably won't heed any advice in this book; however, you would be doing yourself a disservice not to at least experiment with a few of my techniques. Humor me. No one has to know.

Sincerely,

Mike Swedenberg

Preface

Imagine having the opportunity to earn an unlimited income in a job where you set your own schedule and your own objectives. For the most part, you enjoy the independence and reward of those who are self employed. Imagine the benefits of working for a major corporation with perks including a company car, computer, expense account, free trips, gifts, full benefits, and a generous retirement package. You would also have a complete staff to support you. What if there was a comprehensive manual to show you step by step how to find, get and succeed in such a job?

What I've described is a career in field sales. There are tens of thousands of corporations, large and small, that needs salespeople. The unemployment rate is at a twenty-year low and many of these positions go unfilled because of a lack of qualified representatives. They are available to you regardless of your background, race, color, creed or physical limitations. You don't need specialized education, although college is helpful. I know people with only a High School education who became multi millionaires in sales. There are others with advanced degrees who failed because they couldn't get out of their own way.

You don't have to be a born sales representative. Once you master some simple techniques and adopt the right attitude you will discover sales is rather easy and the opportunities are endless. The only limits to your potential are those you impose on yourself. You must ask yourself how much effort you're willing to put in your career.

Field sales is any activity in which representatives travel throughout an assigned territory to visit current customers and to solicit new clients. This is opposed to an inside sales rep who waits for customers to visit a showroom.

Here is how it works. This handbook reflects my experiences of thirty years in outside sales. It is presented in a transactional approach. Chapter One describes the career. Chapter Two explains how to find the right job with the right company. Chapter Three tells you how to deal with management, co-workers and customers. Chapters Four through Seven cover every conceivable aspect of your career. This treatise, filled with practical advice, guides your every step.

This handbook helps more than the novice territory sales reps for large corporations. The fundamentals of salesmanship are covered to such an extent that anyone who sells a product or service for a living, regardless of experience or industry will find the information valuable. Those who will benefit the most are people who are either self employed or work for small companies that don't provide sales training or do so on a limited basis.

Most sales training manuals and self-help books I've read are boring. I've heard other reps recall struggling with a tedious sales book, only to walk away with very little benefit. I'm sure the books contained good advice, but somewhere along the line the author or editor felt that they needed to write a serious textbook. I've taken sound selling principles and put them in a humorous anecdotal format. I've linked each sales point with a real life scenario to show how and why it works. This makes the task of reading my book enjoyable and therefore more helpful. My objective is to be a colleague helping you out and not a stuffy professor delivering a lecture.

Finally, I've tried hard not to take myself too seriously. One secret of my success is that I have a good time in my career, even if I have to laugh at myself to do so. Life is too short to constantly beat yourself up. You can have a great career, earn lots of money and enjoy every minute of it.

The benefit to those starting out in this career is to maximize the opportunities and avoid the pitfalls we all face in sales. For those who have from two to seven years' experience, you will identify problem areas and unleash your potential. For those who have been in sales for eight years or more, there are simple techniques to redirect your career if you're out placed or in a dead-end situation. I suggest that you read this handbook from cover to cover then keep it handy for continuous reference.

Who am I and what credentials do I bring with me? In the fall of 1970, at the age of nineteen, I left my home in Greenville, South Carolina to seek my fortune in New York's glamorous advertising industry. I attended the School of Visual Arts and specialized in design and copywriting concept. The recession of the 1970's devastated the business.

I had worked hard to polish my skills but was never able to put it all together. I held at least sixteen jobs during those ten years, often working for people who knew less about advertising than I did. That is not sour grapes, but a refection of the industry. Most of the upper management in the agencies had little formal training in the creative process. They provided the capital and brought new clients in; however, they had veto power over the creative people. More often than not, they killed great concepts because they didn't understand it or didn't know how to present it to the clients. I tried to open my own agency, but had no money to back me up. When I wasn't on Madison Avenue looking for work, I called on local merchants, looking for any type of advertising and promotional work. After a ten-year struggle to succeed, a wife and three children to support, I had to get, in the words of my family, a real job.

I was bitter about my failed career and was at a loss as to what to do next. I was twenty-nine years old and did not have a college degree. Many recruiters wouldn't even talk to me unless I agreed to stay in advertising.

When I applied directly to companies for a more traditional job, I could never make it beyond the initial interview. I got bogged down trying to explain the job hopping to personnel managers. They didn't understand the world of creative people in a volatile, competitive industry devastated by a decade long recession.

An ad agency would land a new account and then hire a staff of creative people to produce the advertising. When the agency lost the account, or when the project was completed, the agency fired everyone since there was no cash flow to maintain a large staff. My longest job lasted two years; my shortest was one hour. In the latter case an agency hired me on a Friday afternoon and asked me to start Monday as their new Art Director. They had just landed a major pharmaceutical account and I had extensive experience in that area. My wife and I celebrated that weekend. It was the best assignment I had so far and paid more than double any job before. I truly felt I'd arrived in New York advertising.

I anxiously got to work early. My new boss asked me to wait in my office. Apparently the old Art Director had left in a hurry, so I began cleaning up the mess he left behind. After an hour, the partner who had hired me stepped into my office. He stammered a bit and without looking me in the eye handed me a check.

"Mike, we have to let you go. The new account we landed called this morning and backed out of the agreement. They are going with another agency. We can't afford to keep you on. Here's a check for one day's pay. Sorry kid."

I looked at him in disbelief and asked, "Have I accumulated any vacation time?"

He held the check out to me and said, "You have to leave now."

Try explaining that to a personnel manager who has worked for the same company for thirty years.

In deep self-analysis I began to appreciate my ability to get along with people. One aspect of my advertising career was selling my services to my clients. I enjoyed talking to prospects, asking them about their business and coming up with unique solutions to the problems they faced. Unfortunately, jobs in advertising sales were as scarce as the creative ones.

Years later, I realized that my success in sales was due to my advertising training and experiences of the 70's. I can trace it back to one copywriting class I took at the School of Visual Arts. The class was "How to Write an Ad and How to Make It Better." It focused on developing the concept of the ad more than the actual writing of the copy. Most of us in the class failed to grasp the technique; then, one night it hit me like a bolt. From that moment on I've used that knowledge as the foundation of each sales presentation I make. Chapter Four discusses this in detail.

A close friend, Ira, is a very successful salesman in the garment industry. Ira has that magnetic personality that lights up a room when he walks in. He commands presence, and as a result sells a lot of clothes to his clients. When Ira suggested I try sales, I laughed. Ira is a born and bred New Yorker, with a type A personality. I was the complete opposite. I believed that my quiet, southern style would doom me to failure in the New York rat race of business.

Ira pointed out that I had the necessary tools and training to be successful. I'd done years of cold call canvassing to retailers and hundreds of job interviews. I could take a complex concept and quickly boil it down to a simple thought. My genuine sincerity and bulldog determination could open doors.

I took Ira's advice. I revised my resume to emphasize my selling skills and enrolled in evening school at Adelphi University. It took more than eight years of night classes, after a full day in the field selling, but I got my degree in business and management. I've moved steadily up the ranks in sales; have been named sales representative of the year and have made the President's club at two corporations. I've worked as a field trainer, conducted interviews and have read thousands of resumes. I've been on more interviews than I could possibly recall and have worked for Fortune 500 companies and one-man operations. I'm now a sales rep in tax publishing in New York. In spite of the workload, I manage my time efficiently. I was able to write this book and still have a life.

As a buyer for a pharmacy, I saw first hand how some sales reps are their own worst enemies and others get everything they want. I've always been in the top 5 percent of the sales force and with few exceptions have always finished the year above quota.

I sold advertising to businesses; cake mix to grocers and personal care products to druggists. I've promoted pharmaceuticals to doctors, and anesthesia to hospitals. I've sold photocopiers to architects, digital PCS to transportation companies, home infusion to plastic surgeons, medical equipment to nursing homes, law books to lawyers and tax research to CPAs. I've sold web sites to accountants and financial planning software to CFPs.

I've sold face-to-face, over the telephone, on the Internet and through direct mail. I forced myself to learn how to use a computer, and taught weekend classes in sales. I've recruited for companies large and small, interviewed, hired and trained new sales reps. I've been on the top, worked with the best and the worst.

This handbook is an all encompassing guide to sales that covers everything from getting a job to maximizing your income. I got the idea from my earlier days in legal publishing. I walked down the street, carrying a forty-pound sample bag, cold calling on law firms and CPAs to sell them law books. It seemed for almost every legal specialty, we had a treatise or specialized publication that instructed a lawyer how to evaluate a case, take the case through trial and through the appeal process.

These books, filled with checklists and practical advice, help eliminate omissions and errors. Attorneys found these treatises invaluable. They helped win cases and made the attorneys lots of money. One lawyer said that having my "Internal Revenue Manual" was like having an IRS agent at his beck and call to answer all of his questions. Well, why not such a treatise on sales?

This guidebook will take you through the entire process of getting a job and rising through the ranks to become a top performer in this profession. Wouldn't you like to have a seasoned pro at your side to help you get the most out of your day? How about checklists to help you prepare sales presentations that get orders? There is a simple question to ask that will make a customer switch from the competitor's product to yours and then thank you for selling it to him or her. Would that be useful? I'm confident that this handbook will make most aspects of your job easier and more profitable.

You may ask, if this book is so great, then why the cute title: The Sales Rep Survival Guide? As in all sales situations, first I've got to get your attention. I offer a feature, the book with all of its aspects and then a benefit, or what the book will do for you, which is too make a complex and daunting profession easy to understand. Follow my advice and you can become successful in a lucrative career and earn lots of money.

This book isn't the final chapter of a career that has ended; but, a midpoint analysis from someone that will be out selling in the trenches tomorrow morning.

Editorial Method

A NOTE TO ANXIOUS ENGLISH MAJORS

I'm no Fitzgerald or Hemingway, just a salesman with a story to tell. My formal training in writing stems from my education as an advertising copywriter where quick, witty and to the point carries the day. Writing a snappy headline and fifty words of copy for an ad is one thing, writing ninety-thousand words for a book presented a difficult challenge. I turned to several sources to set my editorial method. These include: Career Institute, *The New Webster's Grammar Guide*, 1987. Frederick Crews, *The Random House Handbook*, Second Edition, 1977. Oakley Hall, *The Art & Craft of Novel Writing*, 1989. Many thanks to my editor, Steve Bregman, who kept me on the straight and narrow and taught me never to use a preposition to end a sentence with.

WHY THIS BOOK IS WRITTEN THE WAY IT IS.

When I was a sales rep for a major pharmaceutical company in the mid 1980s, one of the special assignments I had in addition to my regular sales duties was to train new reps in the field. After they completed formal in-house training, I would work with them and show them how to manage their territory, do the paperwork, how to find new customers and so forth. To make their life easier, I put together a checklist of things that the reps should keep in mind. Unfortunately, the new reps were so overwhelmed studying medical information they rarely read my checklists. It was frustrating to see each new rep make the same mistakes over and over. In one example, Hermie, a new sales rep and recent college graduate, had been assigned to a driving territory in Queens, New York. He had just moved to Long Island and was unfamiliar with the city. Queens is a hard territory to work. The street signs are confusing, parking is horrible and the roads are often one-way or come to a dead end at a cemetery or railroad. This forces you to backtrack and make many detours as you learn your territory. I made a point to tell Hermie to pick up a large Queens street map and a roll of quarters over the weekend and to keep them in his car. He was to plan a full day in the field and route his call ahead of time. I also told Hermie why it was important to do so.

The following Monday, we worked together. The closest parking spot to our first call of the day was four blocks away. This was typical. I stood by the one-hour meter and watched as Hermie fumbled for some quarters. It required one quarter for every fifteen minutes and the sales call would take about an hour. Suffice to say he had only one quarter in his pocket. He either forgot my instructions or didn't take me seriously. A meter maid was coming down the block issuing $35.00 parking tickets. I said, "Hermie, you realize if you get a ticket, you have to pay for it, not the company." He dropped the quarter in the meter and ran across the street to a convenience store for change. Most stores in Queens have a policy that they won't give change unless you make a purchase. Hermie ended up buying a pack of gum from three different stores so he could get he change he needed. We went on the sales call and made it back just as the meter expired. He ran into a nearby bank to get a roll of quarters; ten minutes later, he walked out clearly exasperated.

"The bank won't give me change unless I have an account with them. What am I going to do now, buy more gum?"

I opened my sales bag and handed him a roll of quarters. "Give me ten dollars and expense it out. I've been down this road before and I came prepared. Now do you understand why I suggested that you pick up some quarters from your bank ahead of time? Where's our next sales call?"

He fumbled through his route book and picked a doctor's office that he thought was nearby.

"How do we get there?" I asked.

"Well, both doctors are on 86th Street so I guess it's just down the road." He said.

"OK, let's go."

We drove around for half an hour. He was completely lost.

"I don't get it. Why are the street numbers so weird? Aren't the first and second calls on 86th Street?" Hermie asked.

"Nope. The first stop was on 86th Street the next one is on 86th Avenue, a completely different street. We have also been on 86th Place and 86th Road. Sometimes, streets will have two or three different names. That is why I asked you to plan your day ahead of time. Where is your map?"

"I never picked one up."

"How did you plan to find your way around a new territory?"

"I thought you would tell me."

"What about tomorrow when you will be by yourself?"

"I guess I didn't think about that." Hermie shrugged.

Not wanting to waste anymore time, I showed him how to get there. Afterwards, Hermie frantically flipped through the route book looking for another call to make. I suggested we get a map, stop for coffee and I would show him how to plan his day. Territory management was something never taught at the sales training class nor was it anything he learned in business school. I had allowed him to fumble all morning specifically to get his attention.

Hermie was grateful for my help and confessed that he spent the weekend studying the sales brochures. His medical knowledge was quite good for a rookie. He glanced over the checklist, but it wasn't presented in a matter that grabbed his attention. I explained that product knowledge was essential to his success, but that running a territory was just as important. From this experience, I asked Hermie if I could relay the events of the day in my checklist to help the next rep. Hermie was a good sport. From that time on, no new rep I worked with was ever without a plan, a map and a pocket full of quarters. They all laughed about Hermie's experience. Adding the war story worked.

From this humble beginning in 1987, *The Sales Rep Survival Guide* grew to a full fledge sales guide. It is divided in seven chapters. Each chapter has a many short topics that focus on one subject. Rather than just give advice and leave it as that, I tied in a war story to make the point. I have tried to do so with good humor and cheer so it would not read as a dry, boring textbook. In many instances I had three or four war stories for each point. My challenge was to find the one that best illustrated what I was trying to say. The only exception is when I discuss the five steps of the presentation. I believe it is necessary to give more than one example.

I have included the original checklists and have developed more along the way. The checklists are designed to be used on a daily basis as a reference until they become ingrained in you. At that point you will follow them instinctually.

My next challenge was to write a sales manual that would appeal to as many different levels of experience and skill as possible. For beginners, most of this will be new and for the most experienced it will be a review. I have read sales help books only to pick up one good point. It was well worth the effort. I have also rediscovered things that I learned long ago that have since fallen by the wayside. Perhaps when I first learned them, I didn't fully appreciate their importance, but now with three decades of experience, it has new meaning.

My entire working experience has been in the New York market place. New York is a vibrant city. It is crowded, competitive and highly profitable place to do business. I have tried to keep in mind that some things I discuss will not apply to those of you in the rest of the country. I have tried to point out these differences in my war stories. Over the years I have discussed the unique features of the New York Metro area with reps from different parts of the country. Sometimes when I talked about the ingenious ways I use to get past the gatekeeper and into the decision-maker, I got a blank stare in response. A friend from the mid-west said that he tells the lawyer's receptionist that he found a great fishing spot and wanted to tell Hank about it. (He never met Hank; he saw his name on the front door.)

It often worked. That won't get you far in New York and probably wouldn't work in Chicago, LA or any other major city. The key to using this book is to adapt it to your marketplace. The basics are the same. I don't care where you live and work; you must plan your day, put on a professional appearance, maintain control of the sales call, uncover needs, overcome objectives and follow up.

Introduction

PURPOSE OF THIS BOOK: IS SELLING FOR YOU?

The scope of this book is to provide a practical guide for the day-to-day operation of a sales representative in a territory. This handbook is useful to all salespeople regardless of experience. It doesn't matter if you work for a large or small corporation. You could be commissioned, salaried or self-employed. This book can help you.

THE 46 COMMANDMENTS OF SALES

1. Watch out for number one. You are number one and no one else will care for, or attend to your success more than you.

2. Always cover your ass. Document everything in writing.

3. Work harder and smarter. The days of simply working smarter, not harder are gone forever.

4. Don't get mad or even. Life is too short to waste on anger and revenge. Learn from the transgressions of others and go on with your life.

5. Kill 'em with kindness. Overcompensate for your mistakes and they will be quick to forgive and forget.

6. Keep 'em talking to discover the truth. A liar can't keep track of his deceptions for long.

7. Give it to 'em straight. The truth is always easier to remember.

8. Ask for the business and then shut up. There is a time to talk and a time to be quiet. Put the burden on their shoulders.

9. Never criticize the competition. Take the high road and acknowledge their success. You may work for them one day.

10. Beware of New Manager Syndrome.

11. It's not what you have; it's what people think you have. Right or wrong, people still judge others by the cover of their book.

12. Address a problem when it happens. When ignored, it will fester and grow in proportion.

13. Never argue with a customer. You will win the battle and lose the sale.

14. Never drink on the job.

15. Beware of the gossip. When he talks about others behind their back, he's talking about you behind yours.

16. Charm will carry you for about fifteen minutes, after that, you better know your stuff.

17. There is no excuse for bad manners.

18. Never discuss religion, politics or sex with a colleague or buyer. You will inevitable step on someone's toes.

19. Believe in the 60/40 rule. In most situations, 60 percent of the people will go one way and 40 percent will go their other way.

20. Believe in the 25 percent rule. 25 percent of the people you meet won't like you for any number of reasons.

21. Believe in the 100 percent rule. Those with money, prefer 100 percent natural products.

22. Don't assume-ask. When you ass/u/me, you make an ass out of u and me.

23. Make fun of yourself not others. No one will ever argue with you if you point out your obvious shortcomings, but they will come to the defense of others.

24. Follow the style not the trend. The style is dependable; the trend fades by evening.

25. Never burn your bridges. You never know when your old contacts will crop up next.

26. Never condemn others in public. To do so will make you look bad and will illicit sympathy for your opponent.
27. Never be afraid to ask questions. It shows your concern for others.
28. Always try to resolve problems yourself. When your boss has to do your job, he doesn't need you.
29. Admit your mistakes. Never defend the indefensible.
30. Speak positively of your employer.
31. Always have fun. Don't take life too seriously. Enjoy the fruits of your labor.
32. Put yourself in your customer's shoes. Practice total empathy. Would you buy something from you?
33. Don't get distracted from your goals. Treat each hurdle and road-block as another step to your goal that you didn't anticipate.
34. Always take a vacation. No one can be on stage all of the time.
35. Understand the rules. You will be a mile ahead of the competition.
36. Quality doesn't guarantee success. Your product may be the best, but that doesn't mean it will be number one.
37. Nothing sells itself. Companies need salespeople to take their message to the customers.
38. Always bird dog. Pay others to open doors for you.
39. When it works, keep doing it. Nothing beats a system that brings results.
40. Remember, if sales were easy, they wouldn't need you.
41. Do someone a favor long enough and they will expect it.
42. You can't make money sitting in a coffee shop. Get in front of your customer.
43. It's not how much you make. It's how fast you make it.
44. Never dwell on your failures, look forward to your next success.
45. Get up one more time than you fall down.
46. Time is not money. Time is time and money is money.

Chapter One

THE LIFE OF A SALESMAN, THREE EXAMPLES

In Greenville South Carolina, an insurance agent spent fifty hours a week cold call canvassing his territory looking for customers. He met a young couple with two children. He devoted the bulk of his week presenting, talking, listening and trying to sell them a policy. The husband thought life insurance was for old people. The wife would not even discuss the possibility of death and left the room when the agent brought up the subject.

The insurance company had spent $85,000 training him during his first year, and it showed. He was persistent. He worked hard to win their confidence and understood their reluctance and their needs. In the end the young man gave in and purchased a $50,000 policy, half of what the agent thought was needed. In part, he bought it to get rid of the "pesky salesman" that wouldn't take "no" for an answer. Besides, he knew he could always cancel the policy. His wife was furious. The premium payments cut into their tight budget and would postpone an upcoming weekend vacation.

1

That autumn, the young man developed non-Hodgkin's Lymphoma, a fatal form of cancer and within three months he was dead. The young widow had no job skills and only a junior high school education. She now had to raise two children alone. When she received the insurance check, she called the agent to apologize for her shortsightedness and to thank him for being so persistent. She and her children would have been destitute without the money. She asked about a policy to cover herself to protect the children if anything should happen to her.

In Little Rock, a car salesman pushed a customer to purchase the optional driver's side air bag. (This was before air bags were mandatory.) In marketing terms, the customer was a low perceiver of risk. He was young, invincible, and a good driver. He never had accidents; besides, bad things happened to other people. The salesman was the opposite, a high perceiver of risk. He was proud of the safety options on his cars. It wasn't the few dollars in bonus for selling the air bag. It was the principle of doing his job and watching out for his customer.

In the end the salesman won by showing that the air bag would only add a dollar or two to the payment but would increase the resale value. The customer gave in. He just wanted his new car so he could get away from the "pesky salesman." A few years later, the customer returned to the showroom to replace his car. He had been involved in a head on collision when another car crossed the medium. The other driver died instantly. He didn't have an air bag. Our customer walked away with only a few bruises. He had forgotten the hassle of the purchase and the "pesky salesman." He told the salesman that he was glad he ordered the air bag.

On Long Island, a pharmaceutical sales rep tried repeatedly to call on a doctor that specialized in infectious diseases. The Food and Drug Administration had just approved his drug for use in a rare and debilitating disease, the type of disease that this doctor would see.

His first visit resulted in a meeting with the office manager. She prided herself in being able to get rid of "pesky salesman." She only half listened to what he said. Her mind was on other things. She had little medical training and most of what the sales representative said was gibberish to her.

Whenever a salesman asked to see the doctor, her pat answer was: "The doctor is busy now, he doesn't like to see reps anyway. Just leave the information and if he's interested, he will call you back."

The rep had heard that answer hundreds of times. He knew that when he left; she would forget he was there. The literature would sit on her desk for a while then would be dropped in the garbage along with the literature from all the other reps; the doctor would never know he was there.

He knew from experience that if he left the literature and followed up the next week; the receptionist would offer another pat response. "Well sir, if you left the literature last week, I'm sure the doctor would have called by now, if he were interested." The rep stressed the importance of his visit and tried to set an appointment, but to no avail.

This scenario repeated for weeks. The office manager was patient with the rep. She realized he had a job to do, but felt her job was more important. She was known as a "gate keeper." The office manager screened everyone that wanted to see her boss. She protected the doctor from those who would waste his valuable time. After all, the doctor cured sick people; sales reps just sold stuff nobody wanted.

Finally, the rep walked in when the office manager was away from the desk. The doctor looked out of his office. The rep seized the opportunity and said, "Doctor, I know how busy you are. However, this is important. The FDA has just approved our drug for paracoccidiodiomycosis. May I take a moment to tell you about it?"

The doctor said, "That sounds interesting. In fact I have a patient from Brazil with that and I have gone nuts trying to help the poor guy. Come on in."

The "busy" doctor spent twenty minutes reviewing the medical data and asked questions. He pulled a file, called the patient, and told him to go to his pharmacy to get a prescription. The doctor said, "Mr. Lopez, I think I finally found a drug that will help you." The doctor thanked the rep for coming in and asked him to stop by in a few weeks.

As scheduled, the rep dropped in to see the doctor. Again, the office manager tried to get rid of him. This time the rep said, "I saw the doctor two weeks ago. He specifically asked me to follow up on Mr. Lopez's condition. This is important. Would you please tell him I'm here?"

Reluctantly, she walked back to the doctor's office. A moment later she came out, "The doctor says to come right in."

The rep learned that the patient responded well to the treatment. The infection cleared and Mr. Lopez was able to return to work. As the rep left, the doctor quipped, "I wish you had come by sooner with this information."

The rep was careful not to make the office manager look bad. The doctor had told her not to let any "pesky" salesmen bother him.

The rep said, "Well I have a large territory and it took me awhile to get around to everyone."

On the way out, the sales rep stopped to thank the office manager for letting him in to see the doctor. She responded with a cheery voice and a wave of her hand, "Anytime at all—no problem."

The rep started the process again at the next office.

Why do we have a negative reaction to salespeople? They force us to make decisions and that's the one thing most of us try to avoid. The insurance agent forced the young couple, just starting out in life, to face their own mortality. The car salesman convinced a driver he wasn't invincible, that accidents happen to good drivers. The third sales rep found an opening in the wall of protection the doctor had constructed so he wouldn't have to decide to buy a new photocopier or a yellow page ad. This doesn't make the customers bad people, but it makes the job of a salesperson harder.

IF SALES WERE EASY, THEY WOULDN'T NEED US.

WHO SHOULD BE A SALES REPRESENTATIVE?

The most important aspect of these three stories isn't how the sales representatives overcame the objections. That is easy for me to teach you. However, it is difficult to teach the personality traits that enabled them to persist.

The sales profession isn't for everyone. Working for a company as an outside rep is the closest thing you will ever experience to running your own business.

In the first example, would you spend the time trying to sell a policy to a reluctant couple? Would you try a few times, and when it becomes obvious that it will require a lot of time will you think: "I'm not wasting any more time with these losers. I hope the guy drops dead, then they will be sorry they didn't listen to me. I'll move onto the next prospect."

How would you react in the second scenario? As a new car salesman, eager to make as much money as possible, you would offer the customer the air bag. You would do your job and stress the safety issue. Once the buyer said no, what would you do? Would you take the easy road and drop it? Would you worry that pushing an air bag to someone with so little interest will jeopardize the entire sale? I will teach you when to back off during a sale, and to care enough about your customers to try again.

Consider the third case. Would you drop off the literature with the office manager and leave it at that? Perhaps you should consider another profession, if you answered yes.

I don't suggest that salespeople concern themselves with improving society, and working toward the betterment of humanity. I'm a very assertive individual. I'm money motivated and always strive to be the best I can be. I aggressively pursue the business with the attitude that if you don't want my product or service then I will sell it to your competitor.

I have the patience of a saint, bulldog determination and I usually get what I want. I don't suffer fools, yet I will patiently explain my program until my customer understands. I will accept his decision either way. I see business people make stupid decisions because they refuse to open their minds to something new. Sales can be a richly rewarding profession. If you understand my points, I suggest you use the information in this book to pursue this career.

HOW SALES DRIVES OUR ECONOMY

When someone sells something an entire chain of events with an incredible ripple effect, takes place. It would take an entire book just to report every conceivable impact that one sale has on our economy.

Consider this scenario. A salesman sells a machine to a business. The order generates work for the employees of both the buyer and seller. On the seller's end the machine is produced, packaged, shipped and serviced. On the buyer's end the machine is received, unpacked, installed, operated and paid for. Each step on both sides requires hundreds of man-hours by many employees.

To do his job, the sales representative must purchase a new suit, shoes, shirts, a tie and accessories. He buys a nice fountain pen, appointment book, and attaché case. He either drives a car or uses public transportation to get to the customer. When he writes the order, he faxes the order to his company. Another salesperson sold this company one-hundred fax machines to improve the company's productivity. The fax machines use telephone lines that generate income for the telephone company and for the company that sells fax paper. The clerk enters the order on her new computer and sends the information to both the shipping department and accounts receivable.

The shipping department uses a forklift to load the machine onto their delivery truck. Both machines use fuel, oil and tires, purchased from local vendors. The truck uses public highways, pays license and registration fees, pays tolls and parking charges.

On the buyers end, their receiving department uses their forklift to unload the machine and the necessary personnel to install the machine in the proper department. All along the line, people work, using materials, making telephone calls, photocopies, and all generate income.

Consider the insurance policies for the trucks, buildings and equipment. The printer bought the stapler and staples used to bind the order pads together from a sales rep. There are the post-it-notes used by the secretaries to attach notes to the paperwork. At noon everyone breaks for lunch at the local diner that purchased food from a food broker that morning. The machine is turned on and produces a product that the buyer sells to his or her customers. The cycle begins again.

Multiply this by the millions of sales made every business day and you can come close to grasping the importance of sales on our way of life.

IT'S ALL IN YOUR HEAD

There is an old adage; "Salesmen are born, not made." I'm not sure if that's true; however, many successful people I work with display common qualities.

The traits I observe are a natural sense of well being and good cheer. These people, both men and women, have a positive outlook on life and take pleasure in their career. They aren't angry or bitter nor do they feel that any one group has unfair advantage over them. They see the American system to be one that rewards achievers and that this country is the land of opportunity.

One of my college professors in retail management often recounted stories of his father when he first came to this country. His dad loved to say, "The streets of America are paved in gold. All you need is the gumption to bend over and pick it up." His father learned English by reading the New York Times every day with the help of an English—Italian dictionary.

One day he read a story of a South American country that was facing economic disaster. Silt clogged the main river in their country, causing a hazard to navigation.

No one in the region had the equipment, experience or know how to clear the river. My professor's dad picked up the New York Yellow Pages and began calling dredging companies. When he had sufficient information and a clear understanding of the logistics, he placed a call to the South American country. He asked to speak to a Presidential aide. He explained that he had a resolution to their problem.

Amazingly, the President himself, picked up the phone and, through a translator, discussed the problem. He was on the telephone for more than an hour getting the details. After more calls to the contractors, they set a deal to clear the river. The professor's father received a generous commission for his few hours on the telephone. The contractors earned a profit and the small South American country got its river open and materials flowed. What greater testimony is there of a free enterprise system?

In contrast, less successful people walk around with a chip on their shoulder believing everyone is working against them. The buyers are stupid, the gatekeepers have attitudes, their territory is too small and the competition is using some kind of unfair trade practice. It's everyone's fault but their own.

Yes, there are situations where you have legitimate problems in your territory. The most successful of those I know always look toward themselves for a resolution. The buyer may be stupid, so they find a way to deal with his stupidity. Perhaps the presentations are over the buyer's head, so they present them in a simple format.

I worked with a very bright sales rep that had an MBA. He tried desperately to explain the concept of "return on investment" to a grocery manager that I knew never graduated from high school. As we left the store, without an order, my friend asked why the manager didn't buy his program.

I said, "Because he didn't understand what the heck you were talking about! He didn't want to look stupid in front of us so he just said, 'No thanks.'"

When a receptionist won't let sales reps in to see the decision-maker, the sales representative with the right attitude will make more frequent calls. His or her goal isn't to see the buyer, but just to say hello to the receptionist. They may bring her a few pads and pens that their company supplies with the products name imprinted. They may show up one morning with a box of doughnuts for the secretaries. Perhaps it takes months, but eventually they will get to see the customer.

The competition may very well dominate the marketplace. The true test of a sales representative is how he or she reacts to the situation.

I was calling on a drug store in Manhattan, selling personal care products for a large and successful company, when a very angry sales rep from a competing company approached me.

"You people make me sick. Just because you have all of the number one selling products, you think you own the market. Why don't you save a little for the rest of us?"

His approach and the level of his anger surprised me. I didn't know how to respond. Had he no concept of a free and open marketplace? What about the reps that had an even lower market share than he had? Did he voluntarily sacrifice his business to help his competitors? I don't think so. He felt that he deserved a certain market share. Not because of the quality of his products or his company's market strategy or even his own sales ability, but just because he was there.

In summary, if you have a pleasant nature and approach each day with humor and good cheer, then you possess most of what it takes to be a successful sales rep. The rest, I will teach you.

START WORK AT 10 A.M.— KNOCK OFF AT 3 P.M.

I was calling on a drug store chain headquarters waiting to speak with a buyer. I overheard a conversation between two sales reps who were discussing their own success and failures in their territories.

One rep said, "My boss asked why my business had taken a sharp turn upward. I gave him a nice safe answer about better planning and research, but the truth is I simply started showing up for work every day."

That is it in a nutshell. Some of my greatest success stories aren't a result of some secret sales technique or magic presentation or exhaustive market research. It was a matter of me putting in a full day at work, each and every day.

One of the rewards of working all day unsupervised is that your time is your own. There is a temptation to squeeze in a few personal errands during the "slack time." You deserve it, right? You closed a big sale yesterday that put you at quota for the week. You may decide to take a few moments to stop at the bank and the cleaners. It's only 9 a.m., and you can't get in to see any customers. What harm could it do? You just make it to your 10 o'clock appointment. Afterwards, there is time to hit the mall and pick up that gift. While you are there, you see a new bookstore, so you browse around. Everyone knows you can't see customers between noon and one. The next thing you realize, two hours have flown by. Oh well, you can make it up tomorrow. Your 2:30 call went well. Since it's so late in the day, you might as well head home and start work on the proposal and catch up on your e-mail. It's an unwritten law that buyers start packing it in for the day after three o'clock. Chances are no one will see you anyway. You will just be spinning your wheels. Who would know?

YOU HAVE JUST RATIONALIZED AWAY FOUR HOURS OF PRIME SELLING TIME. IT'S YOUR DOWNFALL WHEN IT BECOMES A DAILY HABIT!

A rep in pharmaceuticals boasted that he never worked on Fridays or when it rained. The only time that he put in a full day is when he worked with our manager. Yet, he never understood why he was below quota and missed bonus. He even complained it was unfair that he never won any of the sales contests.

The sentiment is widespread. While I worked as a pharmaceutical rep, I often field-tested candidates for sales positions. After several interviews, if the manager felt a candidate was promising, he would send him out in the field for a full day with an experienced rep. The purpose was twofold. First, it gave the candidate an opportunity to see firsthand what the job was all about. Secondly, the rep could report his opinion of the candidate to the manager.

Once, I'd spent several hours field testing a young candidate when he said, "Boy this job is great! I'll bet you start work at ten and knock off at three. You get paid to sit in doctors' waiting rooms and read magazines."

I asked where he got that idea. He told me that several friends had recommended pharmaceutical sales because you only work half a day, make good money and get a company car. I asked if any of these friends actually worked in pharmaceutical sales.

He said, "No. They were recent graduates and didn't have jobs, but that's what they heard from their friends in the business."

I told him the facts of life: "You will have hospital in-service calls at six in the morning, late night physician dinners that will keep your agenda full. You will have continuous education programs for the weekends and you will study medical journals to stay abreast of the rapidly changing field.

There is paperwork for territory planning, daily reports, weekly summaries, and monthly recaps, expense reports, inventory analysis and fifteen to twenty pieces of mail to read and respond to each week. (This was before e-mail and voice mail got thrown into the mix.)

Every three months, we have a two-day division meeting. You will often be asked to give a presentation on one of our products to the rest of the team. This will take about two days to prepare for, two days of your own time. There is always a comprehensive assessment test on our products, and you had better pass them. It could mean your job.

Your manager will ask that you prepare a detailed business plan for your territory. Monthly, he will evaluate you on your performance and hold you accountable to your plan. You will put in at least sixty hours per week for this job, more at first of course."

That evening, he phoned my manager to thank him for the interview but said that he had decided to pursue other opportunities.

My manager complimented me on my interviewing skills that got the candidate to open up. He was a nice person, but had taken bad advice from people, who frankly, didn't know what they were talking about. The company would have invested thousands in training him. He would have spent a lot of money relocating and time studying for a job he really didn't want. We agreed he would have quit after a short time.

My friend, Tom had recommended me for that job. He was a rep for the company. When he first recruited me, he laid out the job requirements in detail. I decided to pursue it and that's the difference.

KNOW WHAT YOU ARE GETTING INTO!

MAINTAIN GOOD CHEER

Someone once said, "You never get a second chance to make a first impression." Each sales call is an independent act, not a series of acts. What I mean is the last call of the day should be the same as the first call of the day. The buyer you see at five in the afternoon deserves the same level of freshness and enthusiasm as the buyer you see at eight thirty in the morning.

Never let your customers become a victim of your planning. A buyer is only human and will respond in kind to your attitude. When you come dragging in at quarter to five disheveled and anxious to wrap the day up, don't expect your customers to throw orders at your feet and beg you to take their business.

Some managers laughed when they spent a day in the field and saw me "freshen up." At 3:30 I will stop for coffee and sit for ten minutes and clear my mind. I always carry a small travel case in my attaché. It contains a toothbrush; paste, cologne and comb. I wash up, straighten my tie and wipe off my shoes. I feel recharged and ready to see my next customer. The buyer I see at 4:00 receives the same enthusiasm and attention as my first call of the day. I have made one or two extra calls after five that have resulted in substantial orders.

Treating each call of the day as the first call of the day is a mind game I play that prevents any negative feeling from affecting my next presentation. My last call may have been a total disaster. The company shipped the order incorrectly, double billed the customer or some other mistake. Perhaps the buyer canceled my appointment at the last minute. He may have decided to buy from the competition. I simply pretend it never happened. I do what I can to resolve the problem, but I never let a bad call affect the rest of my day. I simply walk out the door head toward my next call and pretend as though it has been a great day and that the last disaster never happened.

WERE YOU EVER PRESSURED INTO BUYING SOMETHING?

Think of the last time some "pesky" salesperson called you on the telephone, knocked at your door, or approached you in a department store. They hammered away at you, never taking "no" for an answer. Perhaps you answered an ad for time sharing and attended a meeting to get a free door prize and find out about the special offer.

Think of how you felt when the Real Estate agent started putting pressure on you. He never asks if you want to buy one week a year in a condominium for the next thirty years, because you may say "no." Once you say no, negotiations become difficult. Instead, they ask how much money you're willing to put down. They focus your attention, not on buying the property, but on the financing terms. They assume you want to buy and are just looking for the best deal.

After the presentation for time sharing, an agent walks to your table and takes a seat. "So can you manage to pay cash or would you prefer to finance?"

You say, "$80,000 is a lot of money for this deal. Let me think about it for a while?"

He gives you a puzzled look, "What's there to think about? What do you consider a fair price?"

You quote a low price to discourage him, "$20,000."

"If I could get this package for you for $20,000, would you leave me a 10 percent deposit?"

"I don't have that kind of cash lying around. Let me get back to you."

"I don't have that kind of money either, but sign right here and we will finance this beautiful package for only $75 per month."

"Gee, I've got a lot of bills this month," you say as you look over your shoulder for the exit.

"How about $50 a month. Surely anyone who calls himself a man can afford a lousy $50 a month to give his family a beautiful vacation for the next thirty years."

This is why they insist both husband and wife attend the sales pitch. They can always challenge the guy's masculinity in front of his spouse. It also eliminates the objection: "Well, let me go home and speak to my wife about it."

The technique is very effective on a certain target market, one that is easily embarrassed or intimidated. It is called low sales resistance. He doesn't want the agent to think he's stupid and unable to see a good deal when it is staring him in the face. In reality, they forget you the minute you walk out the door. The salesman moves onto the next victim and starts again. At the end of the day he will have made at least one sale and earned a sizable commission.

I don't pass judgment on any salesperson doing what he or she has to do to make a living, as long as it is legal and ethical. You must take responsibility for your decisions. No one is stopping you from saying, "I'm not interested." You may feel intimidated and uncomfortable but you are free to leave.

How did that high-pressure sales technique make you feel as a customer? In certain industries such as real estate or car sales, it may be a one shot deal. "If you don't sign 'em, you'll lose 'em."

Consider a sales rep who depends on repeat business and yet puts a lot of pressure on his customers. They may buy from him now, but will they want to see him next time he comes around?

THE SLEAZY SALESMAN

The lowest form of life on earth is a sales rep who lies and steals from his customers, employer and colleagues. They are bottom feeders who hurt the reputation of all sales reps.

When my company divided a territory our manager decided to give the prime section to Jake, although he had originally promised it to me.

My manager said, "Mike, you're doing well for your first eight months, 107 percent of quota. Jake, on the other hand, is 260 percent of quota, so he gets the expansion territory."

A few weeks later, Jake called, begging me for help on his assignment for the upcoming regional sales meeting. Our manager gave each of us assignments to present certain products to the group. Jake's assignment happened to be his number one selling product. He was in the top ten of the country.

I had no animosity for him and credited his success to his superior sales ability. We occasionally met for lunch or talked on the phone and for the most part had a cordial relationship. Jake always had extra catalogues and brochures and he replenished my supplies whenever I ran short. When he called me in desperation, I was willing to help him out.

Jake's panic request that I do the assignment should have sent up red flags in my head. Why would a top rep look to me to prepare a presentation for a product that he was selling like crazy? After giving so many successful presentations he should be able to do it off the top of his head. In fact, he should have been helping me instead. I didn't look at Jake from a manager's perspective, but rather as a colleague who needed help. I did the assignment for him. All Jake did was to present it to the group. Shortly thereafter, Jake's house of cards collapsed.

We learned Jake was holding at least two and possibly three sales jobs simultaneously. He had learned very quickly how to manipulate our ordering process to take advantage of the basic trust the company placed in the sales force. I know how he pulled his scam; however, I can only guess how much he embezzled from the company. The company, understandingly so, set in place safe guards to prevent this from happening again. This penalized the entire sales force by restricting their commission cash flow. Unfortunately, the actions of one sleazy sales rep adversely affected everyone.

THE OLD GUARD

Joe was a sales representative in his early 60's. A member of the old guard. When the company gave each of us a computer to manage our business, Joe's sat in his office for two years, unopened.

Joe was a nice guy, hard working and dedicated. For decades he called on his wholesalers to "pitch his wares." He had no records of prior purchases, and felt paperwork was a waste of time. When presenting promotions, he would just make up the numbers. "Bill, last year you only bought three-hundred cases and you ran out during the sale, you have nothing left in the warehouse, so I want to send in five-hundred cases."

The buyers knew Joe, trusted him and believed what he said and bought his suggested quantities. Besides, the buyers didn't keep records either; they depended on the sales representatives for that information. Joe's based his numbers on what he thought the customer might need as well as what he had to sell to meet quota.

During the late 1980's, most of these buyers retired and turned their jobs over to young MBA's. When Joe used his sales technique on them, they would turn to their computers. Then they retrieved the track history of the product and the current inventory level. The actual numbers would be totally different from what Joe had said and he would end up looking foolish and dishonest. He was neither; instead, he was a victim of progress. This great salesman saw the handwriting on the wall and soon retired. Rather than invest the time to learn how to run some simple software he chose to quit.

NO SALES JOB IS DEMEANING

There's a pecking order in the sales profession. At the top are the straight commission reps who sell high-ticket items like mainframe computers, networks or insurance. In the middle are salaried reps who promote pharmaceuticals and consumer goods. At the bottom are clerks whom a retailer throws onto a sales floor with almost no training.

I've done all three. All have their pluses and minuses and just because you excel at one doesn't mean you can do the others with the same proficiency.

When I was in pharmaceuticals, a colleague believed that the lowest rung on the sales ladder was a rep who sold food to the grocery industry. He rationalized that food was a staple item in constant demand and the reps were little more than order takers. I recounted my days in that industry and the difficulty I faced on a daily basis. The demands and pressure are just as high. It takes dedication and sales skill to succeed. I pointed out that you could say the same about pharmaceuticals. They too are staple items and always in demand.

No matter what you sell, do so with pride and dedication. It's a difficult job and only a few do it well.

ANYONE THAT SELLS FOR A LIVING BELONGS TO AN EXCLUSIVE CLUB AND DESERVES THE SAME RESPECT.

NOT EVERYONE WANTS TO PROSPER.

This is perhaps the most difficult concept I will ask you to accept. Not all companies want to flourish; they only want to survive. There is no interest in huge increases of volume and profit.

Walk into a mom and pop drug store and look at the merchandise shelves. Do they look empty? Are the prices 20 percent higher than you normally pay? Is there a distinct lack of promotional activity? Go into a busy pharmacy that heavily promotes. See the difference? Nothing is stopping the mom and pop store from doing the same thing, except their desire to prosper.

Yes, as a sales rep, you have a quota and will be expected to meet it. However, you may discover that you work for a certain type of company. If any rep exceeds quota by more than 10 percent, management may frown upon it.

I worked for one such company. Several colleagues and I tore our territories apart and delivered huge quota increases. One rep, named Jim, was 200 percent over quota. Jim got a call from the regional manager, who told him to stop the large orders. They were creating problems up and down the line from credit to shipping and it was making the other reps in the country look bad. The manager was getting complaints from everyone, including sales reps who were with the company a long time. The manager's boss was asking, "If Jones can double his sales, why can't everyone else?"

When the rep quit in frustration, the regional manager promptly closed down his territory. It was preferable to leave it vacant than to have another hot shot come in and create more trouble. They preferred the status quo, anywhere between 95 percent and 105 percent of quota, no less and definitely no more.

This policy, "believe it or not," made the job unbearable. All I did was walk around and pick up fill-in orders. There was no challenge; no gold ring to grasp for and it bored me to death.

In contrast, the job I have now is the best I've ever had. It's also the most challenging. Commission sales on a cold call basis keeps me on top of my game. The quotas are high; the products are both complex and sophisticated. The competition is fierce and the rewards are the greatest in my entire life.

Every day I leave home with an empty bag and I live by my wits. Many times I fail, but I win enough times to earn a great living.

CONQUERING THE FEAR OF SUCCESS

Jake Smith strolled into the well-appointed office of Arnold & Sons for his fourth and hopefully final interview for marketing director. This job would double his salary to $70,000 a year and give him the responsibility and rank he had long felt was owed to him.

Arnold was relieved that the long arduous task of filling the slot was near fruition. He and his national sales manager had culled through 3,000 resumes, interviewed 115 candidates and narrowed down the field to five.

The rigorous screening process consisted of many follow up interviews and placement tests. Now the company was down to two choices. Both candidates had distinct personalities that lent themselves to the task.

The company had faced stiff competition from an upstart rival that was systematically chipping away at its market share. Arnold was desperate to find a marketing director to revitalize the sales force and recapture lost ground. All that remained was for him to make a final decision. Smith was the last interview. Arnold liked Smith; he had a cool, composed air about himself. His was well educated, and appeared to have a strong track record. If all went well, Arnold would offer Smith the job.

As Smith walked in, Arnold rose from his chair and extended his hand. "Good morning Jake, nice to see you, have a seat."

"Thanks Mr. Arnold, I appreciate the opportunity to meet with you again."

"Jake, I have a few more questions to ask before I make my final decision."

"Fire away," Smith said with a grin.

"Are you prepared to start right away?"

"Well, I have to give my employer two weeks notice. I can't quit on the spot." Smith replied.

"I understand." Arnold liked the response; it showed responsibility.

"How do your wife and children feel about joining us?"

"Oh, they are excited and happy for me." Smith said.

"Well Jake, this is a tremendous opportunity for you. We are putting a lot of responsibility on your shoulders and the rewards will be great if you succeed. Do you have anything you wish to say?"

Smith thought for a moment, leaned forward in his chair and looked Arnold straight in the eye. "If you don't try to screw me, I won't try to screw you!" As he sat back, a faint smirk crept across his face.

Arnold was stunned. He leaned back in his chair as his mind went blank. He slowly rose from his seat, shuffled a few papers on his desk and without looking up said, "Well, that's about all I have. We have a few more candidates to consider. We will decide by Friday. I'll give you a call, either way." Jake returned home to await a telephone call that would never come.

Surprisingly, this happens all too often in business, not always in such a dramatic fashion, but it happens.

Consider Bill, a sales rep who writes a large order that puts him over quota for the month. Rather than capitalizing his strong position and pursuing more business, Bill goes into semi-retirement for two weeks by going to movies or playing golf during the sales day. When the new month begins, he's right behind the eight ball again.

Bill isn't lazy. Whenever he's behind quota, he puts in long hours and burns up his territory, but when he hits his monthly quota, he slacks off until he loses his advantage. Bill will always finish the year slightly above quota, because he believes he must do so to keep his job. His income is directly related to his sales, so one would think Bill wants to earn as much as possible. That's the reason he gives when asked why he's in commission sales.

Paul, who is a colleague of yours, complains that his bank CDs is paying a miserable 5 percent interest that adjusted for inflation has a net return of 1 percent per year. Therefore, you introduce him to a great mutual fund. He eagerly invests some risk capital and BANG! The fund shoots up 8 percent in one week. Paul quickly sells the fund and puts his money back in CDs.

Paul reasoned, "Well, my CD is FDIC insured, but the mutual fund isn't."

"But Paul, the fund returned more in one week than your CD will for the next year and half. Besides, it was risk capital."

Paul smiled and shook his head. "I like to sleep at night."

I couldn't sleep at nights knowing my money was only earning 1 percent." You replied.

A few months later Paul complained again about the lousy CD interest rate.

There is a distinction between fear of failure and fear of success. Fear of failure is something we all face and must learn to overcome. A rep may hesitate to prospect a new client or apply for a better job. However, if he stumbles into success, he's overjoyed and relieved.

Fear of success is different. It will drive you to the point of reaching for the brass ring and at the last-minute force you to retreat to safe ground. Being content with your present situation doesn't make you a bad person. Many find their level of confidence and comfort and have no desire to venture into the unknown. The purpose of this section is to help you determine if you have a fear of success. Review the following questions and answer them honestly. If you answer yes to seven or more, then I suggest you get career counseling. You may be in the wrong profession.

1. Have you settled into the middle of the pack on your sales team knowing that you can do better?
2. Have you ever walked away from a client or manager wishing you hadn't made some off the cuff remark?
3. Have you ever coasted for a while after a big sale convinced you earned a break?
4. Have you ever closed a sale when you knew you could have increased the size of the order?
5. Does another member of your team constantly outperform you although you consider him or her less qualified than you?
6. If management is watching you for possible promotion, does your performance slip?
7. Do you scoff at self improvement books and motivational tapes recommended by your company or peers?
8. Are you satisfied with your present income level?
9. If a manager works with you and helps you close more business than usual, do you worry that he may ask, "Why can't you do this all of the time?"
10. Have you ever withheld writing business with the excuse, you want to "sandbag" or hold business until next month?
11. Do you ever use the excuse; "I only work well under pressure?"
12. Do you ever feel resentful of those who stay focused on their work and are very successful?
13. Can you name three things about your job performance that you could change tomorrow, would greatly increase your income?
14. Have you ever wished that a customer didn't place a large order with you, because it would raise your quota for the next year?
15. Have you been in the same income bracket for five years or more and think you deserve more?

16. Have you repeatedly applied for better jobs but have turned down although you're well qualified?

When you commit yourself to this profession, you can conquer your fear of success by recognizing its danger signs. Make your advances in small steps. Give yourself a reasonable goal to increase your income by 10 percent each year. It's less intimidating to work toward an increase from $35,000 to $38,500 for year one, with a target of $75,000 after nine years, rather than trying to double your income overnight. Record and plot your success throughout the year. Later in this book you will read how to quickly double your income. It's a strategy for those who don't fear success.

Before you pursue a promotion, talk with your boss and learn what the job is really like. Ask to assume a few temporary tasks in your spare time so you learn the responsibilities. Then decide if it is what you really want.

I conquered my fear of success in 1980 when I left advertising and pursued a sales profession. In those twenty years, I've accomplished my goals ahead of schedule and set new ones, all within a reasonable time. I now earn nearly ten times my best income in advertising, completed my college degree and wrote two books.

I'M JUST AN AVERAGE GUY; IF I CAN DO IT, SO CAN YOU!

Chapter Two

GET THE JOB

The best way to get a great sales job at a good company is when they come to you and hire you away from your present employer. This has happened to me four times and I never regretted the moves.

"Networking" is the second best method. A friend who works for a company recommends you for a job. It's how I got my jobs at both the pharmaceutical and the consumer products companies. Steve introduced me to my future manager and that got me in to meet the divisional manager. Networking got me past the bottomless pit of the Personnel Department and into the decision-maker's office. I still had to convince them to hire me over the thousands of other candidates, but the job was made easier. The advantage of networking is that your friend can tell you what really goes on in a company. You learn who the best managers are, what territories are available, the pay scale and benefits. You can never ask these things on an interview.

The third method is to get hired at your college campus by a company recruiter. This usually happens six months before graduation. The manufactures send managers to various schools to conduct interviews and select candidates. Unfortunately, a recent news report cites that college recruiting is drastically down from prior years. The recent mergers and corporate downsizing have left little need for this practice. The unemployment rate and scarcity of candidates for certain professions also affects campus recruiting. Consumer companies may have enough applicants one year, while software companies go begging for qualified C++ programmers.

Some companies will go so far to hire you on the spot. People that I talked to, who accepted a job after one interview, believed it was a mistake. Any company so pressured for sales reps as to offer them jobs based on one interview, must have a severe turnover problem. They may be cases where it worked out well, but I have yet to meet anyone who stayed with such a company for more than a year.

Some offer you internships until you graduate. An internship is an excellent way to meet the people who may offer you a permanent job and to see first hand how the company operates. You should accept an internship, even if it doesn't result in full time employment at the company. It looks great on your resume and gives you valuable experience and insight.

The fourth method is through an employment agency, better known as a headhunter. They get job orders not advertised in the newspaper and can coach you on different career paths, salary and benefits and what the interviewer is looking for. They can even help you polish your resume. Remember, a headhunter does not work for you. They work for their clients. You are just a commodity they sell.

IF YOU ARE CURRENTLY WORKING, NEVER TALK TO A HEADHUNTER WHO CALLS YOU WITH A JOB OFFER. THIS ISN'T PARANOIA, BUT PRACTICAL LIFE EXPERIENCE.

It could be a set up. Companies have had office personnel pose as employment agencies to call their own sales reps to offer them a new job. They may suspect you're unhappy and looking to move. They will immediately hire someone to replace you and you will be out of work. Talk only to those people you have called first. Never talk to a headhunter's associate who calls you, even if you know the headhunter. To pursue it further, look up the phone number and call them back. Ask for the person who called you, by name. Be wary of out-of-state employment agencies, and always speak well of your current employer to anyone who calls.

The fifth method is through newspaper or trade journal employment ads. *IF YOU ARE CURRENTLY WORKING, NEVER ANSWER A BLIND AD.*

A blind ad is a help wanted classified ad that offers a great job and wonderful pay but doesn't identify the company by name, only by a post office box. There are times that companies place blind ads to see if any of their employees are looking to change jobs. I have worked for companies that did so and fired any rep who mailed them a resume. Of course if you aren't presently working, blind ads are perfectly safe to answer.

A headhunter may place a blind ad. When he receives your resume, he may place a call to your employer saying he has it on good authority that one of their reps is about to leave the company. He offers to send a well-qualified candidate to fill the "soon to be vacant" position. He then works on getting you placed at another company. The recruiter makes two placements at once.

The sixth way is to walk into a company's personnel office and ask to fill out an application. The only sales job I've ever gotten this way was when I applied for a part time sales position at a large New York department store. I don't recommend this method for anyone seriously pursuing a sales career. The only advantage you have over someone being hired through a headhunter is that the company saves the agency fee, which can be as much as $5,000.

MANAGERS NEVER HIRE BUMS

Let me state unequivocally that I DON'T BELIEVE ANYONE UNEMPLOYED IS A BUM. I've been out of work and on the unemployment line several times. Bad things happen to good people.

Several years ago I worked with a personnel manager who believed that a company would never lay off a competent employee. They only fire the "dead wood." This colored his view of anyone who applied for a job. During the telephone interview, he would ask whom the job seeker was working for, and if the applicant was "between jobs," he wouldn't pursue it any further. This is callous and judgmental. It has always stood out in my mind. In an ideal world this would never happen, but you can't control someone's thoughts. Be aware!

I strongly advise you to never quit your job unless you first have another offer. I don't care if you're totally miserable where you work now; stick it out until you find a better job. I've lost count of the people who resigned in the heat of battle. They were convinced that they could quickly find another job. Many were out of work for a year or more. No job is that bad that you can't hold out until something better comes along. You may discover that the problem resolves itself in time and there is no need to change.

You are more desirable to a prospective employer if you're currently working. Even if you were laid off due to downsizing from your last job, the prospective employer may think there is something wrong with you just because you were let go. He may reason if you're as good as you say, then why wasn't someone else fired instead?

With all thing beings equal between you and another candidate, except that you're unemployed and the other one is working, you won't get the job. The personnel manager may perceive the other candidate as being more desirable. He is hiring a winner away from the competition. You are unemployed, and therefore a bum. (His thoughts, not mine.) Why hire a bum when you can hire a winner? Following, is an example of the job requirements for a managerial position that was recently posted on the Internet.

Management Experience
You must be currently employed.
A stable work experience with no more than three jobs in ten years.

How judgmental and shortsighted is that? Why no more than three jobs in ten years? What about six jobs in twelve years and the last three were within ten years? What about an employee with only two jobs in ten years, is that more desirable? Perhaps a candidate held only one job in ten years. He worked for his Father-in-law and had job security no matter how poorly he did. Another candidate had four jobs in ten years. In his last job, he was the victim of downsizing due a company buy out or perhaps going bankrupt. Is that his fault? Does that make him or her a bad person? Why is the number three so indicative of a good employee? How many well qualified candidates does this employer eliminate right off the bat? Is this indicative of the way they run the rest of their business by choosing random numbers to set objectives and standards? I'm not suggesting that job-hopping is a good thing nor should it be ignored; however, it should not be the first qualifier for an applicant. There are too many other considerations. The point is there are people in positions of power that make decisions based on prejudices and pre-conceived notions.

REFERENCES

When you go on your interview, bring a list of nine people that you can offer as references. You should have at least five business references and four personal references. Have their full names, addresses, phone numbers, occupations and most of all, their permission to use their names. Nothing is worse than for your friend to receive a call unexpectedly from a stranger asking personal questions about you.

You should approach each person on your list and tell them you're interviewing with a specific company for a particular job. Establish the time that you have known each other and review any work experience you may have shared. It's a good idea to leave them a copy of your resume in case the interviewer asks questions about your past, such as the year you graduated and where you went to school.

The reason you want to bring extra references is two fold. First, you will be organized with the correct information and can complete the employment application while you're there. It looks bad when you say to the interviewer you don't have your best friend's address or phone number. Remember that an interview is a game of perception. You always want to look better than the other person.

Secondly, when I conducted interviews, I would disregard the three standard references listed on the application and ask for three more. I wanted to know if more than three people would say something nice about the candidate. You look great if you quickly produce more references.

No one will offer references from people who don't like them, so companies expect references to compliment the candidate. They look for the number and type of references supplied. Aside from personal references, list well-placed associates in other companies and include their title. Get a personalized reference from them, addressed specifically to the person who is interviewing you. You want to create the image that you aren't beating the bushes looking for any job, but want to work for their company at one particular job.

WHAT THEY CHECK

Better jobs with added responsibility require intensive background checks. In pharmaceuticals, they supplied a $16,000 company car, a $3,000 laptop computer and printer. They supplied an open-ended expense account, little hands-on supervision, thousands of dollars worth of drug samples and give-aways with a territory that was generating $1,000,000 a year in sales. I had to be bonded, insurable and trustworthy. They checked everything.

In legal publishing, the company was just as large, but I supplied my own car and they limited expenses to $250 per month. I was on draw vs.

commission, so if I didn't sell, I didn't get paid. I learned afterwards, that they never contacted any of my references. The depth of a background check varies from industry to industry. Since you don't know for certain, always be prepared.

TELL IT LIKE IT IS

Most companies will only go back seven years to check past jobs, any longer and the information becomes unreliable. Many companies won't provide references on old employees for fear of lawsuits. When an interviewer calls your old boss, he won't ask if you were a good reliable employee. To say "No!" would be grounds for a libel suit. What they ask is, "I understand Joe Blow worked for you from 1987 to 1993. Given the opportunity, would you hire him back?" If your old boss says, "Yes!" that constitutes a good reference. If your old boss says, "Jeff is a wonderful person, I like him a lot, but I wouldn't hire him again." That's a bad reference.

In today's climate, it has gotten to the point that some managers won't even respond to reference requests. One of my managers told me that if he gives a positive reference for a former employee, he could be personally sued if that employee is terminated for improper behavior on his new job. The position the new company takes in court is that the employee was hired, based on my manger's positive reference. My manager forwards all requests to the Human Resource department. They in turn, may refuse to collaborate any employment information. This may send a subtle message to the prospective employer.

DESPITE THE SILLY LAWS CONGRESS PASSES OR THE NUMBER OF FRIVOLOUS LAWSUITS ATTORNEYS PURSUE; BUSINESSES WILL ALWAYS FIND A WAY TO PROTECT THEMSELVES FROM DISHONEST EMPLOYEES.

FUDGING THE RESUME

A colleague freely admitted to me that he lied on his job application. He elevated himself to the rank of Colonel in the United States Army and awarded himself an MBA from New York University. He also promoted himself to field sales manager for several companies, who have since gone out of business.

I asked him, "Bill, what would you do if the guy interviewing you was a real army officer, or went to NYU? What if he worked for one of those companies and began asking you questions about the old days?"

Bill replied, "I've gotten away with it for twenty years. Listen, if I couldn't fake it or change the subject, I would excuse myself and go to the next interview."

To me there is a distinct difference between "accentuating the positive, de-emphasizing the negative" and out-and-out lying. If they discover you lied on your resume, they have grounds to fire you on the spot. Stick with the truth, polish it up a bit, but go with what you've got. Yes, I've heard of people who lied about their education. They stayed with the company undetected for years. Do you want to base your life and success on lies and take the risk of being uncovered, embarrassed and fired? Try explaining that on your next job interview.

There are companies that provide a new service to employers. They do the background checks for them. You may already be in the database. Your prospective employer calls them, supplies your name and gets a full report. If the information doesn't match to their satisfaction, you probably won't get the job and will never find out why.

HEADHUNTERS WHO COAX YOU TO LIE

We were interviewing a young woman for a sales position in pharmaceuticals. As we reviewed her resume, we explained the sensitive nature of our business and the value of the company car, computer, drug samples, equipment and so forth. We told her we checked all references, experiences, credit rating and education. She wouldn't be hired, if there were any discrepancies.

We admitted that not all companies verify to the extent that we do and we realized in the competitive job search market, people often exaggerate. Therefore, if there was anything that she would like to amend on her resume, this would be the time to do it.

She hesitated for a moment and admitted that there had been another job. It had lasted only three months. She explained, "The owner of the company hired me over the objections of the manager. She had wanted to hire someone else and was furious that I was forced on her. She made my life miserable, until I quit."

We asked why she had omitted it from her resume. She said her head-hunter talked her into it. "He said a three-month job looks bad on a resume and if I stretched out the prior job, no one would ever check." We asked if there was anything else she should tell us. She said, "No. I understand if you won't hire me now, but it is a relief to get that off my conscience."

My manager thanked her for her candid reply and said, "We understand stuff like that happens. We won't hold it against you. Please amend your resume and re-submit it. Everyone is entitled to one mistake in their career." We hired her and fired the headhunter.

CULLING RESUMES

A resume is a sales tool you use to get an interview with a decision-maker. Your entire career depends on the quality of that piece of paper. Culling resumes is when a manager sorts through many resumes to find the few he or she wishes to meet.

Many books and services take you systematically through the resume writing process. I'm sure any number of them are good and I won't try to compete with them. Instead, I will tell you how some companies sort, or cull, through thousands of resumes finding the ten people they will interview in person.

In this section, I can get you into the top 1 percent of candidates they choose to interview. The final step, getting the job, will be discussed later.

One of my selling techniques is "Total Empathy." In a situation where you're trying to convince someone to do something for you, whether it is to hire you or buy something, always look at it from their point of view. Put yourself in the place of a harried divisional manager who must fill a vacant sales position quickly.

You are a divisional manager for a large, well-known manufacturer of consumer goods. Your boss promoted your number one rep and transferred her across the country. Her territory generated 20 percent of your divisional sales and you're in hot pursuit of the division sales contest for the year. You are under extreme pressure. Every day the territory is vacant; you and the company lose sales. The lost revenue hurts your standing with the other divisions, which in turn hurts morale with your sales reps. They have worked hard all year to make "President's Club." To lose that important award at the last moment would be devastating. Unfortunately, this isn't your only priority. You have your own accounts to call on, paperwork to do and two new reps who need close supervision to get them up to speed.

The company won't spend the $5,000 for a headhunter who can send you a dozen pre screened reps. Instead; they spend $100 for a classified ad and let you do the screening. The ad ran last Sunday. You guess that you will get about fifty responses.

Saturday, you return home from the post office with 1,000 letters. You dump the bag of mail on the dining room table and stare at the pile. Your spouse warns you, what will happen if you scratch her grandmother's heirloom table.

One by one, you open the letters, learning quickly the value of a sharp letter opener. You read each resume carefully, deciding if it is someone you want to meet in person. Thirty minutes pass and you have gone through twelve resumes. The pile seems to have grown.

There must be a better way. You get a brainstorm; good reps have several things in common: they are well educated, organized, experienced, polite and professional. They get to the point quickly.

You call in your two teenage children and offer them $5 per hour to help. You tell them, "First, open each envelope. Any resume that's more than one page long, not including a cover letter, should be thrown away." You don't need someone who isn't concise.

What if there is no cover letter? Throw it away. How professional are you if you couldn't bother to enclose a simple letter of introduction? They don't have a college degree—then throw it in the garbage. You need someone who can set a goal and achieve it. No sales experience, trash it. You don't want to hire and train someone, only to have them decide after three weeks that sales isn't for them. Throw away resumes that are poor quality photocopies. What are they doing, making a mass mailings to every ad in the paper? Let someone else hire them. WOW! This candidate enclosed a short, hand written cover letter. That took some effort. You place that one on the side.

"Hey kids, this is working!" After an hour, all of the envelopes are open, and your son has just carried the first garbage bag of resumes out to the recycling bin. You are now down to thirty candidates. You thank the kids and pay them. You can handle it now.

You review the remaining resumes. Some look promising, but are from out of state. There is no way the company will pay for relocation. You will forward these resumes to the respective managers. They are always looking for good people. Why bother? You are a team player and will do things to help your fellow managers, though you get no direct benefit.

You get another idea. Most every one of your colleagues and reps played competitive sports in college and maintained a good average. You look for resumes that list team sports in school. This indicates they understand the "Team concept," people who work together for a common goal. They also maintained good grades. Great! They can do more than one demanding thing at a time, good management material!

You are now down to twenty resumes. OOPS! This guy misspelled the name of your company. It's a common mistake; everyone does it. His resume goes in the garbage. You don't need careless people working for you. He may make an error on an order that costs the company thousands. Another specifies a required salary; he wants too much. This one wants a two-year guarantee. Get a grip. You don't need any prima donnas.

You find a candidate that knows how to use a word processor. His resume and cover letter are custom tailored for your company and for the specific territory. You put that in the select pile of people you want to meet. Another enclosed a copy of a note he received from his company president for outstanding work on a special project. It goes into the select pile too.

You are now down to fourteen resumes. You begin placing calls to arrange appointments. Two people politely decline; they have accepted positions with other companies. Four people weren't home and you left messages. Five more didn't have answering machines. No one ever picked up. You let the phone ring ten times and then moved on. You can call them later if the others don't pan out. The last three were home and you conducted a telephone screen interview. They all sounded promising, so you scheduled appointments for Monday. You have finished culling resumes.

As you stand up to stretch, you look out the window. The Department of Sanitation picks up three large bags, containing nine-hundred resumes. You know that somewhere in those bags are probably one-hundred candidates who would make perfectly fine sales reps, but there was no time for you to sort through the mountain of resumes to find them. Had they known what you had to go through to find fourteen people to interview, they would have done things differently.

Monday, the post office calls. They have another bag for you to pick up. You decide to have your kids cull through them to find the top three-hundred. You will hold them in reserve in case these fourteen don't work out. They are probably great candidates too, but they are a day late.

What you have just experienced is "Total Empathy" with the person you're trying to reach through a resume. Now that you understand what he goes through, get one of those great "How To" books on writing resumes and you will make it to the top 1 percent. Even in today's tight labor market, where there are more jobs than candidates to fill them, you will still have to compete for the job. There may only be twenty-five responses to an ad as opposed to the two-thousand in the above example. They will, however, only hire one person and you won't have a chance unless they first call you for an interview.

THE INTERVIEW

A company of fifty employees or fewer that has a small sales force may decide to hire you after as few as two interviews. A large corporation may ask you back seven times before they decide.

There are several reasons for this:
1. The decision-maker at a small company may be untrained in conducting lengthy interviews.
2. A small company may not have the luxury of time to dwell on who to hire.
3. Since a small company can't attract the quality and number of candidates, so the selection process is easier.
4. Small companies may consider sales representatives a necessary evil and one rep is as good as another.
5. The competition for quality reps in a small company is fierce and if a good rep should come along, they want to make an offer immediately.

I can't predict the number of interviews you will have nor the exact questions they may ask. I can't tell you how to answer those questions, other than truthfully. I can tell you the types of questions I asked during an interview and those asked of me while I was being interviewed. No matter the size of company you interview with, be prepared for the worst-case scenario and you will do fine.

On my first interview with a pharmaceutical company, I brought photocopies of my driver's license, marriage certificate, children's birth certificate, social security card, college degree and last transcript. I also brought a territory manual from my old job.

My purpose was twofold. First, I wanted to do something different from the rest of the candidates. Secondly, I was confident I would be asked back for additional interviews and they would eventually ask me for documentation. While the other candidates would be scrambling through their records, mine would already be in the interviewer's hand. It demonstrated my "Empathy" with his job. It worked. The manager interviewing me thanked me for my foresight and consideration.

NEVER CLAIM PAST SUCCESSES OR PERFORMANCES THAT YOU CAN'T DOCUMENT.

When you go through multiple interviews, they will ask you more intricate questions requiring specific detail. Often, they repeat the question during different stages of the interview process. This technique helps detect inconsistency in your story.

One rep we interviewed made many claims about his past performances. By the third interview, he had contradicted himself on almost every one of them. He saw us take notes and refer to them. He either couldn't remember what he had told us before or he thought we wouldn't remember.

DRESS CODE

In the final consideration the smallest detail can sway a decision-maker to choose you over a competitor. Don't let that detail be a wrinkled suit, scuffed shoes, or worse yet a loud distracting tie and sport coat.

The safest route is the conservative one. Assume that you're applying to the most uptight, stuffed shirt organization in corporate America. Once you have the job, you can loosen up.

DRESSING CORRECTLY WON'T GUARANTEE YOUR SUCCESS. DRESSING INCORRECTLY WILL GUARANTEE YOUR FAILURE!

Following are guidelines for interview attire:

1. Don't be so cocky about your qualifications that you think an eccentric appearance won't matter.

2. The decision-maker wants to know how you will present yourself to their customers as their representative.

3. For men and women, the best color is navy blue, followed by navy blue pin stripe, then dark gray or dark gray pinstripes.

4. Never wear brown, black or green.

5. Never wear loafers. A $50 pair of department store wing tips is better than $400 import high fashion loafers.

6. White; long sleeve, button down collar, oxford shirts. Cuff links are great. Never wear short sleeve shirts.

7. Suits should be 100 percent natural fiber, wool is preferable; ties should be pure silk, shirts, all cotton and shoes should be 100 percent leather and in good repair. (My manager watched as the candidates walked out of the interview to see if they had run down heels.)

8. Ladies should wear dark blue suits with white blouses and navy blue heels.

9. The only jewelry a gentleman should wear is a watch, wedding band, and a school ring.

10. A woman may wear a watch, wedding band / engagement ring, simple earrings and a necklace. Nothing should be gaudy or flashy.

11. A silk tie with a conservative pattern is desirable. Avoid the flashy patterns of the current fad. You don't want to compete with your tie for the attention of the interviewer.

12. For follow up interviews, never wear the same suit twice.

13. Never smoke or chew gum during an interview, even if they say it's OK.

14. If the interview is conducted over a meal, watch your table manners. Never order alcohol, even if the interviewer does.

PERCEPTION MATTERS

I'm not the final authority on any aspect of this book. You can find those with as much or more experience who will disagree with any number of recommendations I've made. I'm confident we agree on one thing, perception matters. During the interview process, they analyze everything you say and do, to determine your worthiness as a candidate. Consider the decision is between you and another candidate for the job. You lose out due to a minor flaw in your interview, then you're as much a loser as the candidate who finished in 300th place.

I was with the national sales manager at a meeting when he discussed the recent firing of a dishonest sales rep. He was reminiscing about the final interview when he decided to offer him the job.

"Something was wrong about this guy. I couldn't quite put my finger on it. I interviewed him in Manhattan, in the middle of the summer. The temperature was in the 90's and the humidity was horribly high; everyone was dying. This guy shows up at my office at one o'clock. He's wearing a heavy wool, winter suit. He was cool, crisp and as fresh as a daisy. Yet he claimed he had been in the field that morning, calling on his customers for his present job. He continued, "This seemed strange. Everyone else in the office was wearing lightweight summer suits. You know, the poplins and sear suckers. Even so, the weather was wearing them down. I ignored my gut instincts and gave him the benefit of the doubt. Perhaps he stopped at home and showered and changed; rode an air-conditioned subway to my office. That is why he looked so well groomed in that heavy suit. I thought that was a reasonable thing to do for an important interview. Well, I should have listened to my gut instinct. He turned out to be a weasel. I will never make that mistake again."

How you dress, your punctuality and your demeanor will determine your success and failure. Even if your credentials are impeccable, that's no reason to take the interview for granted. Remember that when the consumer product company hired me, I beat out better educated and more experienced candidates. Somehow, the decision-maker had a better perception of me than the other candidates.

Perhaps you aren't yet established and don't have the resources to invest in a new wardrobe. When I first interviewed with a major company, I was fresh out of advertising where art directors could wear jeans and tee shirts to work. It was considered campy.

I was broke and the only suit I had was old and ill fitting. After several interview rejections, my wife Pat bought me a copy of *Dress for Success*. I learned the importance a professional appearance makes. I applied for a credit card at a department store. I used the limited line of credit to buy two suits, two white shirts, two ties and an inexpensive pair of black wing tips. I made an investment in myself. I got the next job I interviewed for.

TRADE SECRETS

Never offer a prospective employer any trade secrets from your current job! Legally, they can't accept them. By placing yourself in a compromising position, you send the message that you're unprofessional and untrustworthy.

You may use knowledge you acquire, such as sales technique or territory management, but the secret ingredients to the number one product on the market belongs to the manufacturer. You may also have access to a company's future promotional schedule. If you place that on the negotiating table, you violate the trust of your current employer and probably federal law as well. Maintain confidentiality and your future employer will trust and respect you as a professional sales representative.

Following are typical questions asked throughout the interview process. I selected the candidates' resumes that I wanted to meet in person and would call them to conduct a telephone interview. If that went well, I would invite them in for a face-to-face interview.

TELEPHONE INTERVIEW

"Hello, this is Mike Swedenberg, I'm with (name of company). I just received the resume you sent us. Do you have time to answer a few questions?"

- How did you hear about us?
- Are you working for someone now?
- If yes, why do you want to change jobs?
- If no, what happened to your last job?
- Can you relocate?
- Why are you interested in this industry?
- Why are you interested in my company?
- Tell me about yourself.

I would record the candidate's answers and would decide to set an appointment to meet them. I placed the questionnaire in a folder along with their resume and cover letter. After the interview we could compare the consistency of their responses.

Following are more interview questions you may face. The comments in parenthesis indicate the reasoning for the question.

FIRST INTERVIEW QUESTIONS

1. Looking at your resume, let's start at the beginning. I see you went to Adelphi University. Why Adelphi? (Did you select that college because it was a good school and a challenge or because it was convenient and inexpensive?)

2. Why did you choose not to go to college? (Was it a lack of ability or for financial reasons?)

3. Why did you choose your major? (This shows your decision process. One candidate said he chose his major because his wanted to be with his friends.)

4. Did you help pay for your schooling? (Someone who worked their way through school demonstrates independence.)

5. What extra curricular activities did you participate in? (Can you handle more than one demanding task at a time?)

6. Tell me about your first job.

7. Are there any success stories you can share?

8. Why did you leave your first job?

9. What about you second job? This continues down your resume. (This demonstrates your judgment on your career path)

10. Tell me about your current job.

11. Can you explain this time gap in your resume? What did you do from June to August of 1990?

12. How did you prepare for this meeting?

13. Sell me this pen, or some other common object.

On several interviews, I've been asked to sell the interviewer a common pen. The purpose is to see how you think on your feet and the level of your communication skills. Refer to the five steps of the presentation in Chapter Four.

Immediately after the first interview, mail a hand written thank-you to the interviewer.

SECOND INTERVIEW

The second interview will be intense. It will demand more detail of the influences on your life and how you work in your present or last job. You may be asked these things even if you have no sales experience. They refer to school activities, internships and summer work.

1. How do you manage your current territory?

2. How is your car / trunk / office organized?

3. You are back from vacation with no appointments. What is your first call?

4. You go backpacking to a foreign country. What ten things do you bring?

5. You have four hours to see ten accounts. How do you prioritize?

6. How far in advance do you plan?

7. What type of organizer / day planner do you use?

8. Show me your calendar for the last three months. How do you account for your time?

9. Tell me about a project you handled from beginning to end.

10. (The interviewer hands you a map) How would you organize this territory?

11. Name the three most influential people in your life?

12. Are you interviewing for any other positions?

13. For our next interview, list ten questions you want me to answer to help you decide if you should work for our company

QUESTIONS TO ASK AN INTERVIEWER

I've yet to be on one interview where I wasn't asked if I had any questions for the interviewer. The worst answer you could possibly give is: "No." Following are some suggested questions you may wish to ask the interviewer:

1. How long have you worked for this company?

2. Why is the territory vacant?

3. What is the standing of your region within the company?

4. How did this territory do last year?

5. What do you like best about your company?

6. What is your favorite product in the company line?

7. How long were you with the company before you were promoted?

8. Does the company always promote from within?
9. Who is your number one rep and what makes him or her the best?
10. How often do you work with your reps in the field?
11. Tell me about company training.

QUESTIONS NEVER TO ASK AN INTERVIEWER

Everyone knows you won't work for free, unless you are an intern. Then, you are working for experience and the future opportunity for a job with that company. It's bad form, however, to ask about salary or benefits on an interview. The interviewer will bring those subjects up at the appropriate time, only then should you ask for clarification. Your headhunter is the person to ask about these before you even begin the process, assuming you didn't answer a classified ad.

Never ask:
- Salary
- Benefits
- Perks
- Expenses
- Vacation time or time off

THIRD INTERVIEW

1. Let's review your list of questions. (Assuming he gave you an opportunity to prepare a list after the second interview.)
2. What do you expect from your manager?
3. How would you find a book in the library? (How clearly you can relay information demonstrates how well you can sell. NEVER BLUFF YOUR WAY THROUGH THIS STEP. ADMIT IT IF YOU DON'T KNOW.)
4. What was the best vacation you ever had?

5. Tell me a success story.

6. Tell me a failure.

7. An interviewer asks a confusing question to see if you clarify before you answer. Example: "Of the leading indicators, which, if any, is the most reliable?"

8. Describe your ideal job.

9. Where do you want to be in five years?

10. How do you stay current in your field?

11. Who is the Speaker of the House of Representatives? (This is an indication of how well-read you are. In a recent poll, only 34 percent of those adults asked, could name the Vice-President of the United States, although he had been in office for eight years.)

12. Take one minute to talk about a subject that you know nothing about. Example: Explain the transportation problems faced in Central Africa. (This indicates how well you surmise. This is not to be confused with bluffing. You are asked to discuss a topic you know nothing about.)

FOURTH INTERVIEW

1. Tell me why you have been successful.

2. How does an airplane fly? (Do you admit ignorance or try to bluff your way? A good sales representative will say: "I don't know, but I will find out." Find out and then tell him on your next interview.)

3. How do you balance your checkbook? (Can you handle routine math and accounting chores associated with a sales job?)

4. What are you greatest strengths?

5. What are your greatest weaknesses? (Never say: "I just work too darn hard.")

6. Why would a customer be cynical and tough and how do you overcome that obstacle?

7. You have a pet project that I'm dead set against, what would you do?

8. What if I asked you to handle a problem and you disagreed with my method.

9. A receptionist won't let you see the buyer. What do you do?

10. A customer blames you for a problem you didn't create. What do you do?

11. A customer asks you to bend our company rules, what do you do? (Qualify the question: Does he ask me to steal or simply give some extra service not encouraged by the company?)

12. What paperwork does your company require? How do you handle it?

13. You said you were computer literate. How do you create a file, or copy a file to a disk? (This is another reason you shouldn't lie about your qualifications.)

14. I call you at the last minute to fly to Chicago for a three-day conference. What are the first five things you do?

15. In your current job, what paperwork do you do that isn't required?

16. Describe the various steps of a presentation.

17. How do you overcome an objection?

FIFTH INTERVIEW—THE FIELD TEST

When the company invites you to spend a day in the field with one of their reps, it is an indication you're being seriously considered for a sales position.

My pharmaceutical manager often asked me to field test promising candidates. This often happened after the fourth interview. We tell the candidates that it is an opportunity for them to see for themselves what the job entails and if it's really for them. In reality, it was a daylong interview. The theory is if you keep someone talking long enough, the truth comes out.

I was field-testing a candidate whom I liked from the start. He was a salesman's salesman. He was personable, jovial, well read and a great conversationalist. He had a quick smile, showed up for the field test early and asked the right questions.

At the end of the day, I told Carl that I would recommend that he be hired. He was ecstatic. I told him about our screening process and how we would thoroughly research his background. I gave him the last option to amend his resume. He sat silently for a moment then said, "Nope, everything is 100 percent accurate." That night, I called my boss Gary and recommended Carl for the job.

A week passed when Gary called me to field-test another candidate. I asked, "What happened to Carl?"

"He lied on his application. It turns out that he never graduated from college. We contacted his school for a transcript and he never got a degree. He was one credit shy of the requirement."

"What did Carl have to say?" I asked.

"He admitted he lied. He said he put himself through school. He needed one more credit which meant he needed to stay in Buffalo for the summer. He was supporting himself, out of money and decided to go with what he had."

"He would have been a great rep," I protested.

"I liked him too. The regional manager is furious that we couldn't hire him. Had he told the truth when you gave him the chance, we could have worked around it, you know, let him take the course during the fall semester while he worked. We would have even paid for it, but he never gave us that option."

I defended Carl again; "It wasn't that big a deal. I understand his dilemma."

Gary said, "Does that mean if he fills out a daily report saying he called on twelve doctors, I'm to assume he only called on eleven? His expense report says he spent $3.00 on parking meters, so it really means he only spent $2.00? Where do we draw the line? How else do we judge someone's character? Besides, his little white lie has already cost us time and money. I thought I had the slot filled; now I have to start over at square one.

Another promising candidate I liked has already accepted a job." Gary had made his point.

Other field tests had uncovered people's true intentions. One woman admitted that the only reason she was interviewing in New York for a Florida position was because she wanted to have a job when she relocated. She did not intend to stay with us. Another slipped up and discussed a job he had that wasn't on his resume.

My manager asked me to field test a candidate, Ken, for a territory that had been open for a long time. My boss was eager to fill it and this was his number one selection. If I gave the thumbs up, my boss would send him to the regional manager for a final decision. Before the field test, I met the candidate for breakfast. This gives them time to relax and open up. We discuss the day's plan and what I expect of him or her.

I hadn't seen Ken's resume yet. My boss wouldn't discuss this candidate before hand for fear of prejudicing my opinion. We talked about his background.

Ken mentioned that he worked for the same consumer product company I had. (He didn't know I'd worked there) As he talked about the company, it became obvious he never worked for them. I said, "Ken, I'm ending the field test right now. I'm going to call my manager and urge him not to hire you."

"Why not? The day just started. You didn't even give me a chance."

"Ken, don't you think it's strange that you and I worked at the same company, in the same two man division, at the same time, but sold different products? Do you think it's odd that we worked together, in the same office for five years and we never ran it to each other, not even once?"

THINGS TO REMEMBER ON A FIELD TEST:

1. A field test is a full day interview.
2. Everything you say and do will be reported.
3. Be early for your appointment.

4. Ask the field tester how much you can be involved in the sales presentation.

5. Always introduce yourself to the customers and extend your hand.

6. Never interrupt the sales rep when he is presenting.

7. Offer to pick up your own lunch tab. The company may pay for everything, but make the effort.

8. Never ask to be reimbursed for your travel expenses to or from the field test, unless it involves airfare and you don't get the job.

9. Never criticize your present or past employer.

10. Ask as many questions about the job and company as you want, but be careful not to repeat any questions.

11. Some jobs entail physical work, like building displays; take off your jacket and help. Don't offer to help; just do it. An experienced field tester will look for these things.

12. Don't ask about fringe benefits, salary or anything that relates to what the company will do for you. When the field tester volunteers that information, it's fine, but don't ask.

13. Bring a note pad and take notes of every call you make and any questions you have about the day. Bring this with you for the next interview.

14. At the end of the day, get the field testers business card and address. When you get home, send a thank-you note for the day in the field. (He or she may not be willing to give their home address to a relative stranger, so send the card in care of the company.)

15. Ask for a brochure or catalogue. This will allow you to study the company and its products before your final interview.

16. Decide if this is what you really want to do with your life.

One reason my boss asked me to field test so many people is that I would note everything said during the day. I could call my boss that night and re-count every comment the candidate made. This gave him a wealth of information and often revealed the true side of a candidate.

I should note that it doesn't always work to your advantage. When I interviewed for my first commission job I was invited to do a field test. The shoe was now on the other foot. I showed up early; however, the rep was late. He offered no apology or excuse. We were to spend the entire day together. After each call, I took a small pad and wrote a few notes. I wanted to keep track of whom we saw, what was presented and any other interesting thing I observed. This way, I would be prepared for the next interview.

After the third call, I reached for my pad. The rep gripped the steering wheel, leaned back and in a high, shrill voice asked, "What are you writing? Did my manger send you out to spy on me?"

"No, of course not!" I explained that I had been a field tester in my last job, and this is what many of my candidates did. "I don't want to be embarrassed if your manager asks about the customers we saw and the products you presented. It's nothing more than that."

"Well, just stop! Don't write anything more." He begged.

When we were ready to break for lunch, he abruptly dropped me off at the subway and said, "I'm not spending any more time with you."

"Would you relax? I'm supposed to spend the entire day with you. What do I tell your manager when I show up early? I really want this job." I said.

"Well, go to a movie or hang out at a coffee shop. Tell him we spent the day together and wrote a few orders. I'll back you up."

"I'm not going to lie to him. I promise not to take any more notes, let's get some lunch."

He was visibly shaken and insisted that I leave. He sped away as soon as I got out of his car. I didn't know what to do. I assumed the worst, and went directly to the office to meet with the manager. When I got there, I tried to play down the fact I was five hours early. The manager pressured me and I told him what had happened. (I didn't mention that the rep wanted me to lie about writing orders.) He laughed and explained that the rep was a "Nervous Nelly" and not to worry about it. He said he never thought about giving direction to a rep for a field test, and this was the first time he had used that rep. When I explained my experience as a field tester, he was intrigued. He said his industry wasn't as intense as pharmaceuticals and he was more concerned that I liked the job.

I got the job, but that rep never spoke to me again. In hindsight, I should have asked the rep when we met, if I could take some notes during the day. I would have respected his wishes.

SIXTH INTERVIEW

After successfully completing the field test, the interviewer's boss may invite you to meet him. He or she will combine the previous five interviews in to one, and make a decision to offer you a job. It's important to remember the interviewer has recommended you for the position. He is being judged as much as you are by the quality of people he recruits. You are both on trial.

THE PROFESSIONAL INTERVIEWEE

One type of candidate an interviewer must watch out for is the professional interviewee. This is someone who has the art of interviewing down to a science. They are overly rehearsed and their appearance is impeccable.

Your appearance must be clean, sharp and professional, but I've met candidates that look like they just stepped off the cover of GQ. Normal people just don't look like that. These people are great in interviews but quickly fall apart on the job. "They talk the talk, but can't walk the walk."

Another sure sign of a professional interviewee is that they have a canned answer for everything. The interviewee responds without even thinking, sometimes before the interviewer can finish the question. They can do this because they've heard them a hundred times before. If I were to ask you your full name, address and telephone number, you could rattle them off without thinking. That's fine. If I were to ask you your driver's license number, or your spouses' social security number, how quickly could you answer? You would have to go look them up, unless you've been asked so often, you know them by heart. This is why I didn't list every possible interview question or any responses. You must be genuine and sincere, not rehearsed.

Next time you're watching a political debate, listen to each candidate. Do they sound as though they are speaking from the heart or are they just spitting out rehearsed lines? On an interview, you want to be the former, not the later.

THE SELF-DESTRUCTIVE CANDIDATE

Managers watch for the self-destructive personality. (Refer to Conquering the Fear of Success in Chapter One.) That is someone who, sets a goal, works steadily toward it and when they are on the verge of success, does something to cause themselves to fail. They may give a curt or sarcastic answer to a reasonable interview question. They fail to produce certain necessary documents. They arrive for the final interview with alcohol on their breath or any variety of things that would cause disqualification.

It's obvious that such a person would be unable or unwilling to achieve success and would damage the company. I will always err to the side of caution when I judge someone who has displayed this trait.
PERCEPTION COUNTS.

TAKING THE JOB
DECIDING BETWEEN TWO OFFERS

The ideal situation is when two companies offer you a job. Compare what each has to offer with your long-term goals. Look at every aspect of each offer. Write down the salary, retirement plan, company turnover, management style and the financial status, if they are publicly held. Consider any chance for advancement and the possibility of company mergers or buyouts. Speak to your potential customers and ask which they think is the better company. Choose the job offer that has the greatest long-term potential, even if the money is less. [Refer to Chapter Two, Salary Negotiations, Value of the Fringes.] Determine the relative value of each package. The salary package for one may appear to be higher than the other, but the higher paying job may only cover limited expenses and make you contribute to the health care plan.

Consider the following comparison for two companies, both of which have offered you a sales job.

Compensation Package	Job A	Job B
Base salary	$35,000	$27,000
Commission based on 100 percent quota	$50,000	$70,000
Subtotal	$85,000	$97,000

On the surface, it appears Job B pays $12,000 more per year. Job B is less desirable, because the territory is spread out and would require several overnights per week. This means less time with your family. The manager at Job B appears to be more difficult to work with than the manager at Job A. You may be tempted to accept the offer from Job B based solely on the income potential without doing anymore homework.

Now consider that it costs you $325 per month on average to cover your territory. Job A only reimburses you a maximum of $250 per month. Job B's is open-ended, meaning they cover all reasonable expenses. At Job A you must pay $900 in expenses out of your own pocket each year.

Compensation Package	Job A	Job B
Covered expenses	$85,000—$900	$0 (No cost to you.)
Subtotal	$84,100	$97,000

Job B looks even better. It pays $12,900 more. After further research you discover Job A supplies you with a company car and covers the lease and insurance. Job B requires you to supply your own car and insurance and reimburses you 32.5 per mile. Assuming that is what it costs you to operate your car, there is no net gain for Job B in this category.

This gets a little sticky. Job A supplies you with a new car every three years and you are allowed to drive it for personal use. This allows you to sell your own car and saves you $8,000 per year on the payments, insurance, and upkeep. This adds $8,000 to the value of Job A. Although Job B reimburses you for your mileage. It barely covers the cost of owning and maintaining your personal car and does nothing if you have a major repair. At the end of three years, you are left with a worn out car that you must replace. I have deducted $5000 as depreciation on your personal car.

Some reps at Job B will lease a car for their job, and assume that after five years the company reimbursement has bought them a car. They are left with the residual value as income. You may want to consult with your tax accountant on which is best for you.

Compensation Package	Job A	Job B
Company Car	$8,000 per year	32.5 cents per mile for your car.
Subtotal	$92,000	$92,000

The two job offers appear to be the same. Job A supplies you with a laptop and fax machine which you need for the territory. I have assigned no intrinsic value to Job A, although you have access to the laptop for personal use. Job two requires you to supply your own. Assuming a three year life span, the cost is $1,166 per year, but you must layout $3,500 in year one when you start your job. This assumes you don't already own either a laptop or fax.

Compensation Package	Job A	Job B
Computer, fax machine	$0	$92,000—$3,500
Subtotal	$92,000	$88,500

Now job one looks more appealing. You must have medical insurance for you and your family. This costs, on average, $5,000 per year for Job A, which only offers access to group rates, but does not cover the premiums. You must deduct $5,000. Job B pays the full premium for you and your family.

Compensation Package	Job A	Job B
Medical Package	$92,000—$5,000	$0
Subtotal	$87,000	$88,500

At this point the two offers are almost the same. For the sake of simplicity, both jobs offer you a 401-K savings plan, up to 6 percent of your pre tax income. Job A matches every pre tax dollar you contribute dollar for dollar. Job B matches with 50. Said another way, for each dollar you contribute in Job B the company matches it with 50. Since Job B pays you $97,000 in base and commission they give you and additional $2,910 for your 401K. ($97,000 * 3% = $2,910) For each dollar in Job A, the company matches it with a $1.00 ($85,000 * 6% = $5,100)

Compensation Package	Job One	Job Two
Contributions to 401K	$1.00 on the dollar	50 cents on the dollar
Grand total	*$92,100*	*$91,410*

With all else being the same, Job A pays you $690 more per year than Job B. A dramatic difference from the initial chart above that only compared base salary and commission. This exercise revealed that the two jobs pay just about the same. Now other differences are more important and can sway your decision. Those differences can be many. Is there greater potential in one job over the other? Was one territory neglected for a long time, while the other was covered very well? This may give you a greater opportunity to exceed quota and earn more commission and bonus.

Which job has the best corporate culture, opportunity for advancement and stability? Would you have been willing to accept the less desirable Job B, thinking that the $12,000 extra per year would compensate you? In the final analysis, you have to decide which job will benefit you the most over the long haul. Now you have enough information to make an informed decision.

MAKE NO MISTAKE. COMPANIES HAVE SPENT YEARS FINE TUNING THEIR COMPENSATION PACKAGES. JOB B KNOWS FULL WELL THAT THEIR BASE SALARY PLUS COMMISSION OFFER IS MISLEADING. THEY WANT TO LURE YOU AWAY FROM THE COMPETITION, HOPING YOU WON'T DO THE MATH OR ASK THE RIGHT QUESTIONS.

You may wonder why a company would want someone who doesn't thoroughly analyze a job offer. It's simple; they aren't hiring a CPA. They are looking for a sales rep who can bring in business. Companies love reps who are poor bookkeepers. They save a fortune on reps who don't check commission reports for errors and who don't bother to submit expense reports. More on this later.

As a footnote to the above exercise, I did not know the outcome of the comparison when I started. I choose the base salary and commission at random and worked my way through the problem. I planned that Job A would be much higher paying than Job B. This would show how misleading offers can be. That happened, but not in a way I expected. I was surprised to learn that the two jobs paid almost the same. I decided to leave the example as is. This demonstrates how important this exercise is even for someone like me who has been doing this for thirty years.

ONCE YOU QUIT, STAY QUIT.

Al worked for a boss who practiced management by fear. One by one the best reps were leaving the company. The costly process to recruit, hire and train a replacement took a month.

Al was fed up with the terrible work environment and was actively looking for a better job. When he found one, he resigned.

The manager and his boss, the regional manager, called Al and invited him and his wife, Becky, to dinner at a four star restaurant. The two managers expressed their shock that Al would leave. Al listed his complaints about the company and the great offer from the competitor.

The regional manager said, "Al, you're our number one rep in the region, and we're very pleased with your work. (Al was number one by default; the top three reps had quit.) Whenever we have a special sales promotion, we know that you will do fine. There is never any question, if we forget to tell you that during the heat of battle, well... that's our shortfall. As regional manager I'm here to apologize."

The divisional manager chimed in, "Al, it was only last week that I was telling everyone at our managers meeting, I was lucky to have you on board. When the chips are down, I can count on you to come through. When the other reps have a question, they call you for help, sometimes bypassing me. I admit that makes me a bit jealous, but your grasp of product knowledge and your creative sales technique is about the best I've ever seen. I would consider it a personal favor if you would reconsider your decision."

Al responded, "The offer from the other company is just too good to pass up. My work load has increased steadily but I haven't gotten a raise in two years."

The regional manager said, "Al, I understand. You have a family to support and Becky is expecting another baby in June. It's a very tempting offer. I respect your priorities, so give me a chance to make a counter offer."

The regional manager offered 20 percent above the other company's offer. (He didn't address Al; rather, he focused his attention on Becky.) He threw in a promotion to manager within six months and a work / play trip to San Francisco for a weeklong medical conference.

"Al, decide now, and you can take Becky and your son with you, at company expense. You will have to work the conference, but your wife and son can enjoy the hotel all day long. Then you will have the evenings to yourselves."

"How can you make a counter offer? Last month at the sales meeting, you said all salaries were frozen to comply with the President's wage and price freeze."

"Al, if you want to get into management, you have to understand we take advantage of situations like the President's War on Inflation. It keeps the sales force in line and to keeps our budget down. For special times like this, I have some leeway in salary that's tied to a promotion. Say yes now, and I will handle the rest."

By this time, Al had three quarters of a bottle of wine in him and his head was swimming with the offer. Becky's eyes were bulging and she was eager to accept the offer. Al extended his hand and accepted the counter offer and said he would call the other company the next day to decline the job.

With that, the regional manager excused himself from the table to attend another engagement. The division manager stayed until the end of the meal. The manager made no further discussion about the job.

The next morning, Al called the manager who had offered him the new job and told him about the counter offer and his decision. No amount of persuasion could change Al's mind. He felt obligated.

The other manager warned him that it may be a ruse to keep him on long enough until they found a replacement. He would then be out of a job. Al stuck to his guns.

After the next two paychecks came through, Al still hadn't received his raise or the tickets for his family for San Francisco. He called his divisional manager but never got a straight answer.

The next month, when the San Francisco medical conference was to begin, Al got a call. "Al, I'm sorry to say this, but there was a mix up on the medical conference. The wires got crossed and the rep in San Francisco will attend the conference. We just can't justify the extra cost of flying the three of you out there if we have a rep that lives in the area. I promise that the next trip will be yours."

Seven weeks passed since the dinner meeting. Al had received neither the raise nor the promotion. His manager called him late one night and asked to meet him at a local hotel the next morning. Al was to bring his account cards, price book and special material with him. At nine o'clock, Al entered the lobby and met his boss.

"Al, the regional manager is waiting for us upstairs. Let's go."

When they entered the room, the regional manager said, "Al, I'm not one to beat around the bush, we're disappointed in your work performance during the last two months. I guess the promotion offer went to your head. Today will be your last day."

We met the replacement at our next meeting and learned that the company hired him three weeks before they fired Al. He had already been to the training class. The day Al was fired, the new rep was in place and covering the territory. Al was out of work for sixteen months before he got another job and for less money than his old one.

NEVER ACCEPT A COUNTER OFFER. WHEN YOU QUIT, STAY QUIT.

NEVER BURN BRIDGES

When you resign, give your old company the customary two weeks notice and leave on good terms. They will most likely tell you that will be your last day. They don't want you out in the field telling customers you're leaving. It's in their best interest to fire you as soon as possible.

Your employer may conduct an exit interview. They ask why you're leaving, and to register any complaints that led to your decision. Your former company spent a great deal of money to hire, train and employ you. They want to know what is wrong so they can make adjustments.

Never blind-side anyone and never burn any bridges, no matter how badly they treated you. You never know if a former co-worker or boss may one-day end up in the same company you do. It's a small world in sales. The person you badmouth at an exit interview today may turn out to be your national sales manager in five years. Your old company could buy your new company. You would have to face the same management team. Do you want them to nurse any grudges?

BOOT CAMP

Sometime within the first six months of employment at a large corporation, they may send you to a special school for sales and product training. I call these classes boot camp or Hell week. It depends on the industry. Usually, you stay in a hotel close to the corporate headquarters. They give you a tremendous amount of information on the company, products, services, paperwork, company procedures and sales training.

The classes vary in size, scope and length and intensity. Despite what anyone tells you, everything you say and do is reported to your manager. He or she will see all tests, assignments and video sales presentations you make. This is a final test to see if you have the potential for success.

I know reps at different companies, who elected to party all night instead of studying. Others tried to arrange liaisons with female members of the class. A few people got drunk at dinner and brought a call girl into the hotel. Another stayed in her room each night and ordered expensive meals and wine from room service, although we received a memo expressly forbidding that. She ordered massages, made long distance calls, got a manicure and charged it all to the company master bill. They were all fired.

Another rep rented a car, went out drinking, got involved in a hit and run and drove the car through a show room window. One guy picked a fist fight with another sales rep. Three guys partied all night and went through the hotel, breaking windows, light fixtures and defecated in the hotel pool. They were arrested for disorderly conduct and were fired.

One person left the hotel on the first day of class and didn't return for three days. His excuse was, his manager told him that the sales training class was informal. No one would make reports or take attendance. He used the time to visit his girl friend. He was fired.

I can't stress enough how important it is to prepare for the class. The reason they give you the pre-study material is so they don't have to go over it in class. If you don't know this material thoroughly, you slow the class and make yourself look bad.

TAKE THE CLASS SERIOUSLY. STUDY ALL MATERIAL AHEAD OF TIME. KNOW YOUR STUFF. YOUR MANAGER WILL FIND OUT!

BENEFITS

Sign up for every benefit offered, even if you feel it isn't necessary. These benefits include long-term disability, life insurance, payroll deductions for savings, purchase of company stock and 401K plan, health club membership and automatic deposit of the payroll into your bank account.

The forced saving of a 401K plan is the best. You can place up to 6 percent of your income, before taxes, in an account that earns interest. Many companies match your contribution with 50 on the dollar. With earning of $50,000 per year, $3,000 pretax dollars are set aside and matched with an additional $1,500 from the company. That's an instant 50 percent return on your investment and it's all pre tax money.

Automatic deposit of your payroll check is another benefit that is great. They wire my salary directly to my checking account each payday, deposited as cash. I don't have to wait for the mail, drive to the bank, stand in line and wait seven days for the check to clear.

SALARY NEGOTIATIONS

When you negotiate for an entry-level salaried position, with a medium to large company, a budget determines the salary. The person hiring you has little leeway in how much you will earn. Your recruiter can tell you what the job pays, so you should go into the first interview with a knowledge of your earning potential.

Be careful of how you answer money questions if you pursue the job without a recruiter. He may have a range of $25,000 to $30,000 for an entry-level position. Don't ask for $40,000 without knowing his budget, you will eliminate yourself from consideration. The best response is, "I understand that most companies of this size have salary guidelines. I'm sure they are fair. My interest is in long term growth and potential, not immediate compensation." You have put the ball back in the interviewer's court.

The interviewer may hedge, "Well, give me an approximate number."

Your safest response is, "I'm prepared to accept the average starting salary. I'm anxious to become part of your team." It's what you can do for them, not what they can do for you.

An experienced salaried rep should take his last salary and add 20 percent. This is a guideline to determine the salary range. If you are now earning $30,000 on your present job and wish to make a lateral move to another company, it is reasonable to expect a 20 percent increase to $36,000. This is based on your record of accomplishment. Since you are still employed, you have the advantage of demanding an increase. On the other hand, if you are unemployed, you may feel pressured to take any salary offered. Keep in mind if you're not using a headhunter, the company is saving about $5,000 in fees.

A seasoned pro with at least seven years sales experience and a proven record that is being recruited by a competitive company can negotiate a larger increase. When asked about salary he can reply, "Here is my W2 form from last year. A 30 percent increase would be fair and reasonable."

Remember that they want you. It's time your hard work and good reputation paid off. This is another example of why it is important to stay with your old job until you get a new one. You are working and can afford to shop around until you get the salary you want.

A salary plus bonus or draw vs. commission has little negotiating room, even for experienced reps. All reps may receive the same draw of about $35,000 per year.

DRAW VS COMMISSION

This is a compensation package designed to help you with a weekly cash flow until your commission check comes in. The company subtracts the draw you receive from earned commissions. Consider the "draw" a loan until your commission check arrives.

For example, your draw is $35,000 per year. ($2,916 a month) In January you earn $4,500 in commission. They deduct your draw of $2,916 (Which you have already received.) and pay you a balance of $1,584. Your income for January is $4,500.

In February, your commission is $2,000. You have received $2,916 in draw and are in the red for $916. This is carried over to March. March commission is $6,000 and you receive $6,000 minus the March draw of $2,916, minus February's red balance of $916. Your income for March would be $5,084.

For the three months you have received $8,748 in draw against $12,500 in commission. Your total income is $12,500. Do that well every quarter and your yearly income would be $50,000.

On the other hand if your commissions are less than the $12,500 for the quarter, you will owe a red balance going into the next quarter. Most companies will cut off your draw if your red balance equals one month's draw.

STRAIGHT COMMISSION

Like stud poker, what you see is what you get. There are no wild cards, no bonuses and no draw. When you earn $5,000 in commissions, you receive $5,000. If you earn no commissions, you get nothing for your effort. It is the same as if you are working for yourself in your own business.

SALARY PLUS COMMISSION

This is a base salary plus commission. Regardless of your commission earned, you keep your salary. There is no deduction as in draw vs. commission. As an example, your salary is $25,000 per year and you earn $30,000 in commissions; your income for the year is $55,000. Under this arrangement you may be required to service established accounts and handle various issues that come up. You may have certain products in your sales bag that are not commissioned and you don't get sales credit for selling them. The company considers this work covered under your base salary.

SALARY PLUS BONUS

This is a variation of salary plus commission. You receive a salary, plus bonus every quarter for exceeding your sales quota. This is common in mid-level salaried sales position. Almost every sales position, regardless of commission or salary, offers bonuses. They are all the same; they just make you qualify for the money in different ways.

VALUE OF THE FRINGES

Each company, despite the compensation package, offers fringe benefits. You must understand the value of these when negotiating for salary. By acknowledging their value, you demonstrate maturity and foresight. Examples for a $35,000 salary job:

- A company car: $5,000 per year.
- Health Insurance: $6,000 per year.
- A computer: $3,000 for the first year.
- A 401K plan: $1,500, based on 6 percent withholdings and a matching contribution of 50 on the dollar.

These benefits total $15,500; in addition, your $35,000 salary and your job are worth $50,500 per year.

There are benefits to both you and your employer for this type of arrangement. Instead of simply paying you $50,000 a year and telling you to supply your own car and benefits, they offer you nontaxable income that places you in a lower tax bracket. They, in turn, can negotiate with vendors for volume discounts and can offer you a $52,000 package for $45,000. You may pay $3,000 for a computer, but by buying in bulk, the company only pays $2,500. They may purchase an entire fleet and save thousands per car. A group health plan is far less than you buying an individual plan. Multiply that $5,000 savings per rep times the number of reps in your company and the amount is substantial.

Chapter Three

INTERPERSONAL RELATIONSHIPS

BE NICE TO EVERYONE

In the early 1970's, while struggling in my advertising career, I often worked as a bartender to help make ends meet. I walked into a college pub and approached the woman behind the bar. I asked if she was the owner. When she said yes, I asked if she needed any help. Jenny offered me a job on the spot.

Later, Jenny told me there were ten others who had applied for the job. I asked why she had selected me when others had more experience.

Jenny said, "You were the only one who asked me if I was the owner. Most assume that since I am a woman, I am just a barmaid. I worked hard for this place and invested my life savings to have my own business. It's nice when someone recognizes that, in even a small way."

In contrast, I worked in the field with a rep named Link who held women in contempt and believed they should be home cooking, cleaning and having babies.

We were cold calling on lawyers and Link was trying to bulldoze his way past a receptionist. The woman became defensive saying she was too busy and we should call to set an appointment.

Link said, "Listen little girl, go back and tell your boss I'm here."

With that the woman stood up, fists clinched and through grinding teeth said, "I'm the boss; I'm the lawyer. This is my practice and I wouldn't buy a book from you if you were the last publisher on earth. Now get out of here."

As we walked to the next office, Link shrugged, "Women have an attitude. You just can't deal with 'em."

I remembered that experience. When I cold call canvass and the receptionist seems distracted or just trying to get rid of me, I ask, "Are you the owner / doctor / lawyer?" Most of the time I get a quick smile and a polite "No, I wish I were! May I help you?" Moreover, on occasion, I hear: "Yes I am. My secretary is out sick today and I'm trying to figure out the phone system. What can I do for you?"

One manager complained that I was too nice to people. He said, "Mike, you could socialize with the scum of the earth. It will hold you back in your career development. Many perceive niceness as weakness, and you won't get the support you need to advance in management." He may have had a point, however, that's my nature and it has worked to my advantage.

I was calling on a grocery store when a young man approached me. I knew him from somewhere, but couldn't recall where. He wore a grin from ear to ear and extended his hand. He told me that he was the new store manager and was glad to see me again. I was at a loss, so he explained.

"For years, I was a lowly stock boy and the suits (his term for anyone who wore a suit to work.) would brush by me in the aisles as if I was invisible, all except you. Though I couldn't give you any orders, you always stopped and said, 'Hi kid, how's it going?' We always exchanged a few words."

I still didn't remember him. I say hello to almost every employee in the store I pass, if they respond, I may stop and talk for a moment. The turnover in the grocery industry is so great that faces become a blur after a while.

He continued. "I always appreciated that. Soon I was transferred to another store and was promoted to assistant manager. Now I'm manager and you're my rep." He handed me the store's order book and said, "You own this place; send me what I need."

A few years later, he was promoted to supervisor in charge of seven stores. We had a great relationship and I always got full promotional support from him and his managers.

MANAGEMENT
NEW MANAGER SYNDROME (NMS)

The sales representative general has determined that new management syndrome is hazardous to your career. There is no prevention. The only cure is experience.

Virtually every person promoted to management will experience New Manager Syndrome. It's a condition caused by an otherwise competent salesperson being thrown into a position with new responsibilities.

As a sales rep, you have almost complete control of your territory, or at least as much as your colleagues have. When your sales are down, you quickly look for opportunities to fill and you work on correcting them.

Once, when I was below quota midway through the second quarter, I reviewed my year-to-date sales by product, saw where my strengths were and focused on my weak areas. It turned out that I'd been ignoring a brand because it hadn't done particularly well historically. I focused my attention on that brand for the next six weeks. At the end of the quarter, I'd been able to generate enough business to put myself just above quota. The brand was still weak but I got enough movement to correct the problem.

When you're a new manager, you quickly find out that you must depend on others to correct problems and consequently you may feel inadequate. The skills that made you a successful sales rep are for the most part useless in a managerial position. You must motivate your sales force to concentrate on a particular problem and hope they follow through, whereas in the past, you would simply fix the problem yourself. The tendency is for the new manager to follow the "book" to the letter so as not to be accused of missing something by his own boss.

The "Book" is a written, or unwritten, set of rules and regulations that governs the business's daily activities. The "Book" may say that you may only give one permanent display piece to a customer at no charge. However, a good manager may bend that rule to accommodate a customer in a highly competitive marketplace in exchange for promotional activity.

This is frustrating for a sales force that knew the manager before the company promoted him. They know that as a rep he worked completely different from than the way he tells them to work.

Following is a checklist to determine if your boss suffers from New Manager Syndrome:

1. Forgetting everything he knew as a rep that made him successful.
2. Following the "Book" to the letter of the law.
3. Buying in on "Manager Hype" 100 percent.
4. Becoming a stickler for unimportant detail.
5. Saying dumb things at meetings.
6. In role play: assuming the role of a buyer and being intentionally "hard nosed."
7. Discounting feedback from the experienced reps.
8. Acting as a-know-it-all when working with more experienced reps.
9. Directing reps to do things he or she never did as a rep.

10. Thinking that what worked well in one part of the country will automatically work well in another.
11. Assumes that the sales reps have problems when, in fact, none exist.

Most new managers overcome NMS within a year and go on to be very good leaders. As the new manager settles into his position, he or she gains more confidence and begins to loosen up. They learn when it is necessary to follow the "Book," as with a sales rep that is caught stealing from a customer. Then there are the times they look the other way as when a rep goes through a nasty divorce and it affects his work. However, the first year of "Breaking in a New Manager" can be frustrating.

Some experienced reps see NMS as an opportunity to take advantage of a new manager. A newly promoted manager was transferred to the northeast. The rep heard that we were due for territory realignments and that we were getting new people for an expansion. He pumped bogus business into his territory that had recently fallen on hard times. When the new manager arrived, the rep offered to give up his "prime territory" for the downtown section of Manhattan, to help the region and the new people. The new manager simply compared the latest shipment records and not the territories' history. Being from the South, he was unfamiliar with the downtown section of New York and its potential. The section had been vacant for almost a year and was ripe for picking. The rep easily misled the new manager. The new rep got stuck with a bad territory and the experienced rep made bonus and won every contest the company offered that year. An experienced manager would have made a more in-depth territory review.

The best method of dealing with NMS is to go along with everything the manager asks and slowly bring him around. When he works with you in the field, show him the reality of doing business without sounding like you're simply resistant to change.

If the manager introduces a program that you believe will be counter productive, take him or her to an appropriate customer and experiment with the idea. If it fails then ask, "Well, as you see I tried your program, and it didn't work. What do you suggest I do now?"

This leaves the new manager an opening for a graceful exit and the opportunity to ask what you think. A good response would be, "Well in the past what I've done is..." Then give the manager the chance to reconsider the plan.

Often, my colleagues and I have gotten gung-ho new managers to back off silly programs by taking them out into the field, so they can see the buyer's reaction first hand. This is part of breaking in a new manager.

In the grocery industry, we got a new manager from the Midwest who had a great way to sell displays to grocers. Part of our job was to get each grocery manager to buy a large quantity of our product and put it on an end cap display to support a newspaper ad that we were running. Most retail stores in New York City are limited in shelf and floor space. The competition is fierce and the store managers have little patience for sales reps, especially ones that try to be cute.

Our new manager, Chuck, fresh off the bus from the Midwest, told us how he always got the grocery manager's attention and a sizable order. He took a $5 bill and taped it to a baseball. He would go into the store and tell the manager about the program and say, "Now this is what will happen if you don't put up our display." He would roll the ball out the door and say, "There goes your profit rolling out the door." He would pick up the ball, throw it inside to the manager and conclude, "Or you can toss the profits in your register."

The point being: the grocery manager was letting his profits go out the door if he didn't promote our products with a big display. Chuck swore this was so unique; it always worked. He wanted us to try it on our next ten calls.

We tried to persuade him that it was a good idea to get the manager's attention, but this was too parochial for the New York market. Chuck was convinced that we were just being closed minded to new ideas. He insisted we try it anyway and announced he would work with me the next day. We would report to the region on our success.

Our first call was to a chain store in the heart of a tough Brooklyn neighborhood. This was as about as far away from Kansas City as you could get. When Chuck demonstrated his special presentation to the grocery manager, we certainly had his attention. The three of us watched as the ball rolled out of the door and onto the sidewalk where several teenagers were standing.

They jumped on the ball, grabbed it and began running down the street laughing with delight. We stood there as Chuck chased the kids to get his ball back. After a moment the store manager asked, "Where the heck you find him?"

"Kansas City." I replied.

"Well, you better go get him before he runs those kids halfway to Harlem and back." He shook his head and walked away.

I got into my car and drove about three blocks. I saw Chuck standing on the corner of Myrtle Avenue, with a look of bewilderment on his face. He was completely lost and had no idea how to get back to the store. As Chuck got into the car, he asked if we should go to the police station to file a report. I asked, "How are you going to explain the money taped to the baseball and what you were doing with it?"

Chuck looked at me and said, "Just forget it." He never mentioned his special technique again.

I'm not making fun of the people from the mid-west! Reps in Kansas City work just as hard as those in New York, however they face a different set of problems.

I know if I relocated to Kansas and used my, "grab the buyer by the throat and bang his head against the wall until he buys something" technique that works so well in New York that I would soon starve to death. Things aren't done that way in other parts of the country. Chuck was experiencing New Manager Syndrome. [New Manager Syndrome checklist points: seven, ten and eleven.]

First, is point ten. Our new manager assumed what worked well for him in Kansas would work just as well in New York. All we had to do was try.

His second error, point seven, was that he allowed his enthusiasm to override his judgment. He was so excited about sharing his success story that he completely ignored the feedback from his experienced reps.

His third mistake, point eleven, was that he didn't first go into the field to see if we had any problems in getting the buyer's attention. He assumed that we did and his job was to correct it.

Within a year our new boss had settled down and became a very good manager. Other infractions of the New Manager Syndrome checklist were so minor and infrequent that they don't deserve mentioning.

The other side of the coin is some of his ideas worked and I found new ways to sell. That is why I always say, "Try a new idea at least three times before you pass judgment." Your new boss was promoted because he or she was a top rep in his region. You would be doing yourself a great disservice ignoring his advice without first trying it out.

One way to minimize NMS is for the company to create an intern manager position. A rep would work for several different managers for one year before his or her promotion. This would give the intern time to learn the demographics, sales team and managerial tasks. After the intern period, he or she would be up to speed and ready to assume a leadership role.

THE MANAGER FROM HELL

Early in my career, I had my first encounter with the "Manager From Hell." He wasn't the only one I worked for but he was the worst.

Zeke was a sales superstar who had turned a very weak territory into a productive one. The company stressed the importance of promoting only those with the best sales records to management. However, they provided no training for this new responsibility.

UPPER MANAGEMENT ASSUMED THAT IF A REP CAN SELL, THEN HE OR SHE CAN MANAGE THOSE WHO SELL.

As a rep, Zeke had a great personality. He spoke to his colleagues often and was eager to share his expertise with anyone who sought his counsel.

At the time of Zeke's promotion as our manager, our region was the top producing sales force in the country. Everyone was at or above quota. Morale was excellent and we were confident of winning the national sales contest.

To reward the number one region, the company would send the winning sales reps, their spouses and the manager to a four star resort in the Caribbean. This all expense paid vacation was an incredible motivation.

Zeke wasted no time in establishing himself as the new manager and instituting his policies, which were often contrary to those of the company. There are too many things to list. The worst were calling his reps at five o'clock in the morning to ask about business. Rerouting territories even if the rep knew it wasn't the most effective use of time. Zeke would insist that our sales bags and supplies be arranged similarly to the way he kept his bag and supplies. We may have had account cards arranged in sequential order to match our itinerary. Zeke would place them in alphabetical order because that's the way he worked.

Some of these things aren't bad, if warranted. However, Zeke had no discretion for wholesale criticism. It didn't matter if the rep was new and floundering or a twenty-five year veteran and number one in the country. Zeke spared no one from his micro management. He assumed that we were all incompetents and only he knew the best way to do things.

Upon reflection, I believe Zeke thought this was what a manager was supposed to do. He had no managerial training, and didn't know how to teach. Zeke said if we were doing a good job then one of us would have been promoted instead of him. Therefore, the company promoted him to get everyone to work exactly as he worked. His mission was to create an entire region of Zeke clones.

Zeke used a stopwatch to see how much time we spent driving between accounts and how long we spent in each call. During the sales calls, he interrupted our presentations to the buyer and took over. If he failed to get an order, which was often, he noted in our evaluations that we missed opportunities to get sales.

While driving to an account, Zeke would pepper us with product knowledge questions making it hard to concentrate on our driving. He would ask us to explain expenses from prior months without letting us review the paperwork. He distracted me once and I missed the exit for my appointment. Traffic was slow and by the time I got to the next exit and turned around, we arrived twenty-five minutes late. We had just missed the buyer. Zeke reported to the regional manager that I didn't know my way around the territory, got lost easily, and probably wasn't working the field every day. At the time, I was 109 percent of quota and third in the region in dollar volume.

Zeke spent prime selling time on a pay phone picking up his messages and returning calls. I would have to stand idly by. He then criticized my productivity for the day.

To save time he would tell us to drive the wrong way on one way streets, park in no parking areas or even drive on side walks if the street was blocked. In addition, if we got a ticket in the process, then we had to pay for it.

He began disallowing expense reimbursements normally approved by the company, such as postage, telephone calls, photocopies and parking meters.

When I talked to friends about the hell we were going through, most advised me to simply look for another job. Some boasted that they wouldn't put up with that and would either punch the jerk out or just quit.

That was easy to say. Those were the days of double-digit unemployment and jobs were hard to come by. When you have a family to support, you think twice before you make a rash decision. It was an employer's market. Several of us went job hunting; however, the employment agencies told us that times were bad and we should stay where we were until something better came along. Our division had dropped to third place and several top reps did find better jobs with the competition. Eventually, Zeke was demoted and put back in the field as a rep.

A year later, I ran into Zeke at a company function. He confided that it was a relief to get out of management. He never liked it. He felt that everyone hated him and that he wasn't very effective.

I asked Zeke how he got along with his new boss. He said, "Great! The guy is super. He leaves me alone, never butts in during a sales presentation and is a wonderful morale booster for the region."

Over the years I've collected horror stories from colleagues at other companies that made Zeke look tame by comparison. Many reps resign to the fact that they are trapped until the manager is forced out or promoted. Others pursue available options or leave sales all together.

How do you deal with a manager like Zeke? Unfortunately, it's not easy and I have no clear-cut answers.

My advice to those who are in this situation is:
- Don't fight your manager. You will always lose.
- Document everything.
- Keep your options open.
- Realize that in life you will always meet difficult people.
- Remember, what goes around, comes around. Often these situations have a way of resolving themselves. Don't quit an otherwise great job over a temporary situation.

THE MANAGER FROM HEAVEN

When our manager, Kevin, worked in the field with us, he made us believe his only purpose was to make sure we were happy with our job.

Intellectually, we knew better. Kevin was under the same stress as all of the other managers. There was pressure to meet and exceed quota, merchandising objectives, promotional support and expense management. There were the administrative tasks of paperwork and recruiting. Kevin kept his sales force insulated from that, so we could focus on our responsibility to sell more stuff.

Upper management would deliver a "fire and brimstone" sermon to the front line managers. They yelled, screamed and threatened everyone with their jobs. They in turn would call their own regional meetings and deliver the same threats to their reps—all except Kevin. He would say to me, "Mike, did you get that squeak in your car fixed? I know it was bothering you. How is your daughter doing in school? Does she still want to be a doctor?" Kevin would pass along the important information from his meeting, but it was almost an after thought.

Kevin would tell us about the slump in sales and the company's plan to correct it. He would ask for our ideas but he would omit all of the fear tactics such as job threats and poor performance reviews. We knew about the pressure from the reps in other regions. They told us they felt that the weight of the entire company rested on their shoulders and if they didn't perform, they would be out.

At one point, I had a bureaucratic nightmare that involved my purchase of company stock through a payroll deduction. Simply put, I had $70 per month, $35 every two weeks, deducted from my check to purchase company stock. I could buy fractional shares and the company paid all expenses including the sales commission. It was a great benefit and I took advantage of it when I qualified.

I received a statement of my account every three months. I reviewed it and filed it away. After nine months I noticed a discrepancy in the statement. The report showed I had exactly one half the number of shares in relationship to the dollar amounts that payroll deducted from my check.

NEVER BRING A PROBLEM TO YOUR MANAGER'S ATTENTION, UNLESS YOU FIRST TRY TO CORRECT IT YOURSELF.

I called the payroll department and they said that everything was in order and I should contact the brokerage firm. The firm said all money sent to them from my company was used to buy shares. They suggested that I go back to my payroll department. They passed the buck back and forth; each saying it wasn't their fault.

This went on for another six months. I was getting nowhere and the discrepancy was more than $1,000. When I got my next statement, the problem still existed. I waited until I was working with Kevin to ask for his help. We were driving into the city and I said, "Kevin, I've got a small problem. I've tried to resolve it myself, but I've run into a brick wall." Kevin looked a bit annoyed and he asked me to explain. I told him about the account balance and the run around I got from everyone. I could see Kevin doing a slow burn. I thought he was mad at me for bothering him with a problem that I should be able to resolve myself.

"How long have you had this problem?" Kevin asked.

"About twelve months."

"How much money are we talking about?"

"About $1,300 plus dividend for the missing shares; then there was the two for one stock split. I've tried to document everything. I'm sorry for bothering you with this."

Then Kevin pointed to a pay phone on the service road to the expressway and said, "Stop here, I have to make a call."

He took the paperwork, went to the phone and started dialing. I stayed in my car and watched Kevin's animated actions as he screamed at someone, I presumed, in our payroll department. His arms and papers were flailing about. I was glad I wasn't on the other end of that telephone.

Kevin returned to the car and we headed for the city. He was visibly angry, but didn't say anything for the longest time.

"Why did you wait so long to tell me?" He asked.

"I try to correct problems on my own without bothering you."

"I appreciate that, but a year was too long to wait."

"What did payroll have to say?"

"Nothing. I never gave her the chance. I told that idiot you have been dealing with, that she had until two o'clock to resolve the problem. If she didn't, then my next call was to her boss."

We continued with the day and didn't discuss the issue again.

At exactly two o'clock, we were in the middle of a sales call when Kevin abruptly left the store. Later, I met him outside, where he was waiting for me.

"Mike, the problem has been resolved. They now acknowledge the mistake was on our end. Your account has been fully credited with all shares and dividends. Our residential CPA in the home office is verifying the numbers. You should receive written confirmation by Friday—if not, call me."

That Friday, I received an apology letter, signed by the head of the accounting department. He said when my account was set up; two payroll deductions were entered, as prescribed by the plan. The first was on the 15th of the month and the second, on the 30th. Unfortunately, the keypunch operator had transposed numbers in my social security number. This resulted in the correct dollar amount being deducted, but the second payment was put into a different account. This resulted in the discrepancy. He apologized for the inconvenience.

I called and told Kevin about the letter. He knew about it already. He had accounting send him a copy as well. I thanked him again for his help.

"That's as much a part of my job as shipping product each month." Kevin replied.

In later years, my colleagues and I've run into similar problems at other companies. No manager has taken control and responsibility the way Kevin did. At another company some reps complained that they hadn't received expense reimbursement check for six months. "That's because they are sitting on my desk waiting to be signed. Your expense checks are on the bottom of my priority list," the manager replied.

Kevin was the greatest when it came to his people. He was demanding in every aspect of the job but he was always there for us when we needed it. That is why we would go the extra mile for him, put in the extra effort and follow Kevin through the gates of hell. At the time, Kevin had two reps working for him. In 1983, my colleague was the sales rep of the year. The following year was my turn. I believe Kevin was the only manager to have 100 percent of his team win this award.

To the cynics who say, sure, with only two reps, he had time to attend to such things. I say that my current manager has a dozen reps and always has time to help us out.

MANAGERS: WORKING VS NON-WORKING

A few years ago, I was planning a hunting trip. Larry, my brother-in-law, offered me his prize hunting dog, named Sales Rep. Larry boasted that Sales Rep was the best hunting dog ever born, so I stopped by to pick up the dog.

When we got to the hunting field, Sales Rep bolted into the thicket and began scouting for quail. I barely got out of the car when the dog flushed a prize bird from the underbrush. I shot the quail and Sales Rep took off into the marsh to retrieve the game. Within two hours I had my limit.

When I returned the dog, I raved about how great he was. Larry promised I could use him any time I wanted.

Before my next hunting trip, I called Larry and asked if I could borrow Sales Rep. He said, "No, that dog doesn't hunt any more."

I insisted, recounting our last great outing. Finally Larry relented, "Alright, but you will regret it."

When I got to Larry's, Sales Rep wouldn't budge. I had to physically pick the dog up and put him in the car. When we got to the field, I had to drag the dog out of the car. He just sat there all day barking and nipping at my heels. He wouldn't move nor would he flush out the quail. The trip was a disaster.

That night I returned Sales Rep and asked what was wrong.

Larry lamented, "Someone called him 'Sales Manager' by mistake, now all he does is sit on his ass and bark." (–Unknown)

There are two types of managers. There are those who, besides managing their reps, call on major accounts. Then there are those who do nothing but manage. I don't mean that in a pejorative sense. The role of upper management is to motivate and delegate. The role of front line management is to get into the trenches with the reps and join the battle, but different industries have different ideas on how to do that.

In my career, I've worked for both types of managers. The ones who maintained an active account base were by far the best. I could call upon these managers for practical advice anytime. They faced the same problems, rejection, competition and company bureaucracy, that I faced on a daily basis.

When I sold high-speed photocopiers, I told my boss, Pete, that I faced a certain objection on a new copier that I couldn't overcome. He said, "I know, I hear it all the time at my accounts. Why not try this approach next time you hear it." He explained how he overcame the objection. "It has worked for me a few times. I spoke to the manufacturer about it and they are getting more info for us."

This contrasts with the pharmaceutical industry where managers didn't have their own account base. Typically when I had a problem selling a medication, my manager gave me a rehash of the company line, written by the product manager.

We had introduced a new medication that had benefits that the leading product did not have. However, once we began detailing the new drug to physicians, many of us in the field ran into skepticism over a particular claim. When we reported to our managers, they simply reaffirmed the original claim. In the product manager's opinion, we either didn't understand the claim or we weren't working hard enough.

First, the product manager had no sales experience. Secondly, he didn't have to go out in the field and sell the product. When isolated from the front line, many managers tended to buy in on the company hype about the product.

At our next regional sales meeting, the product manager addressed our concerns by showing us a slide of a sales rep, wearing a suit and pole-vaulting. The analogy was that this objection was an easy one to overcome, if we just tried. Again, he repeated the original claim supported by the weak data. He said that we weren't showing enough enthusiasm during our presentations.

"Give 'em the facts with enough gusto and those doctors will jump over the desk to thank you."

I asked a colleague, "How would he know how much enthusiasm we have? He has never been in the field with any of us."

The company gave us no additional ammunition to support the claim. Eventually, many of us simply omitted the claim from our presentations. The physicians weren't buying it without better supporting data and we were damaging our credibility. Even our competitors began to tell the physicians we were exaggerating our products benefits.

When I worked for Kevin, the manager from Heaven who was a working manager, we were introducing many new products and line extensions. Kevin advised us to make sure we followed the product manager's introduction strategy to the letter. We should document as much of our work as possible with copies of circulars, photos of displays and so forth. This would be insurance in case the product failed in its introduction. Kevin had full confidence in our sales ability, but he knew that the reps would be blamed if product management didn't do its job.

We were introducing a new shampoo nationally and the company planned to support us with a media blitz of advertising. The major campaign included a $1 off coupon in local newspapers, the week of the launch. The sales force went into the field and did its job. We secured major account support, window displays, cut case displays and circulars to support the $1 off coupon. The product took off like a rocket everywhere except in New York City. Product management was quick to blame us for the dismal results, citing the strong sell-through elsewhere in the country. Kevin never told us of the pressure he was under, but many of us in the region knew he was in trouble.

Fortunately, we had taken his advice and documented sales and the merchandising support to insure the products sell-through. I'm sure Kevin used this information in his defense.

Several months later, Kevin discovered why sales were so weak in our market. Product management had neglected to order the $1 off coupons for the New York City newspapers. The rest of the country got them, but we didn't. We all lived outside of the city and our local papers had the coupons. We didn't realize that the major market had been neglected. Without the coupons, the customers didn't respond and the merchants withdrew their support.

WHEN THINGS GO WRONG, PRODUCT MANAGEMENT'S KNEE JERK REACTION IS TO BLAME THE SALES FORCE.

THREE MANAGEMENT STYLES

Management by fear is when a manager uses outright threats to motivate reps. Two examples are: "Do this or you're fired." and, "If you don't achieve your quota, we will find someone who can."

Zeke practiced management by fear. He believed that sales reps acted like children and therefore he treated them as such. He watched over our shoulders to the point of distraction. Zeke, and those like them, failed to realize the consequences of their actions.

A manager who micro manages the sales force will quickly demoralize everyone on the team. The best people know that they are good reps and don't have to put up with any aggravation. They can get a job anywhere. The first consequence is that they leave the company, often going to the competition. The reps who stay are the mediocre people who put up with the harassment because they know it would be difficult finding a job elsewhere. They make a game of pulling things over on the manager. The belief that reps act like children becomes a self fulfilling prophecy.

When an organization practices management by fear long enough, they get a reputation for being a lousy company to work for and they can no longer attract good people. They also become a resource from which their competitors can steal experienced people.

Management by objective, (MBO), is when a manager and the rep, together, set goals for the territory. This results in a plan that both parties agree on. [See S.M.A.C.]

My Manager From Heaven subscribed to MBO. Since I always played an essential role in setting the quotas and objectives for my territory, I worked with confidence and a complete understanding of the goals expected of me. I never felt that a quota was unrealistic because some manager in the home office pulled a number out of thin air just because it sounded right.

Others took the easy approach and divided the company's goal in equal quotas for each rep. No consideration was made for individual territory characteristics. As an example, the company wants to achieve a sales goal of ten million dollars for a new product. They have ten divisions, so each division gets a quota of one million dollars. Each division has twenty reps, so each rep gets a quota of fifty thousand dollars. Some reps may have an easy time hitting their goal; others will work just as hard and struggle. Strong reps with a poor territory may end up losing their job because they could not hit an arbitrary quota. Weaker reps could easily surpass their quota and reap huge rewards for doing less work. [For further discussion see: S.M.A.C.]

Management by example is a manager using a hands-on approach to demonstrate his or her selling skills and objective setting approach.

Jeff practiced management by example. During the eight months that I had the privilege of working for him, Jeff took me into his territory several times. His instructions were simple: "Mike, keep your eyes and ears open and your mouth shut." I followed him around his territory and watched him work.

I saw how Jeff planned his day, organized his trunk, sales bag and how he canvassed a building. I saw first hand how he got past receptionists. I learned how he found the decision-maker, asked probing questions and walked out with orders. Afterwards, we analyzed the call. We discussed our success or failure and determined if "we" learned anything to use on our next call. By observing Jeff work in the field, I knew he completely understood what I faced in my own territory. He was demanding but totally empathetic. It gave me satisfaction to occasionally share a success story with him that helped him in his territory.

I once came with an idea to sell our bankruptcy desk guide to CPA's. For the most part, bankruptcy is a legal issue but CPAs handle the accounting end and it's important for them to know the legal ramifications. No one had done that before. I shared this idea with Jeff and the next week he called to thank me. He sold three sets to CPAs.

THE CO-WORKER

I've always had an easy time making friends. I often make the first overture, and go out of my way to help someone who is new and struggling. I treat everyone as a peer. Therefore, whenever I joined a new organization, within weeks I'd made several "corporate buddies."

A corporate buddy is someone you meet and work with on the job. Usually, the driving force that maintains the friendship is the common bond of work. Often, if you leave the job, the friendship dies a sudden death. People who talked to you regularly for years no longer return your phone calls. You move onto other jobs and make new corporate buddies.

These buddies not only serve as a source of companionship but a wonderful source of information and insight. Often I've called on colleagues when I had difficulty in selling a product. They in turn ask for my help in various ways.

Watch for the gossips! The company rumormongers are the worst. They are negative, manipulative, selfish troublemakers. I've seen them pit co-workers against each other and get people fired.

A colleague called me with news from a reliable source of his, that our organization would be merged with a sister company. After the merger we would all be out of a job. This concerned me. I thanked him for the information but I didn't act on it or tell anyone else.

The next morning, I received a call from a buddy in our sister company telling me the same scenario. Later, I got a call from an out-of-state headhunter asking if I'd put my resume together in light of my forth-coming termination. My concern grew.

That week we left for a national sales meeting. On the bus to the hotel, I sat with two vice presidents of the company, both whom I'd gotten to know. I expressed my concern over the rumor. Both assured me that it was false. They had heard it too; but, there was nothing to it.

At the meeting, the national sales manager spoke to us about the rumor and reassured us that there were no plans to merge and our jobs were secure. I let the matter drop and heard nothing more on it during the meeting.

Several weeks later, upper management called me into the home office for a meeting. They confronted me with the charge that I started the rumor and had continued to spread the rumor after the sales meeting. They claimed I was calling people up across the country and fanning the flames. I asked who made these charges, but they wouldn't tell me. They asked if I was working with a headhunter to recruit our sales reps for one of our competitors. I denied all of this, asking what possible motivation I could have. I loved my job and territory and was earning more money than anytime in my life. I was doing extra assignments and was giving computer instructions at sales meetings. They admitted they were at a loss to explain why, but were sure I was the root of the rumor.

I understood their concern. A rumor like that could decimate a company. The best reps know they are good and won't hesitate to jump to another position. The company is left with the bottom 2/3 of the sales force and must hire new reps who must be trained. That can set a company back six months or more. It could even cripple them for years until the new sales force gains experience.

They didn't fire me because I was over quota and in the top 20 percent of the sales force. The Vice-president said, "Mike, you sell a lot of books for us. So, I won't cut off my nose to spite my face; however, if I hear your name mentioned one more time with this rumor, you're fired!" I never revealed the name of the rep that first called me with the story. I took the heat, knowing that he was young, inexperienced and would lose his job.

Several months later at a national meeting, we learned from the same senior V.P. I had met on the bus that such a plan was under consideration. They killed the idea when word leaked out and they saw the reaction from both companies.

I also learned that I wasn't the only rep called in and accused of spreading the rumor. Apparently, they were on a fishing expedition trying to discover who in management leaked the story. I believe that being associated with this rumor affected my career since I was passed over for a promotion. Ironically, a less experienced rep got the job. He was the one who originally called me with the rumor. That was one reason I decided to leave the company the following year.

IF ANYONE CALLS YOU TO SPREAD A RUMOR, WHETHER IT'S GOOD OR BAD, HANG UP THE PHONE!

TEAM PLAYERS VS THE LONER

The most effective sales force I ever worked for had a strict policy that all reps, both men and women, must have participated in a team sport in school. Whether it was football, basketball or baseball, you must have been on a team. Therefore, you understood the team concept. That was one key to their success.

A team player knows that selfish behavior hurts the entire organization. They have a desire to do the best possible job, to work with fellow reps to help the team win. A team player will do what is necessary to help the team accomplish their goal even if it means he doesn't win the spotlight.

A team player would never participate in destructive behavior on or off the field because of the consequences it would have on the team's ability to win. This philosophy lends itself directly to a sales force where sales results are subjective. In the grocery industry, a sales organization may have ten representatives covering several different chain stores in a geographical area.

Management would call on the headquarters to place large orders into the warehouse and to secure promotional support. The sales force would then canvass the individual stores to get the store managers to pull merchandise from the warehouse.

As an example, the sales manager would call on the headquarters of three different grocery store chains in his region. He would sell each, ten pallets of soap to support an upcoming newspaper ad. The sales reps then go to each store to tell the store manager of the ad and get them to support the promotion with a multiple case display. This is "promotional support of an ad."

The sales force's reports with the results to the manager on a daily report. These are "turnover" orders. That means the sales rep writes an order and then "turns it over" to the store's warehouse for fulfillment. A "direct order" is one that goes from the manufacturer "directly" to the store.

Turnover orders are based on the honor system. The reps report to the manager that they each called on fifty stores from four different chains and sold an average five cases to each store that week. The manager can't drive to each of the 350 stores to personally check that all reps reported their sales accurately. He would be so busy being an auditor; he would have no time to do anything else.

That is why the interview process is so important. A manager must have people working for him that he can trust without question. The team player understands this and wants to participate to help the team win. He or she wants to belong to a winning sales organization even if they receive no credit for their personal contributions.

The pharmaceutical industry works in much the same fashion. Reps cover their territory to detail, or promote their drugs to doctors and to leave samples. The number of calls made and the results of the calls are difficult to document. Having team players that motivate themselves toward the success of the sales team assures management that they are getting accurate feedback on sales activity.

Unfortunately, some companies placed no emphasis on teamwork. They may pay lip service to encourage you to work with your colleagues; however, they are for the most part a loosely knit group of specialty reps who have little if any business experience. The results are individuals known as loners. The Pharmaceutical industry is an example.

A loner isn't concerned with the success or failure of the sales team, only with his or her own success. A loner might even sabotage the efforts of other reps to make himself look good.

When I first joined the pharmaceutical company, I was still in high gear as a team player. I called a colleague that I'd met at my first sales meeting to ask if he could explain a complicated pharmacological concept in more simplistic terms. I also asked if he could spare a few brochures, since mine hadn't arrived yet.

He said, "No. Figure it out for yourself. I'm not paid to teach you. And as for the brochures, I'm keeping what I've got." With that, he hung up.

I could understand his reaction, if we had been in an argument, or had a bad relationship, but I just met the guy. As time passed, and I got to meet more people in the company, I learned he treated everyone that way, but he didn't hesitate to ask you for help if he needed it.

Loners have made it to management, and I've seen them sacrifice their entire sales team just so they could get a promotion. This attitude, I firmly believe, is destructive to the company as a whole. Perhaps there is a place for them somewhere in the organization, but definitely not in a sales team.

OFFICE POLITICS

I'm sure that there are books devoted entirely to office politics. To this topic, however, I will devote one paragraph.

One benefit to outside sales is that I don't have to deal with office politics. There are people in certain departments that I will go out of my way to befriend, such as order entry, credit and shipping. I need them on my side to get business processed and into the customer's hand. Whenever they try to draw me into one of their cliques spread gossip or take sides in a dispute; I distance myself as fast as possible. My territory is my home office, my fellow sales reps and managers are my corporate buddies and that policy has served me well.

THE PUZZLE PALACE

"The Puzzle Palace" is a pejorative term I use to describe the home office when they are incapable of doing their job correctly.

One of the top one-hundred national accounts in my company happened to be my number one account and responsible for 20 percent of my volume.

Long before I joined the company, the credit department erroneously placed the account into collections for past due invoices. The account didn't owe us the money. For two years they tried to resolve the problem. In spite of the dispute, they continued to place orders with us.

The territory had been vacant for several years due to a merger and I was the first rep they had in a long time. Understandably, I caught the brunt of their fury my first day in the account. Without giving me the opportunity to try to correct the problem, they abruptly closed their account and refuse to do business with us. This became the prime focus of my job. I spent at least five hours in the account and on the phone with the credit department documenting the case. Each time I called, the credit department acknowledged the error and promised to correct it that week. Nevertheless, the following month, the account would receive another collection notice, threatening legal action for the past due amount. The account would then leave a blistering message on my answering machine. I would return to the account and spend most of the day trying to resolve the issue.

When I called the credit department, I found that there was a reorganization of the department. The last person I spoke with had quit, been fired, reassigned or promoted. The new person couldn't find the records of my last call, so I would have to fax them my copy. This all took several days for them to get back to me with the same acknowledgment that the account didn't owe the money. Again, the credit office assured me they would resolve the issue that week. At the end of the billing cycle, the account would receive another collection letter, and I got another blistering phone call. This scenario repeated itself for months.

I reported the problem to my manager and documented the situation and how I tried to resolve it. Each month we went through the same process. Eight months later, I got a new manager, a Manager From Hell. When I asked for his assistance, he said, "Mike, you must try to resolve problems on your own. You can't come crying to me every time there is a little snafu in your territory."

The situation went unresolved for another three months. In the meantime, I was trying to make up for the lost business elsewhere in my territory. When you factored out this large account I was over quota, but since the company wouldn't do that, I was quickly slipping below quota.

In the spring, my new manager finally got involved, "Mike, now let me show you how to get things done." He called the office and spoke to the newest credit manager. The credit manager acted surprised that such a glaring problem could possibly exist for as long as I claimed. He questioned my manager if I had even tried to resolve the issue. He went said that the credit department had no records of my previous contacts and asked my manager to fax him copies of all documentation.

When my manager got off the phone, he assured me that he had fixed the problem conclusively. A month later, the account got another collection notice. My manager was incredulous. He immediately called credit only to learn that a new person was handling the department and that they had no records of the dispute and that he would have to fax them copies of everything. The account folder had grown to more than two-hundred pages of documentation.

The following month when the account received their next collection notice, my manager called the national sales manager and he got involved. It was to no avail. He got the same promise that both my manager and I received and that too went unfulfilled.

The lost business from this account was affecting my year to date sales figures. I was 20 percent below quota. After a sales meeting, my manager pulled me aside to tell me that I was now on probation. He told me that if I didn't bring my sales up to quota by the end of the quarter, he would fire me.

I reminded him that the reason I was below quota was because of the credit problem with my major account. He should understand that since he was helping me to resolve it. He said, "Mike, it's your territory and you're responsible for it. I have to follow the book to the letter of the law. If you're below quota for three months, you go on probation."

When the national sales manager got involved the second time, credit finally resolved the problem. They sent the customer an apology letter admitting the mistake and assuring them it would never happen again. I took my copy of the letter to the account and personally delivered it to the buyer and he thanked me for my efforts. He didn't know that I was on the verge of losing my job.

I walked out of the account with an order that instantly placed me at 118 percent of quota. In the next company newsletter, my manager praised my hard work and my above quota performance. He paraded me around like a conquering hero. At months end, the account received another collection notice, this time including the amount for the large order they had just given me. The company hadn't shipped the products and refused to do so until the customer paid all past due invoices plus the current invoice in advance. I was once again below quota and immediately placed back on probation. The puzzle palace was hard at work.

The error was finally corrected when the account's legal department threatened my company with a multi-million dollar lawsuit. The company promptly shipped the product with a corrected invoice. I was taken off probation and reinstated as a hero. My manager encouraged everyone to talk to me about my success; however, he pulled me aside and said, "Mike, if anyone asks you the details, just make something up that sounds good."

LET THEM OFF THE HOOK

In that situation, it would be understandable if I became enraged at the credit department for their incompetence. They had all but cost me my job and the buyer at my number one account thought that we were a bunch of idiots. He told every sales rep, from every company, of the fiasco. The story spread throughout my territory and other major accounts were hesitant to place large orders for fear that the same thing would happen to them.

I let the credit department off the hook. I called the new credit manager who supervised the latest credit mishap to thank him for all of his efforts. He didn't create the problem and I needed his support for other account problems.

I've had buyers place substantial orders only to cancel them after shipment. I let them off the hook. I let them know that I was doing them a favor, but I never lost my temper with anyone.

As a buyer for the pharmacy, I called a vendor who serviced a display rack in our store. The rep came in and went right to work cleaning the rack. After an hour he said that he had written a minimum order to refill the display. I asked how much the order came to and he said, "About $200."

I was new and we had just taken delivery of several large COD orders I asked him to wait while I cleared it with the owner. The rep rolled his eyes up to the ceiling.

The owner said he couldn't spend $200 off the bat, and wanted to review the order. I went to the rep and said, "We can't go for $200 right now."

The rep shouted, "Well I've been screwed again."

He turned and stormed out of the store. He never gave us a chance to review the order or ask if there were any options. He should have told us up front about the order requirements. We would have asked him to wait before he serviced the rack. It was just bad timing and we needed a few weeks to place an order.

The rep lost his temper, created a scene in a busy store and lost his credibility. The owner called the company to complain, which made the rep look bad in front of his boss. We learned that the minimum order was the rep's guideline, not a company policy. How much business does this rep throw away every year because of his temper?

"Let them off the hook" applies to every aspect of your business, from your customers, their staff and your own co-workers. Besides, one day they may return the favor and let you off the hook.

THE BUYER

CLIENT VS CUSTOMER

TREAT A CUSTOMER LIKE A CLIENT, NOT LIKE A CUSTOMER.

This is illustrated by the way two dermatologists treat their patients. My company pioneered antifungal therapy. An antifungal is a medication that treats common but painful conditions such as athletes' foot.

We had the latest generation of an antifungal that was the most potent, most effective and most economical brand on the market. It was available by prescription only and my job was to visit dermatologists and convince them to prescribe our product. (A dermatologist is a doctor who specializes in diseases of the skin.)

JUST BECAUSE YOU HAVE THE BEST PRODUCT ON THE MARKET, DOESN'T MEAN IT WILL BE THE NUMBER ONE SELLING BRAND.

Doctor's are just like you; they are creatures of habit. They may have prescribed one product for years and are reluctant to change brands. That is why pharmaceutical companies need sales reps to call on doctors to present them with new information, product samples and to ask them to prescribe the product for their patients.

The first dermatologist I called on treated his patients like clients. His concern was to give the patient the best treatment and medication possible. All other considerations, such as costs, fees and brand loyalty were far down the list. The doctor, after carefully reviewing all of the test data, agreed to try our drug on his next dozen patients with fungal infections. He would monitor the results and then decide. That was exactly my sales objective for the call.

The second dermatologist treated his patients like customers. After presenting our new antifungal, I asked the doctor if he would try our product.

He said, "No, I can see by the trial data that it works too well."

"Doctor, I don't understand."

"Your drug is very effective, and clears the infection in as little as seven days. The fungus usually doesn't come back." He said.

"That was the whole idea. Our product is the most effective on the market. It is used once a day versus twice a day like our competitor's product and is more economical."

"Mike, that's the problem. You see, I get $45 a visit from my patients. If I use your product, it will work so well and so fast I will never see the patient again. I'll stick with the other drug, and get two, maybe three visits out of them. That's up to $135 in my pocket. Your cream will cost me business. Why should I use it?"

He was in it strictly for the money. With this insight, which doctor would you want to care for your family?

Think of this when you call on your accounts: Do you treat them like clients where you have their best interests at heart, or simply as a cash cow to be milked dry?

I've always looked at things from my accounts point of view. This is "Total Empathy." Yes, I want to earn a lot of money. I want to be the number one rep in my company. I also want to build long term relationships where I can count on repeat orders. The only way you can do that is to treat your customers like a client, the way the first dermatologist treated his patients.

BUYER ASSISTANT

The buyer assistant is one who is in a training position for the position of buyer. The assistant will help plan promotional strategy, search for vendors and make suggestions for types of products and qualities. The average tenure for assistant buyers is about two years. After that time, the assistant will be promoted to a buyer in that department.

It doesn't always work out the way it was planned. I met a newly promoted buyer for hospital pharmaceuticals. He spent two years as assistant buyer in the hospital's medical equipment department. When the position in pharmaceuticals opened, the hospital placed him there. He knew everything about medical equipment and hospital procedures, but nothing about pharmaceuticals. The poor guy was struggling to learn a myriad of complex drugs and obscure terminology in a short period. Since there was no one to guide him, it quickly turned into a disaster.

He made many costly mistakes and the hospital suffered. He was in a position that he wasn't prepared for. He was bright, hard working and well trained, but for a different department. After six months, he lost his job. Rather than putting him back into the job he was trained for, the hospital simply fired him.

WHEN YOU TALK TO THE ASSISTANT YOU MAY BE TALKING TO YOUR FUTURE BUYER.

The relationship that you develop now may affect your future business. There are several advantages and disadvantages of working with assistant buyers.

Advantages:
- Eager to do a good job.
- Open minded about all vendors.
- There is an opportunity to build a long-term relationship.
- Few, if any, preconceived notions.
- More contemporary.
- Not jaded by experiences.
- Establish your product as his "Product of Choice," and he will remain loyal to it for years.

Disadvantages:
- Easily swayed by your competition.

- Little, if any, real decision making power.
- Unable to cope with internal bureaucracy.
- Little experiences in decision-making.
- Fear of making mistakes.

When I sold copiers, I received a call from an account that I'd recently cold called. They were in the market for a new photocopier and wanted a proposal.

I was new in this industry and asked my boss to go along in case I got in over my head, or if a buying signal came up. He would be there to make a decision on the spot.

When I told my boss that we wouldn't be seeing the buyer, but his assistant instead, he was wary. After some pleading, he agreed to come along. The assistant buyer was working as a gatekeeper. A gatekeeper is someone who insulates the buyer from sales reps. The gatekeeper said that no rep was allowed to meet the buyer and if we tried to contact the buyer in any fashion, we would be eliminated from consideration. This often happens with a weak buyer who has low sales resistance. Someone who has low sales resistance will use an assistant to collect all information so they can review the material at their own pace. Buyers who use gatekeepers may have little self-confidence and may fear appearing ignorant in front of an experienced sales rep.

The disadvantages in our case were threefold. First the assistant had no knowledge of photocopiers, nor the terminology of the industry. She possessed little, if any, mechanical knowledge. To her, a copier was a copier.

Price and features were the only way she could discern between the various makes and models. As an example, we stressed that our machines were constructed with metal gears and levers, while the imports she was considering were made of nylon. That is why they were cheaper. We explained that nylon parts wore faster and would lead to more breakdowns. She understood that; however, she said that the imports had a service contract that covered everything.

We told her that the nylon parts wore quickly causing a decrease in quality and efficiency. If the machine still worked, regardless of the quality, they wouldn't replace the worn parts. Our copier, on the other hand, used metal parts that wore much slower and delivered a consistently higher quality copy. Our warranty specifically guaranteed that the quality would be consistent. This was important to the customer because they mailed out the copies to their customers who need quality photocopies. Unfortunately, she was unable to grasp this concept.

Our guarantee was specific as to what it covered. The competitor's warranty was designed to confuse. It listed certain exclusions, such as the standard water and fire damage and miscellaneous items. We pointed out that the word "miscellaneous" could include anything. If the machine broke, she had to pay to fix it. Our service contact was free; the competitors included a monthly fee. When you factored all of that in, the cheap import was more expensive and less reliable that ours.

Secondly, she had no knowledge of financing. She was confused by all of the options, the leasing structure, the difference between rental contracts, purchase of used machines, and service contracts.

Thirdly, we were unable to survey the office to determine their actual needs and budgetary constraints. Since we couldn't interview the decision-maker, we couldn't uncover and overcome any objections. We couldn't stress the superiority of our lease and equipment and help him choose a copier that fit his needs and budget.

My boss and his father were tough businessmen, highly competitive and successful. However, I never saw them sell someone a machine that didn't fit the customer's needs or renege on a contractual agreement. They always cut themselves a good deal, but never sacrificed long-term growth for a quick buck.

For the next six weeks, this assistant buyer ran me ragged. She changed her mind from leasing to buying, from new, to used, to rental. Each required a new written proposal. In the end, I didn't get the order. She went with the cheapest copier with the worst service contract.

When I discussed this sale with my boss, he explained that he had run into this customer before and knew that we would never get the business.

"So why did you let me waste my time?" I asked.

"Experience is the best teacher and you had to learn the hard way. Next time, when you run into this situation, give a quote over the phone, send a written proposal, but don't let a gatekeeper waste your time. I guarantee they will always make the wrong decision."

Within a year, I heard the gatekeeper's company was suing the people who sold them the import. The machine worked fine for six months and then began to malfunction. The machine was too small for the volume of copies that they made. The service company made her to pay for the repairs and held them to the contract.

KILL 'EM WITH KINDNESS

When you have a buyer who is mad at you or your company, even for something that isn't your fault, "Kill Them With Kindness."

My company had shipped an order in error to one of my customers. The buyer was furious. They needed the product for a special project. She left me a message on my voice mail, saying how this error made her look bad in front of her boss and she promised never to do business with us again. I returned the phone call immediately to see if there was anything I could do to resolve the problem.

"No! Not unless you're willing to get in your car and deliver the product to the branch office in New Jersey by two o'clock," she said in a sarcastic tone.

I told her that was exactly what I planned to do. I got the information and cleared my calendar for the day. I drove to our warehouse, picked up the correct item and drove to New Jersey. I got there at 1:45 and delivered the product to the customer's warehouse. I called the buyer from the loading dock and told her what I'd done. She was relieved that I fixed the problem, but she was still upset.

That evening I wrote a note to her boss, taking full responsibility for the error. I said that I understood how important accurate and timely deliveries were and that I understood if they didn't want to use us again. To compensate them further, I arranged for the customer to receive the product free of charge. (It was under $50.) I sent the letter express mail, with a copy to the buyer and my manager.

Several days later, she called to thank me for everything I'd done. She appreciated the effort and admitted that mistakes happened. "What is important is that instead of shuffling the blame onto someone else, you took immediate action to correct the problem. The product was delivered on time and the project went ahead as scheduled." She then gave me her largest order to date and she remained a good client.

TREAT AN ANGRY CLIENT WITH MORE URGENCY AND SERVICE THAN ONE WHO CALLS TO PLACE AN ORDER.

WHEN THEY WASTE YOUR TIME

The most difficult decision to make as a sales rep is when to pick up your bag and head for your next customer. I try to get at least three "Hell Fire No's" from a buyer before I accept rejection, but there are situations where buyers aren't up front about their intentions.

The types of time wasters are those who can't make a decision. They may lack authority or are afraid of making a mistake. Then there are those who use you to make themselves look busy.

A classic time waster is an administrator who constantly calls in reps to submit proposals for various products and services. Their objective is to have a constant flow of people and mail flowing through the office. The buyer's worst nightmare is for their boss to walk by and see him or her with nothing to do.

The time waster will note that the photocopiers are several years old. There may be nothing wrong with them, but will contact everyone on the Rolodex who sells copiers to come in and do an on sight inspection.

Reps, smelling a nice size order, stampede through the door, meet with the buyer and get the guided tour. The reps run back to their office and prepare proposals. Each vendor invites the buyer to their showroom for a demonstration and a free lunch. After the dust settles and the reps wait for the decision, the buyer decides that the new machines are just too expensive and their current machines will just have to do for another year. Worse, he tells each rep that he decided to purchase their competitor's machine. To maintain the pace, the buyer turns his attention to replacing the fax machines.

The second type, are those who use your brochures and proposals to keep their present suppliers in line. A vendor calls on a regular customer and finds that the competitor's brochure or proposal is on the buyer's desk. The buyer will step out of the office for a minute, giving the vendor time to "peek" through it.

THE ONLY REASON YOU WERE ASKED TO SUBMIT A PRO-POSAL WAS SO YOUR BID COULD BE USED TO SCARE THEIR CURRENT VENDOR. THEY HAVE NO CONCERN ABOUT WAST-ING YOUR TIME AND EFFORT.

The third type is the "Buyer Wanna-be." This type of buyer wants to make decisions, but lacks authority and is too embarrassed to admit it. This is common in small family run businesses where the owner won't let the kids make any important decisions. A variation is a company with two partners where only one partner controls the purse strings.

After you spend your time on proposals and try to close the sale the "wanna-be" may say, "Sorry pal. I was all ready to go with your copier but the 'big guy upstairs' won't go for the dough. I fought like crazy to get it through. We'll try again next year." Of course your proposal never left the "wannabe's" office. The "big guy upstairs" doesn't even know you exist. He is unapproachable and you can't see him to close a sale.

The fourth type is the one who won't make a decision for fear of making a mistake. This type may work for an unforgiving boss who doesn't tolerate errors. Therefore, your proposal gets kicked around the office because no one wants their fingerprints on it.

The fifth type is the most pathetic. They just are incapable of making a decision. When a crisis arises, they just sit back and wait to see if the problem will resolve itself. They may lack the experience or mental capacity to analyze information or cut through red tape to get something done.

In the last three cases, some good questions to ask are:
- "Are you prepared to make a decision now or in the next two weeks?"
- "What time frame are we looking at for a decision?"
- "Is there someone else I should talk to, or are you the final decision maker?"
- "Who else is involved in this process?"

In the first two cases, only experience and good company records can protect you from time wasters.

BUYING CYCLES
One of your customers can give you a $500 order every month and the next can give you a $6,000 once a year. Where do you spend your time? I suggest that you spend equal time at both.

See each customer once a month. The first gives you consistent small orders and therefore requires constant attention. The second, however, can only buy once a year, but for the same dollar amount. Drop in to see the second account every month. Check to see if they have any problems you can help resolve. "Hi, I was in the neighborhood and stopped in to see how you're doing. Is there anything I can help you with?"

When the end of the year rolls around, you will be like an old friend to the buyer as opposed to your competitors who come by only once a year for an order.

I did this in pharmaceuticals and legal publishing with excellent results. My territory included the East End of Long Island and the resort area of the Hamptons.

Things were very quiet during the winter, but I always found time to go out and see my clients. Business was slow and I often left without getting any orders. When the summer crowds arrived and things were very busy, my clients always found time to see me. I got the choicest display spots for my summer goods and most of the physicians used my prescription products as their drug of choice.

In legal publishing, my large state libraries could only spend money once a year. That is when most of the other companies showed up to meet with the librarians. I dropped by once a month to have coffee and small talk with them. I was quick to resolve any billing problems and to replace missing volumes at no charge. The librarians had to call my competitors' customer service department to resolve any issues. When the end of the fiscal year rolled around I was first in line and got the largest order.

People like to be treated as someone special. Try to cater to their needs even if they can't give you orders right away. Your payoff will come down the road.

LET THEM KNOW YOU ARE DOING THEM A FAVOR.

I had a good customer who placed a large order to fill a contractual agreement with one of their new customers. The order put me over quota for the quarter.

After the order shipped, the buyer called me and said that their new customer abruptly canceled their contract. He said that without the agreement the order would do serious damage to their cash flow. They had no other use for the product.

Contractually, we had no obligation to take the merchandise back; however, I went to the "well" (to retrieve favors) and got my manager to authorize the return and without the standard restocking fee.

My customer was very grateful. I made a point that it was a one-time deal and I had called in several favors to get the return authorized without a penalty.

My reward was a solid relationship with the customer and repeat orders. Whenever we came out with a new product, they agreed to take in a large display. There was no guarantee that they would appreciate my efforts and others certainly took advantage of me. However, I will always give my customers the benefit of the doubt.

TOTAL EMPATHY

My policy is to place myself in my customers' shoes, to look at things from their perspective. When I talk to the buyer, I assume I own the store and it is my money. I present the right products in the right quantities and follow up after each delivery to ensure everything is OK.

I've done this for so long that it is second nature to me. A few customers have picked up on it and said they always felt comfortable when I came to visit. They never felt as though I was trying to sell them something that they didn't need or want.

I learned this in the grocery industry when I had a tough store manager who wouldn't give me any business. I would stop by once a week and say, "Hi George, I'm not here to sell you anything. I just want to check to see if you have any returns." I would check inventory levels; hang a few shelf talkers and leave. I never approached him with a presentation. After a few months of this, George walked over and said in a low authoritative voice, "From now on, before you leave, let me know about your weekly specials."

The initial orders were small but over time they grew and I recouped the business I'd missed out on at first. We never had a cordial relationship. George was strictly business There was never any small talk with the reps.

We often stood in line to speak with store managers and could hear each other's presentations. I saw him brush off new reps. Most of whom, never got any business from him. Only a few of us had earned George's trust.

STOMPING OUT FOREST FIRES

This expression represents your attempt to resolve a crisis that has sprung up in your territory and detracts you from your day-to-day attempt to write new business.

Example: You wrote an order for a customer for a promotion that will run next Tuesday in the customer's store. Your credit department held up the order for a past due invoice. It's Friday morning before the sale and you're facing a three-day weekend. You scheduled delivery for today.

This forest fire sprang to life because no one in your credit department told you the account was on credit hold. To compound the problem, the customer waited until the last minute to let you know there was a problem. You are the sales rep, so both the credit department and the customer hold you responsible. This happened to me in the 1980's before cellphones, auto redial, e-mail, voice-mail and pagers. Although communications have improved since then, problems still happen.

9:30 a.m.: *You receive a panic message from your customer. To stomp out this forest fire, you plan to call the credit department and ask how much the customer owes. The second step is to call the customer and ask if they will cut a check. If they say yes, you can fax a copy to the credit office as proof of payment so they will release the order. You mail the check overnight express. It sounds simple enough until you call the credit department.*

9:45 a.m.: *You call the credit department several times. Either the line is busy or everyone is out on a coffee break or in a meeting.*

11:50 a.m.: *You get through to credit and get the information.*

11:55 a.m.: *You call your customer. He says he doesn't owe the money because he paid the invoice C.O.D. The customer wants the shipment for Tuesday's sale now, or he will never do business with you again.*

Noon: *You call credit, but everyone is out to lunch.*

1:15 p.m.: *You get through to credit, but they need to research the problem. They say to call back at 4:00.*

1:20 p.m.: *You call the customer to let them know the status of the order. Meanwhile you have had to reschedule one appointment and missed making three cold calls while handling this. You are on commission and have earned no money for the day.*

3:58 p.m.: *You call credit and the person you need has stepped away from his desk. They suggest you call back in five minutes.*

4:05 p.m.: *You call credit and the line is busy.*

4:10 p.m.: *You call credit, but they don't have an answer for you yet. They say to call back in twenty minutes. You hop in your car to drive to your next call. You hit traffic.*

4:30 p.m.: *You get to a gas station to call but the phone won't accept your credit card. Your company won't accept collect calls even from a sales rep. You drive to the diner down the road.*

4:37 p.m.: *You call credit and they acknowledge the mistake. They promise to release the order and to rush it to the customer.*

4:39 p.m.: You call the shipping department to expedite the order. Everyone has left early for the three-day weekend.

4:42 p.m.: You call the customer to tell him the good news / bad news. He is angry. He knows he didn't owe the money and is furious that the order won't arrive until after the sale starts. The buyer hangs up on you.

4:45 p.m.: You have a brainstorm. You call a wholesaler who owes you a favor. Last month you stomped out a forest fire that he started and kept him from being burnt. The wholesaler loads his truck with the merchandise your customer needs and sends it out. You promise to replace the merchandise Tuesday.

4:55 p.m.: You call your customer and tell him the delivery will be there in fifteen minutes and to please keep his receiving department open.

5:10 p.m.: Your customer gets his delivery. You go home, get a cold drink and enjoy your weekend until the next forest fire springs to life.

Hindsight is 20/20. I could have monitored my deliveries to catch any problems early; however, I had 250 accounts. I would never have time to go out and sell. Besides, 95 percent of the orders go through without a problem.

I could have called the wholesaler earlier, but I had no way of knowing it would take all day to resolve the problem. Moreover, I didn't think of it until the last minute.

I could have ignored the whole situation and let the customer and the credit department straighten out the mess, but the customer would never buy from me again. This isn't an option. I was on commission and have worked hard to cultivate this top account. I always look at my business long range.

My customer thinks I'm a superman for resolving the problem so quickly and creatively. My credit department is mad because I uncovered their mistake which made them look bad. They will remember that the next time I call. I keep in mind that the customer pays my salary, not the credit department.

LOOKING FOR NEW OUTLETS

Finding new outlets is when you look for new places to sell your products or services. These are outlets not normally covered by other reps in your company or industry. This doesn't mean that you simply look for new customers in the traditional marketplace.

In legal publishing, I faced a problem in my Long Island territory. Because of the horrendously long recession that drained the budget of every local municipality, the town attorneys weren't allowed to purchase any new law books. They had to travel to the local county court libraries to do their research. This reduced my customer base by two-hundred. However, my quota included the two-hundred town attorneys buying books from me.

I was browsing through my local Franklin Square public library one Saturday when I noticed they had a limited legal reference section. I learned that all of the two-hundred or so local libraries purchased their books through either of two purchasing departments.

I visited both; presented my idea that the libraries purchase some of our single volume and small reference sets to build their own legal reference centers. About 45 percent of the libraries were large enough to do that.

I could solicit two-hundred libraries by simply making two calls. The volume compensated for 80 percent of the lost volume of my town attorneys.

In pharmaceuticals, I had a co-worker who read every medical journal and article about our products and the types of diseases they were effective on. We called on Dermatologist plus a few other specialists who might see these types of conditions.

My colleague read some obscure article that veterinarians treated dogs for a skin disorder that's also common to man. The thought of calling on vets for our product was unheard and the competition certainly wasn't doing so. He had at least fifty vets in his territory. He called on them and presented our product with success.

When I sold office supplies, I only called on stationary stores. My territory was in Manhattan and I was walking through a large office complex. I stopped in a drug store that was on the ground floor. Their clientele not only included the 10,000 employees working in the complex but also the people who walked by the storefront each day.

This drug store sold health and beauty aids, food, candy, greeting cards, cold soda and newspapers but not office supplies. I approached the owner and suggested that he order a small selection of office supplies to cater to the thirty businesses in the complex. He felt that wouldn't be prudent, since there was a large stationary store several blocks away that delivered.

I said that there are times that companies run out of basic items when the commercial stationary was closed. He tried a small order, and it went well. Although I never found exactly the same situation again, I managed to expand my customer base into a new area.

Look closely at your customer base and your product. Are there other outlets that might use your product or service, one that your competition has never considered? You have nothing to lose by asking.

REVIVING LOST CUSTOMERS

I know reps that stopped calling on customers because they fought with the buyer some years ago and held a grudge. There are customers, who fell on hard times and just stopped buying, so the reps dropped them from their route list. Others had credit problems or were buying from the competition exclusively. Some were mad at us because our company had messed up on deliveries or on their credit accounts. Sometimes the buyer and the rep hated each other. Now, both the rep and the buyer have moved onto other jobs. I walk in to meet the new buyer and business flows again. The reasons are many but the point remains; time heals all wounds.

Early in my career, an experienced rep was training me in the field. We called on a grocer who didn't like one of our company policies. It was out of my control; I had to adhere to the policy. He got mad and threw us out of the store. I thought that I would never get another order from him. My trainer laughed and said not to worry. "Simply wait two weeks and go back in. Pretend nothing ever happened. He will have forgotten all about you. He sees at least ten reps a day."

It worked. I went in, acted as though the last call never occurred. He had apparently forgotten or just cooled off and I left with an order.

Some in sales take rejection personally. Buyers get mad at companies for their policies and the mistakes they make. You represent the company and therefore catch the blunt of their anger. Intellectually, the buyer knows that you have no control over the decisions made by your company. They have their own bureaucracy to navigate. Let them blow off their steam. Tell them that you understand their position, even if you don't agree to them, and come back another day.

I've called the credit department and negotiated settlements on past due accounts to get a lost customer back in the pipeline. I've gotten the shipping department to send a letter to a customer apologizing for some error that happened years ago. I've done whatever is necessary to discover why someone no longer buys from us and tried to correct it. There were times I was unable to change anything, but the customer appreciated my effort enough to resume business.

Once, I had caused a problem with a new client. I was entirely at fault. I walked into the buyer's office and he just glared at me. I extended my hand and said, "My fault. What do I have to do to make things right?"

The buyer looked at me for a moment and said, "Forget it, everyone makes mistakes." He soon became a very good customer.

ORGANIZATION

One key to a successful, stress free work environment is how you organize yourself. The key to organization is having information and equipment in an easily accessible location, even if you rarely use it.

Consider the tools you need to change a flat tire. When you purchase a new car, it comes equipped with a spare tire, jack, tire tool, and instructions. Since the equipment remains in your trunk, you can find it when you need it. However, if you use the tire tool in your workshop as a crow bar, you may forget to put it back in the trunk. One day you may have a flat in the middle of nowhere and will be unable to change the tire.

Keep a special folder for credit problems in your brief case. Keep your customer records in a file system by name or geographic location. Carry an envelope for travel receipts so when you do your expense report, you can account for everything.

Keep your attaché and car trunk well stocked and in order. Never be embarrassed that you don't have a brochure or product sample. This is especially important if you're working with a manager. Nothing is more stressful than telling your manager that you're missing a key brochure during the middle of a presentation.

In my sales bag, I have an emergency supply pocket. In it, I have twenty-five extra business cards, several pens and a spare calculator. I carry a spare price book and brochures in my trunk. More than once, I've had to use them because I was not prepared for a sales call.

Chapter Four

READ THIS CHAPTER AND DOUBLE YOUR INCOME

Despite your territory planning, expense management and relationship with your manager, your selling ability has the biggest impact on your income.

Following are the sales techniques I've used to dramatically increase my earnings. Read, adopt and practice the art of probing, the seven steps of the call, the five steps of the presentation, overcoming objections and closing. You will double the number of sales you make.

A commission rep earned $35,000 last year by closing one out of every ten presentations. He will earn $70,000 this year by closing two out of every ten presentations. That is a tremendous increase in earnings for a minor increase in sales.

A salaried rep would see an increase in bonuses and raises for doubling his or her sales. By establishing a proven track record, he or she can move to a more lucrative position and, in time, double their income.

I believe many reps lose sales because they give up too easily or don't understand the buyers' objectives and goals. Use the strategy outlined in this chapter, and you can close more sales.

YOU DON'T HAVE TO MAKE A LOT MORE SALES TO HAVE A DRAMATIC IMPROVEMENT IN YOUR INCOME.

I don't like to talk about failure, but here I will, just to make a point. I mentioned the $35,000 a year rep that closed one out of every ten presentations. Said another way; he earns $35,000 by failing nine out of ten times. By reducing the number of failures to eight out of ten, he would double his income to $70,000 a year. Isn't it worth $35,000 for you to read this chapter carefully?

Read each section thoroughly as I've described them. Try each point at least three times to see if you feel comfortable with it. Then decide if it is worth adopting into your daily action plan.

My brother, Clyde, owned the Candy Factory in Mooresville, North Carolina. On a recent visit, he gave me a tour of the store and asked my opinion. My background in sales, merchandising and point of purchase gave him a new perspective:

"IT'S EASIER TO INCREASE THE AMOUNT OF CANDY EACH CUSTOMER BUYS AS OPPOSED TO GETTING MORE CUSTOMERS TO SHOP THE STORE."

Obviously you want to increase your traffic flow, but it is more important to maximize the customers you already have. If thirty customers a day buy candy, my brother would have to find an additional thirty customers a day, or more than 11,000 a year, to double his income.

I recommended that he take all of the back room stock and fill the display racks to the point of overflow. I also set up small counter displays and placed the more profitable items near the register. With proper merchandising, it was possible to double the average purchases of his present customers from .50 to $1.00. The theories that apply to retailing also apply to direct selling. In the economies of scale, you will receive a large reward for a small increase in effort.

WRITING GOOD ADVERTISING AND SALES

Advertising is a close cousin to direct selling. They employ many of the same principles to achieve the result: selling something. In the forward, I promised to teach you to write good advertising and how to apply it to sales. You may think of sales as an entirely different industry from advertising. Actually, they're closely related. Selling through a piece of paper, e.g., a newspaper ad, is the most difficult type of sale. You can't probe, uncover objections or do more than suggest that the customer take action. There is no guarantee that your intended market is being reached. The things you take for granted in face-to-face selling are missing in print advertising.

In face to face selling you would never try to sell dental equipment to a plumber, but in advertising you often have little control of whom your audience is. You pay for circulation in a particular geographic area and expose your product to as many people as possible. You hope your potential customers will see the ad, and respond by purchasing your product. Even if you run the ad in a specialty magazine or newspaper, you still are paying for exposure to readers who aren't potential clients.

When a soft drink company runs an ad, their objective is for you to buy a cola, any cola. Their expectation is that the ad will generate a large volume of sales in the entire category of cola and that they will get some of that volume in proportion to their market share. This form of generic advertising is an expensive and inefficient way to sell.

When I was in advertising and there wasn't a lot of work to do, the agency would have its creative people produce generic ads. The agency would place these generic ads in a file and when an unsophisticated client came along, they would just stick his name and logo on the ad. The client thought we created it just for him.

I worked for a small agency and each week we created one generic car dealer newspaper ad, complete with a rough drawing of a car racing down the street. We ran them off on the photocopier and I customized one ad for each dealer in the area. We presented the same ad to every dealership in town. The dealer, who said yes first, got the ad. Each dealer thought the agency created it just for them.

The following week we repeated the process with a new generic ad. Unfortunately, these generic ads weren't very effective. The way to write good advertising is to make it specifically for a client's product or service. In the above example, we should have studied a particular dealership, the way they run their business, their pricing, service and customer relations. From this, we would spend several days to develop a unique concept for a campaign, work up fresh ad dummies and then present it to the dealership. This type of speculative work is labor intensive and expensive for the agency, but it's the right way to do it.

I discussed this with the agency owner, who just laughed. "Mike, I used to work that way and it almost cost me my business. I picked up the technique from another 'ad man' who was retiring. The bottom line is that it works. The dealerships buy them, and I can in turn meet your paycheck each week. In all honesty, I don't see a big difference from one dealer to the next. I'm not going to change as long as it works."

The sales technique worked well for this small agency, but how did the ads work for the dealership? Did they really increase sales? It was impossible to determine. The dealers were too afraid not to advertise and ran something almost every week, so there was no benchmark to measure the ad's effectiveness.

How then, do you write good advertising? I learned a great technique at The School of Visual Arts, to determine if an ad is good or bad. First read the ad out loud. Second, reread the ad and substitute the competitor's name for the sponsor's name. If the ad still makes sense and is a true statement, then it is a bad ad. Why? If you can substitute the brands that easily, then the consumers, in their rush, will certainly do so. They may remember the ad but not the product name. How many dramatic or funny ads can you think of and have forgotten the product's name? I have seen ads that were so broad and generic that they could be used by the competition and by products in entirely different industries.

Try this test. Take a weekly magazine and flip open to a car ad. Find another ad from a competing car company, cut out the photo of the car and the logo, and place them on top of the first ad to cover the original car and logo. Now read the ad substituting the name of second car for the first one. If the ad had appeared that way originally, would you have known the difference?

Both manufacturers want to sell you a car, but may have nothing unique to say about their product. Their respective agencies create an image of a guy and girl, with wind blown hair, cruising through the mountains or by the beach. The ad suggests, to a male reader, that if he wants to get the beautiful girl, he needs a new car, so he should go to the nearest showroom and buy one. The ad entices you to shop for a new car—any car. Each manufacturer hopes you choose theirs, of course. If the entire marketplace sells 1,000 cars a week and a manufacturer has a 20 percent market share, he will sell two-hundred cars. If his ad can increase the total volume to 1,100 cars a week, then he will sell 220 cars. This represents his 20 percent market share. If, at the same time, he can increase his market share to 21 percent, he will then sell 231 cars.

Most creative people know when they are producing bad advertising. It's not, however, always in their power to decide which campaign runs. Instead, the client makes the final decision. The agency may produce two or three different ad campaigns for a product, then show them all to the client to choose. Frequently the client will pick the worst ad, because he or she's not trained in the creative and persuasive process.

The agency tries to do good work, but in the end it's the client who pays the bills and the one they must please. It seems ironic that a company will hire creative people, spend millions on an advertising campaign, then tell the agency how to do its job. These same people would never think of telling their family doctor how to practice medicine.

ADVERTISING IS LIKE SALES; EVERYONE THINKS THEY CAN DO IT.

I was working at an agency when a client presented us with a sketch drawn by his eight-year-old daughter. It was a cute drawing and deserved a prominent place on the refrigerator. He wanted us to use it in the campaign. We did our best to discourage him without insulting his daughter's work, but he insisted.

Would this client let his eight-year-old come to work and balance his books, or give him legal advice on a patent infringement suit? Would he let her reprogram his computer? Of course not! However, she was allowed to develop the concept and create the artwork for a $200,000 advertising campaign that could determine the success or failure of the company.

I believe 99 percent of the advertising you see is generic and bad. This has led to the downfall of companies with good products. You therefore want to avoid generic presentations in sales. Let's concentrate on the 1 percent and how it will help you sell better.

J. Walter Thomson, the founding father of modern advertising, called it a "Unique Selling Proposition" (USP). Find a unique aspect of the product, something no one else could say about their product, and make that the focal point of the advertisement.

Perhaps yours is the only product of its kind made in America. Perhaps a testing lab rated it as the best made in the world. It could be something as simple as the only product without some scary sounding ingredient.

Invent a USP if you sell a "me too" product. A "me too" product is one that is identical to other products on the market. Examples are hairpins, book matches and thumbtacks. There is no question of quality and they all do the same thing. Assume you make a glass cleaner. It's identical to every other glass cleaner on the market. You take the basic ingredient ammonium hydroxide that every window cleaner contains and give it a special name: Clapp-a-san. Then you register it as a trademark. You can now advertise your product as: "The only glass cleaner with Clapp-a-san." Does that sound familiar?

Later in this chapter we will discuss the elements of a presentation, for now, concentrate on discovering the USP for your product or service. Focus on that difference when you sell.

Never assume that the flashy brochures the company gives you are good. What if a product manager with absolutely no sales experience selected them? No thought was ever given to asking the sales force what they thought. Apply the substitute test I described above if you're unsure. Substitute your competitor's brand for yours in the brochure. Does it still make sense? Are the claims so broad that they would apply to practically any competing brand on the market? You are probably holding a generic brochure that an ad agency sold to your company.

I've learned that if you read through all of the fluff, you will find the USP buried in the small print. Use that hidden feature and benefit to promote your product. Refer to the five steps of the presentation to see how you can develop your own advertising campaign.

You may sell the identical product for the same price as everyone else, if so, make the USP "you" and the quality of service you provide.

While I was working a small town on Long Island, I stopped into a pizzeria for lunch. New York has the greatest pizza in the world and a pizzeria on every corner. Perhaps the crust is a bit thicker or the sauce is spicier from one place to the next, but they all taste about the same.

I ordered two slices and a medium soda. The owner dropped the plate on the counter and barked: "$4.80!"

"$4.80? That's a bit steep. In my neighborhood, it's about three bucks."

He slapped his hand on the counter and yelled: "You don't like my pizza, go someplace else."

"Good idea!" I said as I left.

Life is too short and there are too many restaurants to put up with rude service. One day he will hang up the "Out of Business" sign and padlock the front door. He'll scratch his head and wonder why nobody liked his pizza.

ME TOO PRODUCTS

A "me too" product is a copycat of another product. All of the service stations in a small town sell name brand gas at the same price. They all clean the customers' windshield and check their oil.

To differentiate himself from the other "me too" stations, one station offers to vacuum the customers' cars free with each fill up. He has now set himself apart from the pack and the others must play catch-up to maintain their market share.

Look closely at your product and service and what your competition offers. How can you make yourself different and better?

One manufacturer I worked for had a product that was a cash cow. A cash cow is a product that generates profit with little or no investment of advertising. Unfortunately, this cash cow had a minuscule market share and was difficult to keep on the shelves at major chain stores. These chains would not stock any product that had a market share below a certain percentage. The company reclassified the cash cow as the "Number One Adult Product." Their market share went from near zero to 100 percent since it was the only product in that category. No store wanted to be without the number one adult product. They succeeded in stabilizing their cash cow.

Sometimes all you need is a little service to set you apart from the crowd. In retailing, I had a snack rack that sold well; but because of poor service, it was usually empty. I had to phone the company every two weeks and ask for the rack jobber to come in to refill the display. My boss would constantly complain about the rack being empty. My workload was overwhelming. It quickly became a thorn in my side. A new rack jobber cold called our store. He said, he would provide full service, build the display and come in each week, clean and refill it. I said, "Yes, bring it in."

I called the old jobber and told them to come pick up their rack and why we were changing vendors. They offered us a 20 percent discount on our next order, if we kept their service. I told them that it wasn't the money: it was the lack of service.

WHEN ALL THINGS ARE EQUAL, MAKE SERVICE YOUR UNIQUE SELLING POSITION.

SELLING

Selling, as defined by the Harcourt Brace & World Standard College Dictionary, is "The transfer of property to another for money or some other consideration." It's how you make a living.

You take your product to customers. You ask what their needs are, tell them what your product will do for them, and ask them to buy it. Then you deliver the product or service in exchange for money. You've earned part of that money as your compensation. Amazingly, there are those in this profession who have not grasped this simple concept.

There are sales managers who think selling is a bunch of reps that call each week and report their sales numbers to him. He adds up the numbers and calls his boss and says, "I sold $35,000 this week. Isn't that wonderful?"

There are sales reps that go to their customers to pick up orders that the customers decided on their own they needed; call their boss and say, "I sold $2,000 this week. Isn't that wonderful?"

I met a customer at a convention whose office was outside my territory. I asked what his needs were; presented a solution and he agreed to buy the product. Then the rep, who covered that particular territory, returned from his break. I handed him the signed order as my company policy required me to do. He used his cell phone, and right in front of me called his boss and said, "I just wrote a $3,000 order, isn't that wonderful?" The rep was acknowledged in the company newsletter for writing the largest order at the convention.

Selling is a very pro-active profession. You leave the house with an empty bag, (meaning you have no signed orders) and hopefully, return at night with a full bag. You never know who you will meet during the day. Life may impose many obstacles on you that you must surmount.

ALTHOUGH THINGS ARE BOUGHT AND SOLD EVERY DAY FEW PEOPLE TRULY UNDERSTAND THE PROCESS.

THE RECEPTIONIST

The reps who call on professionals and on office managers must overcome an obstacle other reps don't have to face, the office receptionist.

Before you can get past the receptionist, to see the decision-maker, you must first understand the receptionist's position and responsibility. While preparing this book, I took the opportunity to speak to many receptionists about their job and what they face on a daily basis. By understanding their role, you can learn to overcome this obstacle.

In legal publishing, I called on one office seven or eight times before I got in to see the lawyer. I commented to him what a tough task I had getting past his secretary.

"Good," he said. "I'm glad she's doing the job I hired her for. I would never get any work done if I stopped to see every salesman who came by."

Some reps believe the only reason a receptionist exists is so they can announce to the attorney, "Joe Blow is here to sell you something."

Do you read every piece of junk mail that comes into your home from cover to cover, or just the ones that grab your attention? Do you listen to every commercial on TV, or do you run to the kitchen to grab a snack? Do you listen to every sales pitch on the telephone, or do you ask your spouse to get rid of them? Why then, should a busy professional be any different?

Use "Total Empathy" and place yourself in the position of a lawyer commanding $300 per hour. You are paying a receptionist $18,500 a year to take care of basic office duties, one of which is to shield you from time wasters. What would your reaction be if she allowed every rep that stopped in, to see you?

A responsibility of the receptionist is to screen out those who would waste the boss's time. You must convince her that your message, product or service is of value to her boss. That takes time and many repeat calls. I've become so jaded that if I get right in to see a professional on the first try, I believe he's either broke or in retirement.

My guidelines are simple:

Take the title "Sales Representative" off your business card. You are advertising your true mission, to sell stuff. Put only your name, company and phone number on the card.

- Never be rude or condescending to a receptionist.
- When you're turned down, ask how you might get in to see the boss.
- Don't give a receptionist too much information. If they can figure out why you're there, it becomes easier to get rid of you.
- Think of it as a game. Their job is to say no. Your job is to make them say yes.
- The receptionist or office manager may say you must have an appointment. Open your appointment book and say, "Great, how about 2 p.m.?"
- Create a sense of urgency, you won't be back for a year and stress this is the only time you have.
- Never leave literature in lieu of a sales call. The buyer will never see it. There is an exception. While selling tax research to CPAs I had to call on corporate tax departments. In many cases the receptionist would not divulge the names of the tax manager. I checked annual reports and their Internet pages for the names, but to no avail. In this case I would visit the company and explain my dilemma to the receptionist. If I could not get the contact name or see the tax managers secretary, I would leave a brochure and business card. In a few cases it worked, but it is time consuming and frustrating.
- In a sales position where you have a defined territory and see the receptionist on a regular basis, bring a candy dish for the desk. Then you have a reason to return, to refill it. Use a glass dish with your business card taped to the inside, facing out. Sometimes they will even call you for a refill when the jar is empty. As you refill the jar ask, "Since I'm here, can I see Mr. Smith for a moment?"

- In a service job, as in selling subscription law books, say you're there to audit the library to insure the attorney is getting everything he is paying for.
- A pharmaceutical rep may say that he or she needs to check the supply cabinet for expired drug samples.
- Bring breakfast in for the staff; a box of doughnuts or a bag of bagels goes along way.
- Acknowledge the receptionist's role: "I know your job is to get rid of reps, and you're doing a wonderful job. However, what I have is important and will help your boss do a better job."
- Makes the receptionist think twice: "Are you sure you want me to leave? What if your boss finds out I was here and she needs my product?"

SEVEN STEPS OF THE CALL

Tailor these seven steps to your industry and memorize them. Follow the procedure on each call. After a short time they will be second nature and part of your everyday conversation.

Step 1. PLAN YOUR CALL. Know who you will see, how you will get there and what you will sell them. Have a plan prepared before you walk in the door. Prepare a suggested order in case you meet the buyer walking out as you walk in. You can hand him or her the suggested order and ask if you can stop in later. Have a brochure with your card and details of the promotion in your hand.

When you meet the decision-maker in a hallway, parking lot or standing next to the receptionist desk, it is a selling opportunity. I call them, "hallway" presentations. I've written many orders on the spot. Always acknowledge the decision-maker's valuable time. Walk with him or her down the hall and say, "Hi Ms. Jones. I'm Mike Swedenberg. I can tell you're in a hurry. May I leave you this brochure? I believe it will help you in your practice. I will get back to you at two o'clock to follow up." I didn't ask if I may see the customer at two o'clock. I said I would be back.

Think positive and assume the customer is interested. Don't give them the opportunity to say "No." Once they say "No," negotiations become difficult and in a hallway presentation there is no time to overcome objections. Instead, focus on what time you will come back, not if they want the product. The customer may say "No" again. Assume that they disapprove of the time, not the product. Then ask, "Would three o'clock be better?"

Step 2. INTRODUCTION. At some point of the sales call, you must introduce yourself to the decision-maker. In many industries, there are things to do before you make a presentation, like taking inventory. Before you do that, take a moment to say hello to the buyer and let him or her know you're there. They will expect you when you come back for a presentation.

Years ago, when I was a pharmacy manager, I had reps walk up to me and hand me suggested orders that they had written. They had been in the store for twenty minutes taking inventory and building displays. They were angry to learn that they had to tear down the display because they put them in the wrong area or we had postponed the promotion for a week. Simply put; let the buyer know you're in the store or office before you proceed with the call. If the store manager says he doesn't have time today to see you, ask if it's alright to check the shelves and inventory and that you will come back later. Leave a suggested order when you leave. That way, most of your work will be done when you return.

Step 2. CHECK INVENTORY. Nothing is more embarrassing than to give a buyer a presentation and suggested order, only to have them say that there are thirty cases of your stuff in the back room. You would have seen it if you had bothered to look. You may think that they don't have any inventory, but they may have bought your merchandise from a wholesaler since your last visit. Taking inventory also allows you to look for "out of stock" situations, competitive activity and empty areas for displays.

In cases where you sell office equipment, instead of taking inventory, you do an on site inspection. You take the time to look at traffic flow, volume needs and special requirements. When you make your presentation, you have a greater understanding of the buyer's needs and can recommend the proper equipment.

Whatever the type of selling you do, taking inventory or stock of the situation lends authority to your presentation. You aren't just there to sell something, but as a consultant to help resolve problems. It's part of treating your buyers like clients rather than customers.

Step 4. PRESENTATION. Please refer to the next section for the five steps of the presentation.

Step 5. MERCHANDISING. Whether you write an order or not, you may have an opportunity to merchandise the product you already have in the store or office. This could entail building displays, point of purchase merchandising, cleaning an existing piece of equipment, or talking with the accountant to rectify a past due invoice. Do this after the order is written. The buyer may leave or no longer have time to see you if you delay the presentation.

Step 6. PAPERWORK. Do your paperwork, while the information is fresh in your mind. This includes call reports, changes of phone numbers or personnel changes. You will forget important details if you wait until the end of the week. The file you're creating will be totally useless. Do your paperwork after each call; your paperwork will be done by the end of the day.

Step 7. ANALYZE THE CALL. This is an important mental step. As you drive or walk to your next call, reflect on the success or failure of the last call. Think about each step of the call. What did you do that was right or wrong? Were there things that the buyer said that you didn't act on? When you find something new and useful, try to repeat it on the next call.

OPENING

The purpose of an opening is to start a conversation. When cold call canvassing, you need to introduce yourself, your company and the purpose of your call.

An example would be:

"Hello. My name is_____ and I'm with _____, the number one manufacture of_____ in the United States."

Our product can reduce your costs due to a 6.4 percent reduction in electric power needs and increase your production with a 15.5 percent increase in productivity. I need only four minutes to explain the system in general terms. At that point, you can determine a need for further discussion. "May we talk now?"

Let us examine each section of the opening:

"Hello. My name is_____ and I'm with _____. We are the number one manufacture of_____ in the U.S."

This tells the customer who you are, what company you work for and the success your product has achieved. I didn't mention the title of "sales representative." That sends a red flag up in the customer's mind. Instead of thinking about what you're saying, they are wondering what you're trying to sell them and how they can get rid of you. This isn't a presentation. The purpose is to open lines of communication.

"Our product can reduce your costs and increase your production due to a 6.4 percent reduction in electric power needs and a 15.5 percent increase in productivity."

Your product delivers this benefit to the customer. This assumes that the customer has older, less efficient equipment and that saving money and increasing productivity is a goal of his. There are two safe assumptions to make at this early stage of the sales call. To determine what things to say about your product or service in an opening, see the following section on "Features and Benefits."

"I need only four minutes to explain the system in general terms. At that point, you can determine the need for further discussion."

You aren't there to waste their time and the decision to continue discussion is entirely theirs. I use an odd time like four minutes because everyone says, "I only need five minutes." I once had a prospect take his desk clock and turn it around so we could both see it. He said, "OK, you now have three minutes and fifty-three seconds." I was able to finish in time.

Practice your short hallway presentation, time yourself and use that time frame. Stick to your word! Don't ramble and don't try to get into a full presentation until part four of the opening and the buyer says, "This would be a good time, right now."

"May we talk now?"

Ask if you may begin the first part of the sales call known as probing. You don't ask if they want to buy the product. You ask if you can take time now to begin discussion of the product. This assumes that they are interested and are deciding if now is a good time. As an alternative, use the "Strategy of Choice."

If the buyer seems busy, then offer a choice of time: "Would now be a good time? How about two o'clock?" They then decide WHEN, not IF they want to see you. Use the "Strategy of Choice" throughout the sales process. A cold call becomes a set appointment. You have a reason to return and the buyer is expecting you.

PROBING

Probes are questions you ask the customer about their needs and objectives BEFORE you begin a presentation.

I received a phone call at home from a woman who launched into a prepared script about the oil heat company she represented. She spoke very quickly and was obviously reading. She talked about the low cost, free service contract and free burglar alarm given to each new customer. The spiel went on for about a minute and concluded by asking if a sales representative, who just happened to be in the neighborhood, could stop by. I believe she delivered the entire presentation without once taking a breath. I politely declined.

"Why not?" She asked incredulously.

"I have gas heat," I replied.

"Oh. Thanks for your time sir."

DON'T ASSUME; ASK! WHEN YOU ASS/U/ME, YOU MAKE AN ASS OUT OF U AND ME.—Unknown.

Many reps make assumptions about customers. They assume that everyone is looking for the lowest priced item. They assume that everyone is unhappy with their present service. They believe everyone is willing to drop what they are doing and make a snap decision because a sales rep walked in the door.

Not everyone is price conscious; some are willing to pay more in exchange for service and reliability. Some people have dealt with the same supplier for years and have had many reps try to switch them. Others simply hate change. It's too much bother, even if it means a few extra dollars in savings.

Finally, there are those who equate high price with quality. They gladly pay full or an inflated price because that's the only way they can distinguish one product from another. This may be true sometimes. There is no question that a $60,000 luxury sports sedan is higher in quality than a $7,000 econobox. A quick spin around the block in each can tell you that.

What about sister cars? Identical cars manufactured by the same company and sold through two different divisions. The only difference is the plastic trim and name, but the price difference can be $10,000. Some buy the more expensive version because it costs more and they reason it must be better. It also may be a status symbol.

This leads us to the concept of probing. Had the oil company telemarketer asked if I had oil heat, instead of assuming I did, she could have saved herself time and embarrassment. What do you think her frustration level is at the end of the day?

Depending on your product and service, you may approach probing in a variety of ways. You must find out what the customers' needs and goals are. They may not know that they have needs. It's your job to uncover them and then provide a product or service to resolve those needs.

When I sold consumer goods, I generally had to ask only one probing question before I gave my presentation. "Mr. Grocer, if I could show you how to increase your volume and profit, would you be interested?" Volume and profit are two goals I knew from experience that my grocers wanted to achieve. Depending on his marketplace, he may wish to achieve higher volume at the expense of profit or vice versa; however, most would like to achieve both simultaneously.

A question I could ask a car owner is, "Would you be interested in increasing your miles per gallon and your horsepower without spending extra money?" To say no would make the owner look foolish.

Remember two important guidelines when probing:

1. Know the answer before you ask the question. If I'm selling an attorney a set of books for an area of law he normally doesn't practice, I may ask: "Counselor, are you tired of sending clients to your competition?"

2. Deliver on your promises: "We have a great set of law books on New York State Wills that take you through the process step by step. This will enable you to retain new clients who may bring you more important work in the future. Besides, if you send your client to another attorney, next time they have a problem, who are they going to call, you or the last attorney who helped them?"

When selling a sophisticated product like pharmaceuticals, you must ask the physician a series of probing questions.

When I sold an antifungal cream, to dermatologists, I had a prepared list of thirty probes. I asked five or six from the list below, before I began my presentation. I could then tailor the presentation to the doctor's specific needs and expectations.

Following are some of those probes I worked from:

*   "Doctor, can you tell me about your practice?"
*   "What type of fungal infections do you see?"

- "How do you like to treat them?"
- "Are you always pleased with the results?"
- "Is cost ever a factor?"
- "How many cases are recalcitrant?" (The rash keeps coming back.)
- "What do you do then?"
- "What product have you been using?"
- "Does it always work to your expectations?"
- "Tell me what the ideal antifungal would be like."

Even if you aren't trained in pharmacology, I'm confident you get the drift of my questioning. Each question sets the stage for my presentation. I developed my probes based on my product's features and benefits. My product had distinct advantages over the competition and before I begin my presentation I have the doctor's attention focused on these key areas.

Reps who sell photocopiers would ask questions about the customer's copier needs. They ask about traffic flow, number of employees and so forth. Once they gather the information, the reps can tailor their presentation to the specific needs of the customer. They would emphasize the relevant features and discount the irrelevant ones. If the customer indicated that the bulk of the copies made are single sheets, there would be little use in presenting the built in stapler. On the other hand if the customer needs six page reports, the stapling feature becomes an important selling point. Why present a feature the customer can't use?

A rack jobber selling snacks may ask the store manager about traffic flow or clientele. "Is there a busy office or a high school nearby?" That would help the buyer decide how to position the display and what snacks to stock. If the store sells a lot of cold soft drinks, the jobber would want to place the rack near the soda machine for strong tie-in sales. It drives me nuts when I walk into a convenience store to buy a soft drink and then have to walk around looking for the pretzels. I feel like screaming at the owner: "Put a stupid display of snacks by the soda, for crying out loud." I understand that retailers spread thing around the store to encourage you to shop around. This drives impulse sales, but it still drives me nuts.

For other types of products and services, look at the features and benefits and use them to help build a list of probing questions. As you gain experience, you will add new ones and discard others.

NEVER BE AFRAID TO ASK CUSTOMERS ABOUT SPECIFIC PROBLEMS OF THEIR BUSINESS. IT DEMONSTRATES YOUR DESIRE TO LEARN ABOUT THEIR NEEDS AND GOALS.

NEVER ASK CUSTOMERS GENERAL QUESTIONS ABOUT THEIR COMPANY. DO YOUR HOMEWORK.

There is a difference between asking a potential client about his specific needs and asking the buyer for International Automobile Steering Wheel Manufacturers for Cars with Right Hand Drive LTD, what kind of business they are in. Use the Internet or visit the local library to learn about your customers. Publicly held companies issue annual reports that detail their products and services. Sometimes, there are catalogues available in the waiting room. The more you know before you walk in the buyer's office, the more professional you will be.

THE MAGIC BULLET OF PROBING

In the Foreword, I promised you one question that would make your customer change from your competitor to your product or service, and then thank you for it. I call it my magic bullet.

During the probing session, you will run across customers who are loyal to your competition. Focus on your one major advantage, for instance, price. The competition and you both have a good product but yours is 20 percent less expensive. The magic bullet to use is: "If you could change one thing about the product you're now using, what would it be?"

You know the answer is cost, but you have brought it up in such a fashion that it is the customer, who exposes the competitors major weakness, not you. For you to say, "The competition charges too much," you invite the customer to defend his purchasing decision. He or she might say,

"They are a few dollars more, but I get great service." By asking an open ended question, you allow the customer to verbalize the objection to the competition.

NEVER CRITICIZE YOUR COMPETITOR. IT'S UNPROFES-SIONAL AND THE CUSTOMER MAY COME TO THEIR DEFENSE.

A potential client, one I had been unsuccessful in meeting, called to set an appointment. He told me the competitor's rep had been in and spent fifteen minutes bashing my product and service. The client was so curious, that he had to see for himself how bad we were. He discovered that our product was indeed superior. He didn't like dealing with an unprofessional rep and thought that we must be doing something right to make our competitor nervous. I want to thank the rep for the order I got that day.

Sometimes reps are tempted to criticize their competitors. Consider this actual conversation between a buyer and a sales rep that I overheard.

As the rep walked through the factory floor, he stopped a worker and pointed to his competitor's equipment.

"Well, who's the idiot who bought the Acme Roto machine?"

"Me! I'm the idiot." The worker quips.

"Didn't you realize that our Mr. Roto machine cost less and is faster?"

"I had other considerations."

"Boy that was a big mistake. I bet you regret it now."

"See the {expletive deleted} door?"

"Yes."

"Leave!"

This isn't an exaggeration. I've heard otherwise good reps openly criticize a buying decision without realizing they were talking to the decision-maker.

Imagine if you drove in to a car dealership and wanted to trade your pride and joy in for a new car. How would you feel if the salesman asked: "I can't believe you bought a Dorkmobile. Let me show you our new Coolride." Would that put you on the defensive? Would you be open to deal with a person like that?

This evolves from pride of ownership. I've never sold anything that I didn't have confidence in. I understand my competition and know the distinct advantages of my product over theirs. The greatest danger of bashing the competition, especially if the customer is presently using it, is that you're indirectly telling the customer that they made a mistake. The buyer will defend his or her decision making process. It's bad form to point out someone else mistake, especially when you're trying to sell them something.

At one publishing company, my advantage over my competitor was in price and format. We approached a legal issue from a different perspective. My job was to get attorneys to cancel their subscription to other publishers and to subscribe to mine.

When I presented books to an attorney who had the competing set, I said: "The set you own is a great publication. I've taken time to review it, and I can see it's many advantages." I've reinforced the attorney's buying decision. By complimenting my competitor, I place myself on the high ground.

I then say: "We have taken a good idea one step better." or, use the magic bullet: "If you could change one thing about the set you now subscribe to, what would it be?"

The door is open if customer mentions cost. If the customer doesn't raise the cost issue, it's O.K. to bring it in the back door as a benefit during your presentation: "Counselor, The benefits to our publication are one, two, and three. In addition our set is inexpensive to maintain. What are you presently paying?" (I already know the answer.)

NEVER ASK A COST QUESTION UNLESS YOU ALREADY KNOW THE ANSWER.

CLOSED END QUESTIONS

These are probing questions used to get either a yes or no answer. Avoid closed ended questions when you're probing to discover aspects of a customer's business or buying habits. They should ONLY be used in the close. Examples are:

• Are you prepared to make a decision today?

- Are you interested in our service?
- Do you prefer to pay cash or credit?

When you ask a closed end question, you may get an answer you aren't looking for:
"Are you happy with your current supplier?"
"Yes I am."
Even if the customer isn't happy with his current supplier, he may be reluctant to admit it, because you are a "pesky salesman" and will try to sell him something. It's easier to say "No!"

OPEN ENDED QUESTIONS

These are probing questions that request more than a yes or no answer. Use them DURING the presentation. They can generate a wealth of information.

Examples are:
- Can you tell me about your business cycle?
- What type of customers do you see most often?
- What type of problems have you experienced in the past?

Keep your open-ended question to two or three; don't give your customer the third degree. If your open-ended question generates interesting information, but not enough for your presentation, you may ask: "Can you tell me more about that?"

FEATURE VS BENEFIT

One of my managers had a great way to explain the difference between a feature and a benefit.

"If you say something about your product and the buyer asks, 'SO WHAT?' it's a feature. If he says, 'WOW!' It's a benefit."

A feature is an aspect of your product or service. An example is that you sell an on-line investment software program that allows you to buy and sell stocks. One of the many features is a "Customized Daily News Update." (SO WHAT?) The benefit is what that feature will do for your customer. The Daily News Update sends you an e-mail on any stock splits, earnings reports and mergers. You can customize it for any stock, mutual fund and news item you prefer. This gives you valuable information that occurred overnight that would affect your investment before the market opens. (WOW!)

Bill is a sales representative trying to sell a shop supervisor one case of disposable ballpoint pens for use in the warehouse. Bill is talking about features; however, the shop supervisor is listening for benefits. See if you can tell when the sales rep stops talking "SO WHAT" and starts talking "WOW."

"Mr. Stevens, unlike any other disposable pen, our ball point pen has a pressurized ink cartridge."

"So what?"

"The ink is kept under constant pressure." Bill replies.

"So what?" Stevens asks again.

"The ink flows at a constant rate."

"So what?"

Bill wondered why the supervisor didn't get it. After all, he has given this presentation a hundred times; the benefit is perfectly clear. The rep tried to make it simpler.

"The air pressure in the cartridge forces the ink toward the ball point at all times."

"So what?"

Bill thought to himself, this guy is thick as a brick; any idiot can see the benefit. I better spell it out for him. Bill continues, "The benefit is that the pen will write at any angle, even upside down. So when you're making notes on a clipboard hanging on the wall, or lying on your back while entering an inspection number to the bottom of a machine, the pen will always write. You don't have to stop every few seconds and shake the pen to make it work."

"Wow! Why didn't you say so before?"

"I thought I did." Bill quips.

"Send me five cases at once," the supervisor exclaims.

JUST BECAUSE THE BENEFIT IS OBVIOUS TO YOU, IT'S NOT ALWAYS OBVIOUS TO THE CUSTOMER.

When self-winding watches were introduced about sixty years ago, the benefit was self evident to anyone who wore a watch. As long as you wore it, the movement of your arm kept the watch wound. Perhaps the mechanics weren't widely understood but you knew you no longer had to wind the watch every day to keep it running.

In the 1970's when the quartz watch was introduced, the benefit of a battery operated watch wasn't obvious. People believed it to be a variation of a successful product that was more accurate; since that was the way it was advertised.

The benefit was that the watch would continue to run even if you took it off and left it on the dresser for a year. That was something a self winding watch couldn't do. The ads only stressed the accuracy. The benefit wasn't self evident to the public.

In the late 1980's, long after the quartz watch was introduced, I met a rep at a training class who wound his quartz watch every morning before class.

"Why are you winding a battery operated watch?" I asked.

"I didn't know it had a battery. Aren't you suppose to wind it everyday?"

"Nope. It's like an electric clock."

"I've wound it every day for the last year and it works fine," he said defensively.

"All you're doing is spinning a watch stem that isn't attached to anything except the gears that adjust the hands. It has no mainspring. There is nothing to wind," I said.

It wasn't until I removed the battery and his watch stopped that he understood the benefit of a quartz watch.

He wasn't the only one who didn't see the obvious. I used a word processor for six months before I discovered what "Spell Check" was. I would type a letter, and then review it with a dictionary to check my spelling.

THE PRESENTATION

The presentation is a sales tool that allows for a two-way conversation between a seller and a buyer. It isn't a one-way conversation where the seller talks and the buyer just listens. Think of a presentation as a radio transmission. A one-way conversation is when you listen to a radio broadcast in your home. It's not interactive. They talk and you listen.

A two-way conversation is like a Citizens Band radio. Both you and another CB operator talk to each other. It's interactive.

ALL PRESENTATIONS SHOULD BE A TWO WAY CONVERSATION.

ASERT

ASERT is an acronym for: Get the buyers' Attention, Say what you want, Explain it, Review benefits and Trial close.

As with many aspects of successful selling, there are steps involved in the presentation. You should progress through the steps in order. Memorize them and they will become part of your thought pattern. You can then expand the system of ASERT to every aspect of sales and negotiations including direct mail advertising.

ATTENTION

First, get the buyers' attention. Say something to peak their interest enough to make them stop what they are doing and devote a few minutes to what you have to say.

I've written an example of each step of the presentation for someone selling a display of candy to a retail store. For this example you should know that dead space is any area of the selling floor that isn't producing income for the store. If a store has five-hundred square feet of floor space and they are paying $2,000 per month in rent, each square foot is costing them $4 per month. If the owner puts a candy display on the floor, it will generate income and the space it occupies will be "live." That is why most retail displays are designed to fit into one square foot. (This is known as the footprint.)

Attention: "I can convert one square foot of dead space in your store to $50 worth of profit a month."

SAY WHAT YOU WANT

It's important to tell the buyer up front exactly what you want to do. Instead of paying attention to what you're saying, the buyer will be trying to figure out what you're selling and how to get rid of you.

Say what you want: "My idea is for you to put this display of candy in your store."

EXPLAIN IT

Explain exactly how the program works. With experience, you will learn to anticipate objections. Address as many of them as possible in this step.

Explain it: "Here is how it works. My candy is a proven winner. We have more than seventy-five displays in this county alone. At full markup, and a volume of only one-hundred pieces a month, which is the average, you will generate $50 a month in profit. The attractive display takes up one square foot of space and holds six cases of assorted candy. The candy is rotated on a monthly basis and is a guaranteed sale." (A guaranteed sale means the store gets full credit for any unsold inventory.)

"I will build the display, clean and refill it each month. There is no obligation or contract to sign; if you ever decide you want it out, just call and I will pick it up."

REVIEW BENEFITS

Emphasize what is in it for the store. Emphasize the benefits not features. The benefits to you are:

"You will turn one square foot of wasted space in to a profit center. You will generate $50 in profit per month. The attractive display will encourage impulse sales and put more dollars in your register. It's a guaranteed sale and I will maintain and clean it as well."

TRIAL CLOSE

A close is when you ask for the business. This is a trial close because you haven't finished with the presentation. In most cases, you will have to overcome objections before the buyer makes a decision; however, a trial close will indicate the interest level and may result in an early sale.

Trial close: "Ms. Jones, I have a display rack in my car and can have it set up in fifteen minutes. How about that dead space by the second cash register?" (Don't ask IF she wants the rack; ask WHERE she wants the rack.)

Another trial close is giving the buyer a choice in quantity, "How about two racks instead of one? We can put one in the candy aisle and the other by the register."

YOU KNOW THERE IS A SPACE FOR THE DISPLAY NEAR REGISTER NUMBER- TWO BECAUSE YOU FOLLOWED STEP THREE OF THE SALES CALL AND FOUND A SPACE BEFORE YOU MADE YOUR PRESENTATION.

Following are other examples of ASERT:

Example 2
ATTENTION: "I can increase your volume and profit without you spending any money."
SAY WHAT YOU WANT: "My idea is for you to move our product off the bottom shelf and place it at eye level."
EXPLAIN IT: "Here is how it works: Any product sells faster at eye level. Since we have a higher volume (or profit) than our competitor, you will benefit by placing us at eye level.

REVIEW THE BENEFITS: "The benefit to you is an increase in volume and profit."

TRIAL CLOSE: "Is now a good time? How about first thing tomorrow?"

Example 3

ATTENTION: "We can increase your productivity and still show a 6 percent savings in overhead."

SAY WHAT YOU WANT: "My idea is for you to purchase our high speed photocopier."

EXPLAIN IT: "Here is how it works: Our copier is faster than any other on the market. This results in less time your staff has to wait in line to make copies. Our superior quality results in lower down time and that's how you achieve an increase in productivity. You achieve a savings in overhead because our machine requires 6 percent less energy to run."

REVIEW THE BENEFITS: "The benefit to you is higher productivity and lower overhead."

TRIAL CLOSE: "We can have the machine delivered and running by Friday. Is that soon enough?"

Example 4

ATTENTION: "Doctor, would you be interested in an effective drug that can be used once a day versus the twice a day one you're now pre-scribing?"

SAY WHAT YOU WANT: "My idea is for you to prescribe my new drug on your next ten patients. This way you can see for yourself how good it is."

EXPLAIN IT: "Here is how it works: Our drug isn't absorbed through the skin, therefore only has to be applied once a day vs. twice a day as in the drug you're now prescribing. You can help your patients save money by prescribing a smaller size tube."

REVIEW THE BENEFITS: "The benefit to you is that you give your patients a good drug that's easier to use and saves them money."

TRIAL CLOSE: "Will you prescribe our drug for the next ten patients who need it?"

Example 5

ATTENTION: "How would you like to stop sending your customers to your competition?"

SAY WHAT YOU WANT: "Counselor, my idea is for you to expand your legal practice into a new area."

EXPLAIN IT: "Here is how it works: Stop sending people who ask you to prepare wills or trusts to other attorneys. Our treatise takes you through each step of preparing simple wills and trusts. We also include the forms on computer disk. You simply pull the will up on your screen and fill in the blanks. This set will pay for itself the first time you use it, the rest is increased profit and these new clients may ask you to represent them in other areas as well."

REVIEW THE BENEFITS: "The benefit to you is you increase your revenues and future potential."

TRIAL CLOSE: "Would you like me to send the books third class mail? What if I send them express mail at my expense?"

Example 6

ATTENTION: "I can reduce your inventory levels without costing you any money."

SAY WHAT YOU WANT: "My idea is for you to build a display of your back room inventory in a high traffic area."

EXPLAIN IT: "Here is how it works: Displays, set up in high traffic areas of your store, increase the number of sales of that item by 250 percent. By taking the merchandise out of the back room and placing it on display, you will lower your inventory and increase your sales. You won't have to spend any money on labor since I will do the work for you."

REVIEW THE BENEFITS: "The benefit to you is you lower your back room inventory and put the cash in your register faster."
TRIAL CLOSE: "I have the time to build the display now. Is that O.K., or do you prefer this afternoon?"

NO ONE EVER DIED ASKING FOR THE BUSINESS

There are sales reps that think it is undignified to ask someone to buy something from them. Reps should find their own comfort level in sales; but I think you're just plain nuts if you don't ask for the business.

These reps think they have done their job by getting into the buyer, uncovering needs and making a good presentation. Then it is up to the customer to express an interest in making a purchase.

Years ago, I worked part time during the holiday rush at a large department store in Roosevelt Field, on Long Island. I worked in the men's department with a woman who was assistant manager. When a customer expressed interest in a sweater, I didn't ask if she wanted to buy it, I asked: "Would that be cash or credit?" More often than not I made a sale. As we walked to the register, I would stop at the shirt rack and say, "Hey, this shirt would go nicely with this sweater, would you like that too?" Many times I made a multiple sale.

The assistant manager, Ms. Thumble, pulled me aside and said, "That is the wrong thing to do. You are a clerk, not some kind of fancy salesman. Don't be pushy."

"I just make suggestions. I don't twist anyone's arm. I ask once, if they say no, I just drop it." She was adamant and finally, one night, I said, "Ms Thumble, look at the register at the end of day. You always have about $600 in receipts and I have more than $1,500. Isn't that the purpose of being in business?"

That was my last day at the department store. The manager said Ms. Thumble found me difficult to work with.

I heard a great story on sales from one of my managers. Frank was an insurance agent and he spoke of a yearlong relationship with a potential customer, named Tom. They met often for golf and had a great personal relationship. Frank waited patiently for Tom to ask him to sell him life insurance. Frank recounted how devastated he was when Tom bought policies for his employees from another agent.

"Tom, after all of this time we have known each other, why did you buy insurance from a stranger?"

Tom seemed surprised at the question and replied, "Well Frank, you never asked me. The other agent showed up one day, made a presentation and asked me to buy the policies. I needed a new agent because I was unhappy with my old one, so I said yes."

"Tom, this won't affect our friendship; but, you knew I was in the insurance business."

Tom shrugged and said, "Of course, but all we ever talked about was family and golf, you never once mentioned insurance."

IF YOU DON'T ASK, YOU DON'T GET.

CHECKING

Checking simply means that you ask for input from the buyer during the presentation. This keeps the buyer's attention focused on what you're saying. After mentioning a feature / benefit, you ask, "How does that sound?" Wait for a response, either a yes or a nod.

Other checks include:
1. "Does that sound helpful to you?"
2. "Would that be beneficial?"
3. "Does that sound fair?"

Checking also opens the door for trial closes. If the response is, "Yes, that's exactly what I need!" then skip the rest of the presentation and go directly to a close. "Great! I can have it shipped in this Friday. Is that soon enough?"

A TIME TO SHUT UP

When you finish your presentation, ask for the business and then SHUT UP. The rule is: The first person, who talks, loses.

This is a game of nerves. You have asked Mr. Smith to purchase ten cases of your product. You sit eyeball to eyeball. He waits a few minutes, while he thinks over his decision. DON'T SAY A WORD! I don't care how thick the tension is or how great the temptation. DON'T SAY A WORD! The buyer has won if you do. DON'T START REPEATING YOURSELF. It's a sign of insecurity. If the buyer talks first, the business is yours. The only questions remaining are how much and how soon.

Zeke, my manager from Hell, never grasped this concept. When we worked together, I would ask the buyer for the business and then shut up. Zeke was unable to stay quiet for more than five seconds. He would start the presentation all over again. We rarely wrote any business when we worked together.

I tried to tell Zeke what I was doing, but he wouldn't listen, nor would he do what I asked. After all he was a "sales manager" and to him reps were just "scum of the earth."

Once, he interrupted my silent treatment and blew a major presentation. Afterwards, I politely said, "Zeke, I'm the sales rep. This is my territory, and I'm ultimately responsible for the success or failure of it. Please don't interrupt during a presentation. When I ask for the business and then shut up, I'm using a strategy that has worked very well for me in the past."

Zeke replied, "You are bordering on insubordination. I'm the manager and I will do as I please."

I never took Zeke to an important customer again.

I've seen reps talk themselves into a sale and promptly talk themselves out of one, simply because they wouldn't shut up.

I was watching a sales rep present a promotion to a store manager that involved one-hundred cases of shampoo for a large end cap display. He gave a competent presentation, overcame several objections, found a great spot for the display and asked for the business. The buyer was running in circles trying to unload a truck and said, "OK, send it in."

Instead of shutting up and writing the order, the rep kept selling. He brought up new topics about the promotion he hadn't mentioned before. This generated more questions from the buyer. The rep tried to answer them but succeeded only in placing a seed of doubt in the buyers mind. In a matter of moments, the buyer changed his mind. "Ya know what? Let me think about it. Call me on Friday and I will let you know what I will do."

I never saw the display in that store.

WHEN THE CUSTOMER SAYS, "YES." SHUT UP AND WRITE THE ORDER! YOU WON.

LISTENING

One of the most difficult things I had to learn as a sales rep was to listen to the customer. One training class I went to was a great exercise for developing this important skill. We each choose a partner, sat face to face and told each other our life story in about one-hundred words or so. We had to rely on our memory and couldn't take notes. We then had to stand in front of the class and describe the other person's life. Our partners could correct us if we made a mistake.

We continued this around the room until we had met with everyone. That day, during role-play, we gave presentations to each other in front of the class and had to throw in the personal information we had learned. This forced us to concentrate on what the other person was saying.

When our manager worked in the field with us, we would pause after each call, and repeat everything that had happened during the call. This is part seven of the Seven Steps of the Call, Analyzing the Call. This included whom we met, their names, their positions, any small talk, the presentation, the buyer's reactions and any questions asked.

In the beginning it was difficult and frustrating. However, as I gained experience, I learned to recount the entire sales call in total.

My boss would say, "Mike, during the presentation you mentioned the special sale and the buyer said last time he sold out early. You went ahead and suggested the same quantity as before. You know you should have increased your suggested order. Did you not hear him or was this some sort of secret strategy?"

The fact was, I heard him say that. I recalled it clearly once my manager mentioned it. I focused so much on delivering my presentation that I didn't pay attention to what the buyer was saying.

If you work for yourself and have only me as a trainer, I suggest you sit in front of the TV and listen to the evening news. At the end of the broadcast, recount how many details you can recall. Either tape the show and replay it or have someone take notes and ask you questions.

STRIKE WHILE THE IRON IS HOT

Many times a customer will give you a buying signal that indicates he's sold. You must listen carefully and be prepared to act quickly to take advantage before he changes his mind.

When I was a pharmacy manager, a sales rep called on me and launched into a product presentation. Although he did no probing and apparently spent no time looking the store over, I wanted to place an order. It was for merchandise that I'd been trying to locate. Several times during the presentation, I gave a buying signal.

"OK, that sounds good, when can we get it?"

"In about three days," He answered, then continued with his presentation

Again I gave him a buying signal: "That would be great, I've been looking for those. What is the minimum order?"

"No minimum, whatever you need is fine." He continued with his presentation.

I interrupted with another buying signal; "Can I get a display rack? I would like to put it in our window for a sale."

He nodded, "Yeah sure, whatever you want." He finished his presentation, handed me his card and said, "Well, maybe next time," then promptly left the store.

I followed him outside to stop him. "What's the problem? Aren't you going to write an order?"

He looked at me and said, "You didn't say you wanted the stuff."

"Yes I did, three times?"

He came back in, somewhat puzzled and wrote the order.

He was transmitting his message on a one-way radio. He couldn't pick up my buying signals and if it wasn't for me chasing him down the street he would have lost an order. I wasn't playing head games with him. I was a busy manager carrying on a normal conversation. Since I didn't grab him by the collar and shake him he thought I wasn't interested. Don't make your customers smack you in the head with a 2x4 so they can buy something.

IF YOU'RE HALFWAY THROUGH A PRESENTATION AND THE CUSTOMER GIVES YOU A BUYING SIGNAL, USE A TRIAL CLOSE. IF THE CUSTOMER SAYS YES, SHUT UP AND WRITE THE BUSINESS.

In the case where you have misunderstood his signal, the buyer will let you know: "Not so fast, I need more information," or something to that effect.

Examples of buying signals include:

"That will be fine."

"Sounds good to me."

"When can I get it?"

Specific questions about quantity, delivery, prices or promotional support are all buying signals.

THE FUN BEGINS WHEN THE BUYER SAYS, "NO!"

When a buyer says "No." you have the opportunity to distinguish yourself from most sales reps in the industry.

Believe me when I tell you, based on my thirty years in sales, there are precious few who know how to overcome objections. Most just argue with the customer, or worse, pack up and walk out of the door. Of all the aspects of this book, this chapter is the most important and this section is the most critical.

A buyer says "No" because he or she has a reason not to buy from you. It's your job to uncover that reason and overcome it.

The thirty-three reasons buyers say "No."

1. No room.
2. Wrong product or service.
3. Wrong clientele.
4. The buyer is satisfied with his present supplier.
5. The buyer doesn't see the need.
6. The buyer is lazy.
7. The buyer thinks it is too big for their needs.
8. The buyer is in a hurry to go home.
9. The buyer had a fight with the spouse that morning.
10. The buyer has no authority to buy.
11. His boss told him not to place any orders.
12. Your competitor is the buyer's brother-in-law.
13. You have bad breath.
14. The buyer doesn't like your tie.
15. You rub the buyer the wrong way.
16. The buyer thinks he can negotiate a better deal.
17. The buyer never says yes on the first try.
18. The buyer doesn't understand you.
19. The buyer is in a bad mood.
20. You messed up the last order.

21. The buyer thinks you're arrogant.
22. The buyer isn't convinced you understand his needs.
23. The buyer thinks you're a crook.
24. You are a crook, and the buyer knows it.
25. The buyer thinks you want to sell something they don't need or want.
26. The buyer hates all sales reps.
27. The buyer is stupid.
28. The buyer is smart, but thinks you're stupid.
29. It's the wrong day of the week.
30. The buyer has no reason; but, simply loves to give "pesky salesmen" a hard time.
31. You remind the buyer of another rep he hates.
32. The buyer is mad at your company.
33. The buyer is jealous because all sales reps are under worked and over paid.

Now, look at that list of objections. Do you think you have the time or patience to go over each one of them to determine which objection he or she has and then overcome it? You would be lucky to make two calls a day.

I dramatically increased my success level by asking the buyer, "What is the main reason you won't buy this product?" I will describe this multi-step process in detail.

FALSE OBJECTIONS
You have given your presentation to a store manager for a display of cologne. You asked for the business, shut your mouth and waited.

The buyer scratches his head and says, "No!"

"May I ask why not?" you ask politely.

THE FIRST OBJECTION OUT OF THE BUYER'S MOUTH IS PROBABLY A FALSE OBJECTION.

We hear and give false objections during the course of the day. Someone asks you a favor and you think of an excuse to say, "No." You don't want to hurt their feelings by telling them the true reason, so you offer a plausible excuse.

A clerk in a store flags you down in the aisle to show you a new line of sweaters. You smile and politely refuse, "Sorry, not today. I'm in a hurry." The truth is you have plenty of time; you just think the sweaters are hideous. You know if you stop and look you will feel guilty if you don't buy one. You are a nice person and you don't want to hurt the clerk's feelings. A false objection avoids confrontation.

After presenting a display to a store manager, he says, "No."

"May I ask why not?" (Do so politely; don't sound confrontational or sarcastic.)

"I don't have any room in my store for your display."

The truth is, he has plenty of room. If you offered him a display filled with $10,000 worth of merchandise absolutely free, he would manage to find room for it. However, you can't challenge him by saying, "Oh yes you do, right over there. What's the real reason you won't buy from me?"

NEVER CHALLENGE A BUYER.

NEVER DISMISS AN OBJECTION

When a buyer says, "We have no room," acknowledge the objection. Never challenge it or dismiss it. Doing so won't remove the objection; it will only drive it underground. It's better to acknowledge the objection by saying, "I understand. Space is a problem in your store."

FOLLOW UP

Ask the buyer: "Is there any other reason you can't buy the display?"

He may answer: "Well I think it has too much merchandise in it for my volume store."

Acknowledge: "I understand your concern with overstock."

Follow up again: "Is there any other reason?"

He may say: "Yes, it is too much work to build the display once it comes in."

You acknowledge again: "I see, well is there any other reason?"

I hope at this point, he will say: "No, that's about it."

DISCOVER THE TRUE OBJECTION

Instead of trying to answer each objection, simply ask which of the three objections is his real concern. "Well, let's see, you're concerned with space, the amount of inventory and building the display. Of those three things, what is your biggest concern?"

Such a question not only acknowledges the buyer's objections but also illuminates the real concern. The buyer may say, "Well I'm worried that the display has too much inventory and it will take to long to sell through."

CONFIRM THE TRUE OBJECTION

DON'T RESPOND YET! You can determine if that's the true objection by asking, "Well if I resolve that problem, will you reconsider and take the display?" You have challenged the buyer, but not in a threatening manner. When the buyer says, "Yes," then you know that's his real objection. You don't have to address the other two reasons.

If the buyer says, "No, even if you resolve that problem, I still won't buy the display." You haven't uncovered the true objection.

DON'T WASTE TIME ANSWERING FALSE OBJECTIONS.

OFFER A RESOLUTION.

The true reason was the amount of inventory.

"We have a smaller display with half as much inventory. Why don't we bring that one in instead?" You respond.

Now that you have offered a resolution to the concern, the buyer says, "OK, send it in."

IF THE BUYER STILL SAYS NO

You asked the right question, "If I resolve that problem, will you reconsider?" If the buyer says, "No!'" there maybe more than one objection. Start the process over.

"What else is on your mind?"

The buyer may say: "I don't have space, even with a smaller display."

You confirm again, "I understand. If I can find room for a smaller display, would you take it?" The buyer may say yes if those are the two real objections. Again, it is important to have followed the seven steps of the call. You already have scoped out the store and have found several good spots for the display. "There is a great spot in aisle four by the shaving cream. It would fit nicely there and be a great tie-in profit maker." You have succeeded. The buyer says, "Send it in."

USING ANALOGIES

Analogies are the power tools of salesmanship. They get the job done faster by demonstrating the relationship between two things that are similar.

In legal publishing, we had a set of law books that was about $3,000 less a year to maintain than the competition. An attorney I called on was unconvinced that it was worthwhile to change from one publisher to another. I said, "Counselor, keeping your current set of reference materials is like buying a Rolex® every year and throwing it out the window. You get no benefit from the effort."

It enabled me to focus on the cost benefit of our product. As much as the attorney loved his current publication, my analogy asked him if his current set was indeed worth the additional money. Sometimes it worked and I closed a sale.

Other analogies that worked for me varied as to my customer and the benefit I was trying to promote:

- "Mr. Smith, buying the competitor's high speed copier is like buying a brand new Cadillac® and pushing it off a cliff."

- "Doctor, using (our competitors medication) is like prescribing a placebo for your patients." (A placebo is a pill that has no active ingredients and used in medical tests.) NOTE: You may recall my discussion about criticizing the competition. In this rare situation, I had documented medical evidence that the competitor's product was so mild that it was ineffective on most patients.
- In Chapter One we discussed New Manager Syndrome. When the manager taped a $5.00 bill to a baseball and rolled it out the door. That was a physical analogy used to demonstrate profit leaving the store.
- I was trying to get past the receptionist who was the buyer's wife. I said, "He will save so much money with my product, he can afford to take you out to dinner." She smiled and let me in.
- "Our die press is so efficient and economical to run, you could save enough to go to Bermuda every year just to play golf."

Think about your product and service and it's main benefit. Then devise an analogy that the buyer can relate. Obviously the analogy of the Rolex® works better on a doctor who wears a quality watch than on a buyer who probably wouldn't appreciate the watch's value.

ADDED VALUE
Added value is when you express additional benefits to the buyer that aren't apparent. It might include savings in cost, time and additional business.

- The added value is that the money saved could go to enhance the law firm's library by purchasing publications in new areas.
- The benefit of tax books published on CD-ROM is the speed one can access information. The added value is that a CPA can literally carry around a complete library in a brief case and take it to

accounts. That is something that one can't do easily with bulky tax books.

- The added value of my sales book is that it will enhance your communication skills outside of the sales arena.
- The added value of a doctor prescribing an effective medication is that he can earn the reputation of being a good doctor. They therefore build the practice over the long run.

TIE-IN SALES

In the grocery industry, I used tie in sales to promote my brands in two ways. I knew that a huge display of soft drinks in the front of the store at a reduced price would attract a lot of attention. I would suggest that the grocery manager add a display of my potato chips at full price as a tie in. When the customers picked up a bottle of cola, they may buy some chips to go with it. The benefits to the grocer were additional dollars in the register and the ability to turn a low profit end cap to a high profit one.

When my potato chips were on sale, I would suggest that he tie in a display of soft drinks or beer at regular price for the same reason. I would even offer to build the soda display although I didn't work for the beverage company. It's another example of how I treated a buyer like a client instead of a customer.

When I sold copiers, I would suggest that we place a small desktop copier in the buyer's office so he or she wouldn't have to walk down the aisle to make a copy. My competitors hadn't offered this perk. If the order was large enough, I could structure the deal so that the desktop would come in at a nominal charge. Now, the buyer saw that there was something in it for him. I may not have earned much money on the desktop, but it increased my unit sales and helped clenched the deal.

In the pharmacy, half of the end cap displays would be stocked with sale items with no profit. The other half would be tie in items at regular price with a .75 profit. We converted a $1.59 sale with no profit into a $4.18 sale with a .75 profit.

Examine your product or service carefully. See if it can tie in with other products you sell or with other products your customer already uses.

IT'S SO SIMPLE

You are now able to double your sales from one out of ten to two out of ten. You can always close a borderline buyer with simple communication skills. You will succeed where others fail because they gave up too easily or got caught up trying to answer each objection as fast as the buyer threw them out. As you gain experience, you may even increase your success rate to three out of ten. Your income will triple too more than $100,000 a year.

IF YOU HAVE FOLLOWED THESE STEPS, OVERCOME THE OBJECTIONS AND THE BUYER STILL SAYS NO, DON'T GET FRUSTRATED. YOU HAVEN'T DONE A BAD JOB. SOMETIMES OBJECTIONS CAN'T BE OVERCOME. IT'S TIME TO MOVE ON. SELL IT TO HIS COMPETITION ACROSS THE STREET.

Once when I was in legal publishing, I tried everything I could to sell a nationally acknowledged set of law books to an attorney. I demonstrated that our set was recognized by the court and was more up-to-date than the competition. All the attorney could focus on was the price. We were several thousand dollars more than the competition. I could not overcome this objection. I packed up my sales bag and moved on. Several months later the lawyer called our customer service department and placed an order for that set of books. He made it clear that he did not want to speak to me directly. I learned of this when I got credit for the sale on my next commission report. Later, I got a call from another attorney who thanked me for selling him the same set of books. He was in court against the first attorney. The opposing counsel has cited my competitor's set. The second attorney objected, citing that my set noted the case in question had been recently overturned and therefore was bad law. The other attorney lost the case causing him embarrassment and his client a large sum of money.

Chapter Five

DO WHAT IT TAKES TO BRING IN THE BUSINESS

Throughout this book I've recounted stories of how I went out of my way to accommodate a customer. I do it because that's what's required to bring in the business.

When I sold consumer goods, a store manager would often use a false objection to an in-store promotion "My supervisor doesn't want me to put up displays in my store."

This objection let him off the hook by blaming it on his supervisor. To qualify this objection I would ask, "If I can get your supervisor's permission, would you then build the display?"

He would reply, "Sure." He thought he just got rid of me and I wouldn't go to the bother of getting his supervisor's OK.

He was wrong. I immediately called chain headquarters to find where the supervisor was and tracked him down. I gave him a presentation, not based on any individual store, but on all stores in his region. Since I'd built a good relationship with the supervisor by quickly resolving problems, he would usually say yes. I asked that he sign my presentation sheet. I made a beeline back to the manager who brushed me off. I handed him the signed order and built the display.

This accomplished three things. First the manager learned never to challenge me. Secondly, I got my display in his store and thirdly, I went to every other store in the region and got a display. Afterwards, I phoned the other sales reps in my division and gave them a copy of my signed order. They would, in turn, use it to sell the stores in their respective territories. Since my colleges were team players, they often returned the favor to me.

It's important to understand that I never took advantage of my relationship with the supervisor. I used this technique about three times a year and only if it was a major promotion. The managers soon learned that I knew how to get what I wanted.

Other times a customer asked me to survey an entire chain of stores before I got an order. I've brought in breakfast to medical office just so I could meet one important physician. I've set up symposiums that required weeks of preparations just to meet doctors who never see reps.

I once drove from Long Island to New Jersey to make an emergency delivery of medical supplies in order to get an order. I gave a customer a free loaner on a photocopier so he could get out a rush job. I picked it up from our warehouse, drove it into Manhattan, set it up and even supplied him with the copier paper, all free of charge. My reward was an order for a machine although I wasn't the lowest bidder.

I called on a pharmacy manager who had to unload a delivery truck by himself. His stock boys both called in sick. Without asking, I took off my jacket and helped him for an hour. He said thanks by giving me a large order. I did what ever I had to do to get the business.

You can have the greatest sales presentation in the world; however, to distinguish yourself from the pack, go out of your way to accommodate the customer. The customer will reward you with the business.

RETURN ON INVESTMENT (ROI)

You are reading the help wanted section of the newspaper looking for the ideal job and you find eight of them. You have always wanted this perfect job. It offers flexible hours, no stress, no supervision, and they all pay $25. The only difference is the amount of time you must put in to earn the $25.

HELP WANTED: Ideal Job!
We pay $25 for life.

HELP WANTED: Ideal Job!
We pay $25 per year.

HELP WANTED: Ideal Job!
We pay $25 per month.

HELP WANTED: Ideal Job!
We pay $25 per week.

HELP WANTED: Ideal Job!
We pay $25 per day.

HELP WANTED: Ideal Job!
We pay $25 per hour.

HELP WANTED: Ideal Job!
We pay $25 per minute.

HELP WANTED: Ideal Job!
We pay $25 per second.

The first job will pay you $25 to take the job. That's it. You go to work for them for the rest of your life and the day you die, they will pay you $25. Would you take the job?

The second job pays you $25 a year. Would you take the job? The third job pays $25 a month. Based on a thirty-year career it pays 360 times as much as job number one. Would you take that job?

Job number four pays $25 per week, or more than four times as much as job number three. Would you take that job instead? Job number five pays $25 per day. Would you take it? Job number six pays $25 per hour. Would you consider this one? Wait! Look at job number seven; it pays $25 per minute. Whoa! Job number eight pays $25 per second. Bingo, you take that job!

All eight jobs paid the same $25, but in different time frames. Job number one pays you $25 for an entire thirty-year career. Job number eight pays the same $25, but does so every second of every minute of every day for thirty years. The result is job number one pays you a total of twenty five dollars and job number eight pays you twenty three billion, six hundred fifty two million dollars.

THE MORAL OF THE STORY IS: "IT'S NOT HOW MUCH YOU MAKE, IT'S HOW FAST YOU MAKE IT."

Many business people fail to grasp this concept. I met a pharmacy buyer, named Gus, who preferred to promote a shampoo with a low market share that earned him $1 in profit per bottle. Gus wouldn't promote my shampoo, which was number one in volume sales and earned him .25 per bottle. All he could see was that the off brand earned him .75 more for every bottle he sold.

"Gus, how many bottles of the other brand do you sell per month?" I asked.

"About eighteen bottles?"

"How many bottles of my shampoo do you sell per month?"

"About sixteen cases."

"That's 192 bottles at .25 profit per bottle. My brand earns you $48 per month in profit and the off brand earns you $18 per month. Why would you want to promote theirs more than mine?"

Gus was unconvinced; although I used the volume numbers he gave me. He chose to promote the off brand. He couldn't get past the point that one shampoo earned him $1 and mine earned .25 per bottle. I laughed when reps from competing companies ribbed me. They thought selling the number one brand of shampoo was easy.

I never give personal financial advice. I would feel responsible if someone lost money based on my recommendation; however, a friend was bragging that he got a 7 percent return on his investment. I said my mutual fund grew 3/4 of a percent last week.

He smirked, "Mike, that stinks. You bragged you got a great return on your investments."

I said, "I do. You earn 7 percent per year. I earn 3/4 of a percent in one week." He still didn't get it. I continued, "3/4 of a percent per week is equivalent to 39 percent per year. That more than six times what you earn.

A jeweler marked a special necklace up from his cost of $1,000 to $3,000 knowing it would take a month to sell it. The first day the necklace was in the showcase, a customer walked in and offered $2,000 for the necklace. In the jeweler's absence, the store manager thought, "No way, if I wait a month, I can get $3,000 for the necklace. Why should I lose $1,000?"

Later, the jeweler returned to the store and the manager told him of the customer's offer.

The jeweler said, "You should have sold it to him. I could have ordered another necklace for the showcase and put $2,000 in my register." The manager was confused so the jeweler continued, "Forget the $3,000. I could have doubled my $1,000 investment to $2,000 in just one day."

The manager still didn't understand, "But you would have lost $1,000."

"No!" said the jeweler; "I would have $1,000 in profit in my register and a replacement necklace from my wholesaler, delivered tomorrow morning. Now I've nothing in my register and a necklace in my showcase. Wouldn't you prefer to double your investments everyday?"

Never assume that your customer understands return on investment. You may have to spell it out to get him to see the advantage in your product or service.

NEVER GIVE UP

In the first Chapter I told you about a pharmaceutical rep who tried repeatedly to see a doctor to present a new use for his medication. Regardless of the receptionist's rejection, he wouldn't give up. Well, that rep was me. The purpose of the story is to illustrate the rejection sales reps face every day, and to warn you how frustrating the job can be.

Rather than hitting a brick wall once or twice then moving on to another physician, I returned to the office on a regular basis. This wasn't to wear down the receptionist, but to catch the physician when he was either in the parking lot, the hallway or standing by the receptionist's desk. I must have made fifteen calls, but I never gave up. I found my opening and jumped in.

When I sold books to lawyers, the attorney often said to call back the next week for a decision. That is exactly what I did if I couldn't close them on the spot. If they put me off again, I waited a week and called back. I mailed letters and dropped by the office until they made a decision one way or the other. Nine times out of ten the answer was still, "No." However, the one order I got, repaid me for the other nine failures. That helped win me the President's Club. Another benefit was the attorneys learned to make a decision on the spot, if they didn't and tried to put me off, they knew I would follow up.

I once applied for a sales job with another publishing company. My headhunter, whom I'll call Kiko, called and said he had a great opportunity for me. He faxed my resume to the regional manager. I waited for a week and then called Kiko to follow up. The following scenario is bizarre, but true.

Kiko said, "Mike, I'm really surprised at you. I thought you had more professionalism than to do what you did."

"What the heck are you talking about?"

"The phone call you made to the company."

"I never called the company," I said defensively.

"You didn't?"

"No, of course not. Besides, you never told me the name of the company. What happened?"

"Well on Wednesday, someone called the company and spoke with a female sales rep who happened to be in the office. He began pumping the woman for information about the job. He asked how much she made, what the hours were like, the perks, the benefits and what her boss was like. He got her so upset that she hung up the phone and went to her boss to complain. He got angry and wanted to know the guy's name. She said she couldn't remember, but he's from Long Island and his resume is on your desk. The manager looked down on his desk and guess who's resume he saw – yours. The one I had just faxed to him. He said to the woman as he threw it in the garbage can, 'I don't need a jerk like that working for me.'"

"Kiko, I never called the manager's office."

"Well, I don't know what we can do at this point except wait to see if another position opens up."

"I'm not giving up. Please give me his name and phone number."

I called three or four times over the course of the week and left messages for the manager. He never returned my call. I wrote a short note expressing my innocence and asking for a moment to speak with him. I said in my letter, "Even if you don't want to interview me, please allow me the opportunity to clear my name."

I sent the letter express mail and followed it up with a phone call. After being on hold for a few minutes, he got on the phone. I explained my conversation with Kiko and gave him my word that it wasn't me.

He agreed to interview me. He decided to hire someone else with specific sales experience in both the types of law books and the exact territory that was open. The industry I was in was small and everyone knew everyone. Having a bad reputation could hurt you in may ways. I didn't give up until I accomplished my objective: clear my name and get an interview.

SELLING TO A BUREAUCRACY VS A PRIVATE COMPANY

Selling to a bureaucracy is completely different from selling to a private company. A private company's concern is with cost and efficiency and usually makes a decision quickly. In a bureaucracy you have systems set in place for bids and contracts. Things take forever to get done and the strict guidelines often prevent them from making a good decision. In a bureaucracy, like a government office, you may have to go to a separate buying office to submit a proposal. In a hospital, you may have to go to a purchasing department who passes the information along to the correct department head who in turn makes a decision.

Learn the system and follow it to the letter. When they require a typed written proposal, double-spaced on green paper, submitted on Friday morning at precisely 10 a.m., that's what you have to do in order to get the business. The danger in not following the proper procedure is that some bureaucrat along the way will reject your proposal just so they can justify their job.

I submitted a proposal to a health group for my home infusion service. The department head told me that another company had also submitted a proposal. Their service looked just as good, but they failed to submit a signed contract. A simple form that required basic information for their records. The company, for whatever reason, never submitted the signed contract. I ran back to our office, filled in the form and raced back to the group and hand delivered it. The buyers surprised remark was, "Back so soon? I guess you really want our business."

DRESSED TO SELL

Nothing stirs more controversy than the subject of proper business attire. Corporate America is relaxing the standards of dress that dominated the industry since the 19th century. Recently, in the *Wall Street Journal*, a report indicated a nearly 25 percent decline in the sales of panty hose. Women are abandoning them in favor of tights and slacks. There are still parts of the country that are traditional, but in the more liberal business centers like New York and California, the trend is definitely moving toward casual business attire. This is great news for everyone, except the professional sales representative. You must dress to maximize your success.

Norman was a sales rep in the legal publishing business, who was eccentric in dress and manner. Every time the subject of business attire came up, someone who disliked a strict dress code would mention Norman.

Norman was in his early fifties and could easily pass for sixty-five. His 350 pounds were centered in his stomach. In the summer he wore the same rumpled seersucker suit. It was one of those blue and white pin stripes, popular in the 1920's. His shirts were polyester with perspiration stains under his arms. The shirt was too small and the buttons strained to stay buttoned against his massive girth, allowing his chest hair to poke through the gaps. The shirt had short tails and was forever riding out from his pants. He wore one of those massive cowboy belt buckles with a buffalo embossed on it. You could tell what Norman had for lunch by the stains on his tie. It was an old fashioned design that hung loosely, halfway down his shirt.

Norman was mostly bald and used creative combing to cover his head. The hair on his left side was sixteen inches long and combed over and held down with hair spray. On windy days the hair would flop over to the side leaving his bald spot exposed and the long hair, stiff from the spray, sticking out horizontally like the landing deck of an air craft carrier.

Norman perspired profusely, even in air conditioning and was constantly wiping his brow. His shoes were old scuffed oxfords, run down at the heels and tied with frayed laces that he had mended with knots.

Norman would pick up three cases of sample books and march right in to the attorney's office as if he were making a delivery. He would walk right past the receptionist and the secretary. His manner was so confident; they would rarely challenge him. He would barge right into the attorney's office and drop the books on the desk so they spread over the top, some falling on to the attorney's lap and the floor. Without so much as an introduction, Norman began presenting the books, flipping through the pages pointing out features and benefits. For the most part, the lawyers sat as students in a classroom and listened to what Norman said. In many cases, Norman left with an order, leaving with the same abrupt manner that he arrived. Norman was always in the top 10 percent of the sales force.

Norman was 100 percent genuine. That is the way he sold. That was his personality and demeanor. His product knowledge was the best. He knew his product, as well as the competitor's, inside and out. I would never succeed in selling like Norman, because that's not me, nor is it 99 percent of those in the business. Don't use Norman as an excuse to dress down for the job. You would have to be Norman to make it work; you couldn't fake it.

IF YOU SELL TO LAWYERS, DRESS LIKE A LAWYER.

Your clothing is as much a part of your communication strategy as your speech. They should complement each other to deliver a consistent message. Observe the way your customers dress and emulate them. The objective is to dress as their peer, not their superior nor their subordinate. I knew I'd accomplished that when I was waiting in the lobby to meet with an attorney when a client asked me if I was a lawyer. In pharmaceuticals, people asked if I was a doctor. Even the lawyers and physicians sometimes asked if I belonged to their profession.

The word of a colleague carries far more weight than that of a salesperson. When your neighbor with the beautiful lawn recommends a particular brand of grass seed, aren't you more likely to heed their advice than that of a sales clerk at the garden shop?

When you sell to grocery managers, you should dress in a shirt and tie to emulate them. They will feel more comfortable than if you dress like their boss. Never dress like their stock boy, in blue jeans and a tee shirt; they will have little confidence in what you have to offer.

Obviously, if you cold-call canvass an office building, you can't run home and change clothes to emulate first the doctor, then the lawyer and then the architect. You must modify your appearance to blend in with a generic professional group.

OBSERVE THE 100 PERCENT RULE

Doctors and lawyers dress similarly, but not identically. A doctor dresses clinically, clean and soothing. A lawyer dresses for power. He wants to intimidate his opponents, reassure his clients and impress the judge.

There are some professions that I've never called on with any consistency but I'm confident that their dress code conforms with their professional environment. An architect must look professional yet be able to walk around a construction site without appearing to be a Prima Donna.

A rack jobber is a nickname for a wholesaler who sells to retailers. They often drive vans and have merchandise with them. The rack is an in-store display, like one for inexpensive, bagged candy. They travel throughout their territory refilling empty displays. It is a hard, dirty job. Rack Jobbers can easily soil their clothes; therefore they should wear appropriate clothing. Don't dress too casual. Never wear jeans and a tee shirt. You don't want to look like you are cleaning out your garage. Choose clothing that resembles a uniform. Watch what the route sales reps for large companies wear and emulate them. Even in a labor-intensive job, you must appear clean cut and neat. You don't want to ruin an expensive pair of dress pants or shirt, so choose clothing that's suitable for the type of work you do. Make sure they are clean and presentable.

Professionals observe the 100 percent rule. Their shirts and suits are natural fiber like cotton, wool, silk or linen. Shoes, belts and attaches are leather. They wear only pure silk ties. They are successful in their own right and shop in the best of stores. These stores cater to a class of people with high incomes and rarely if ever carry clothes made with synthetic materials. They may not be aware of styles but when they shop, the clothes presented to them are up-to-date.

STYLES

When I lived in the south during the 50's and 60's, you could judge someone's station in life by their clothing. The educated and successful dressed far differently than those of lower standing. This was a caste system designed centuries ago to help those of the upper class distinguish themselves from the common folk.

A wealthy person would never drive a flashy luxury car. That was for the nouveau riche. The old money bought obscure foreign cars or rare domestic cars that only a hand full of people recognized. The middle and lower class envisioned themselves acquiring money and driving big flashy cars and wearing gaudy jewelry. This is exactly what happened if they acquired money. Their children were born into money and developed refined taste.

The same held true for clothing. The wealthy had a few reserved stores that catered to them. The middle class had their department stores and off the rack clothes.

When I moved to New York, I was quick to learn that those rules didn't apply. New York is the fashion capital of the world; anyone can walk into a department store and pick out a suit off the rack that's the latest style. They don't even have to be socially aware. You discover their class when they open their mouths. This is why fine-tuning your wardrobe, your manners and your speech to be in tune with your customers is so important.

SUITS

The best way to understand the quality of clothing is to go into a high quality store and look at the suits they have in the $700 range. Examine their construction and the material. Note the stitching and how the sleeve is attached to the jacket. It should be a smooth seam. In a cheaper jacket there will be a bump where the sleeve is attached.

Check to see if the jacket is fully lined. Are there pockets within the pockets? Check the details of the buttons. Look underneath the collar. Is it lined with felt? Take the sleeve and twist it as if you were ringing it out. When you release it, the sleeve should fall back into place with no wrinkles.

Go to the department store that has $100 suits. Notice that the jacket is lined only halfway. Check for the sleeve attachment. Twist it to see how easy it wrinkles. Even if the suit is freshly pressed, it will look a mess by two in the afternoon. The face of the jackets in cheap suits is often glued to the shell. After several dry cleanings the suit may start to pucker. It's very noticeable and makes a poor impression.

Now that you're armed with information, go to one of the outlet stores or larger men's clothing discounters. Go for the best possible quality you can afford. It's better to have two well-made suits than five cheap ones. When selling to professionals they will spot the difference immediately. They may be too polite to point it out, but it does leave an impression of your success. Dressing correctly will have an affect on the receptionists and may help you get into the buyer's office. A well-made quality suit will stand the test of time and deliver more wear than a cheap one. Please don't tell me about Norman. He was one in a million, an exception to the rule.

TOP COATS

Avoid black and dark brown raincoats. They don't show dirt as easily and therefore you don't have to clean them as often. This is why these colors are associated with the working class. Your customers who are professionals wear light tan or green raincoats. They can afford to have them cleaned more often.

Depending on your climate, wear a 100 percent wool topcoat in the winter. Get the light gray color or hounds-tooth. Black and brown relay the wrong image.

SHIRTS AND TIES

Never wear a short sleeve dress shirt; it's too casual. All cotton is the best. Button down or straight collar shirts vary from industry to industry. If in doubt, see what your CEO wears. I prefer white shirts with cuff links, but pastel colors with button cuffs are just as good.

The sleeve may have an extra button below the cuff; keep it buttoned. Have your shirts professionally washed and starched for optimum effect.

Ties are an accessory of self-expression. Go with the latest fad of power ties if you wish, even a bow tie if you dare as long as it's pure silk but, never wear a clip on tie.

SHOES

Cheap shoes look like cheap shoes, no matter how much you polish them. Buy oxfords or wing tips that are all leather. It's better to have a pair of well made comfortable leather shoes that cost $150 than several pairs of $30 shoes with man made materials.

Stay away from the fashion colors like gray or blue. Keep them polished, even if it means carrying a polishing cloth in your car to wipe the dust off. Have your shoemaker put rubber taps on the heels. They keep the edges from wearing down and you won't have to re-heel them as often.

ACCESSORIES

I believe that the only jewelry a man should wear is a wedding ring, a school or service ring and a watch. If you need a flashy pinkie ring to feel confident, then wear one. My confidence is in my sales ability, not flashy jewelry.

A nice gold pen, leather organizer, cuff links and modest jewelry, portrays you as being successful, reliable and dependable. Don't go into debt to buy things you can't afford. I believe if you invest the time shopping around, you can acquire the items you want. Invest in yourself.

If you can't afford a nice new dress watch, go to your local jeweler and ask to see the estate watches. You can pick up a beautiful gold plated watch with a leather band, from the 1940's, for less than $125. Not only will it be classier than the new ones you buy at a department store; it will hold its value. Keep the receipt and in a few years you can take it back and exchange it for as much, if not more, than you paid for it.

IT'S BETTER TO WEAR A REAL TIMEX® THAN A FAKE ROLEX®

People who own a real Rolex® watch resent those who have the cheap counterfeits and can spot them a mile away. A fake watch suggests your product or service may be fake too. Avoid the plastic sport and digital watches. They are fine for casual wear, but not for professional attire.

HYGIENE

Until I worked as a retail manager, I would never think I would have to lecture sales reps about their hygiene. Reps who had bad breath and body odor have taken me back. They had dirty hands and nails and look as if they slept in their suit. When reps grinned at me with stained and broken teeth, I had to force myself to concentrate on what they were saying. A filthy appearance will cost you business. Use cologne lightly; women should use care in makeup as well. If you smoke, remember that the tobacco smell lingers on your breath and clothing and may be offensive to buyers who are non-smokers.

One rep called on me on a Monday and had a food stain on his lapel. I assumed that he spilled something during lunch. He returned the next day for a follow up call and wore the same jacket with the same caked on food stain. I bought from him because I needed the merchandise, but how many people does he turn off every day?

I'm sure if you questioned him, he would say that it doesn't affect his success at all. My question is, "How does he know that?" You can be successful in spite of yourself, but why make your job so much more difficult? And please don't tell me about Norman.

TAKE OFF YOUR HAT AND COAT AND STAY AWHILE

New York winters are brutal, wet and bone chilling, but when I step into a buyer's office, I take off my topcoat.

I had a rep call on me in the pharmacy. It was one of those miserable cold and rainy Long Island days. He stood there giving me a presentation with his hat and coat on. Water dripped off his cap and onto his brochure as we spoke. I got the feeling that he was going to sell me a bill of goods and bolt for the door. He needed a clean getaway and didn't want to stop to get dressed. I didn't buy from him. If asked, I'm sure he could have come up with any number of excuses not to remove his topcoat and hat:

- It's too much bother to take them on and off.
- It doesn't matter; I've done it for years.
- I'm in a hurry.
- It never came up before.
- You're too picky.
- Hey Einstein, it's raining outside. (Yeah, but it's not raining inside.)
- What do you know? I'm the salesman; you're just a "pesky store manager."
- I was out selling when you were in diapers.
- Hey, I never thought about it.
- You're the first one to mention it.

Try to park close to the door so you can leave your topcoat in the car. If you can't, then take it off when you first get inside. When you wear a topcoat into an office, it immediately tips off the receptionist that you're an outsider. You don't look as though you belong. Leave it in the car or in a closet of one of your customers.

BUSINESS CARDS

Your business card is a silent salesman who works for you. When a receptionist takes your card and walks it back to the decision-maker, the impression the card makes on the buyer may determine if you get in.

You may have no choice in your card design if your company provides them. However, consider these guidelines if you have input or must provide your own cards:

- Spend the extra few dollars and get a good quality card.
- Choose a top of the line card stock, with embossed ink. Don't use vellum; it's too flimsy.
- Make sure the company logo is sharp and clear for good reproduction.
- Keep it simple. Don't try to list every product or service your company has. Use a lot of white space in the design.
- Whether it is a company provided card or your own, delete the title, "Sales Representative" or "Area Representative." When a receptionist sees the title, they know exactly why you're there and may brush you off. Without the title you may look like a potential client for the company. The receptionist may be more inclined to let you in to see the boss.
- If you work for yourself, give yourself a promotion. Titles like, "President" or "Director" gives an impression that you're important, not just another salesperson.
- Carry a metal business card case, preferably sterling silver with a monogram. They make a nice impression when a client asks you for a card. Never use the cheap plastic cardholders that come with your business cards.
- Never give a customer a card that's soiled or bent, unless you want your customers to think of you that way.

- To save money on expensive cards, ask the printer if there is a quantity discount. Tell the printer to save the plate for your card. The next time you reorder, you won't have to pay a plate charge as long as there are no changes.
- Collect several business cards from your customers and use them for a guideline. Your card should emulate the profession that you call on. If you call on doctors then your card should look like a doctor's.

I HATE TELEPHONES

I admit it; I hate telephones. It's too easy for a customer to tell you no. I hate looking up numbers and I hate getting someone's voice mail three times in a row.

I hate the "Fake phones" that won't accept my credit cards, or worse yet, when I connect to my 800 call to voice mail and they won't let me use the touch-tones to access my mailbox. I hate broken phones. In Queens, I had to make an emergency call; seven phones in a row were broken. The eighth one wouldn't accept my credit card. (This was before cell phones were cheap and popular.)

Get an 800 number, if your budget allows and put it on your business card. A customer will be more inclined to call you if it's free. An alternative is a professional answering service to give the personal touch, or the answering service provided by the phone company. That makes it appear as though you're in a busy office and have voice-mail.

Consider an answering machine for your home. Make sure the message is clear and business like. Please, no cute music or Elvis impressions. Your customers won't take you seriously.

Get a separate business line if you work at home. When I was a retail manager, reps gave me their home numbers as a main contact. Their spouse or child answered the phone and took the message. Usually the rep never knew I called, and they lost an order. The spouse starts screaming at the kids or the dog barks. It sounds unprofessional. Therefore, I use a private line with an automated answering service.

An alternative to telephone credit cards is a prepaid calling card. It is less expensive and the used cards provide an accurate receipt for your accountant.

Get an e-mail account and put the address on your business card. I now correspond with my established clients with e-mail. It is unobtrusive, fast and you have a permanent record of all correspondents. Never use e-mail to spam prospective customers.

Chapter Six

CAREER DEVELOPMENT

In the glory days of the 80's when business was booming and there was full employment, one of the best ways to advance one's career was to get chummy with the boss. You accomplished this by learning the boss's hobbies and taking them up yourself thus giving you a common interest. You got the opportunity to spend time with the person who would help mold your future, outside the office setting.

Within the last few years, major changes have occurred in the workplace. There have been so many mergers, downsizing and restructuring programs in corporate America that you can no longer rely on one person to advance your career. Your boss may not be there in two years when you need him or her most.

Fraternizing with the boss may alienate you from your colleagues if they think you are the boss's pet. They may withhold important information from you, sabotage your projects or leave you out of critical decision making processes.

Early in my career, I had a great manager named Steve. Several other reps and I befriended Steve and we spent a lot of time with him at his home. He was clearly the man in charge, but was so likable, we considered him one of the guys. This relationship, as well as his outspoken defense of his reps, alienated him from other managers. I believe it was professional jealousy. They never enjoyed that type of relationship or earned the level of respect with their people that Steve did.

Eventually, they drove Steve out of the company. They assigned us a new manager who also hated Steve. He labeled us "Steve's Boys" and one by one, we were driven out of the company as well. Performance was never a consideration, office politics that sealed our future. As much as we enjoyed Steve's friendship and management style, it eventually cost us our jobs.

In retrospect I believe that it is important for reps and management to maintain a cordial but distant relationship. I don't sanction a "we—they" mentality, because a cohesive team effort is essential in business. However, learn to keep a respectful distance from your boss.

DON'T BRAG TOO MUCH

It's important to document your achievements and to let your superiors know that you're making an extra effort, but be careful how you let them know. Don't get a braggadocio's attitude like Franko. He was a human dynamo and let everyone know it. At meetings Franko would pull out a list of accomplishments, from working on Saturdays calling on accounts to how much money he saves the company by changing the oil in his company car himself. His intentions were good, but he became such a bore even the boss made jokes about him behind his back. Be prudent in self proclamation.

THERE IS NO EXCUSE FOR BAD MANNERS

Philip was a young rep from a fine school, well dressed; articulate and hard working, but he had horrendous table manners. Believe me when I say, you're watched and judged by how you conduct yourself.

We were at a formal presentation and Philip was sitting at the same table as the CEO. Philip slouched over the table, with his face two inches from his plate. He held his fork backhanded and talked with his mouth crammed full of food. He had his left elbow propped up on the table with his hand straight up in the air like a claw. He slurped his coffee so loud that people from other tables stopped talking to watch him. You could see the CEO grimace every time Philip picked up his coffee cup. This wasn't a case of someone using the wrong fork for their salad; it was just plain crude. The managers were too polite to say anything to him but it left a bad impression and hurt his career.

THANK YOU

Do you know how Dan Quayle was chosen to be Vice President? I read that when he discovered he was on the short list for the nomination, he sent a thank you to Vice President Bush. In the letter he asked if it was all right if he told his immediate family that he was under consideration. He was the only one who had the manners to do so.

The consumer product company selected me from a large pool of candidates for a sales position, although I didn't have a college degree at the time. Two things I did swung the decision to my favor. First, I arrived twenty minutes early for the initial interview and secondly, I sent a thank you to the manager who interviewed me.

Out of the hundreds of candidates I competed with, I was the only one to do so. It distinguished me from all of the rest. Arriving early signified my respect for his time and my genuine eagerness to get the job. The thank you got me a bit more attention with the decision-maker and allowed me to ask for a second interview.

I send a brief thank you to prospective customers after a presentation even if I don't get an order and to regular customers just to show that I don't take their business for granted.

You may send a typed thank you, but I prefer a handwritten note on personalized stationary. That way it doesn't get confused with junk mail. I know many who use e-mail for thank-you notes. I have sent them too, but I feel more comfortable sending a written note.

SALES MEETINGS

One of the duties of a sales rep who works for a company of almost any size is to attend sales meetings. They can be a rewarding experience or a drudgery, depending on what you put into it and what you take out. It also depends on your manager or the person who runs the meeting.

I attended a meeting about nine years ago when I was selling anesthesia. The company called us into a daylong meeting to discuss some of the side effects and how we should advise the anesthesiologist on dealing with them. We had little medical knowledge outside of the company training, so our managers would invite a medical expert to come in and explain the procedures as simply as possible. This would help us build our confidence levels when we presented our products to the physicians.

At this meeting the lecturer was from a major teaching hospital. She was very bright, experienced and competent. Unfortunately, English wasn't her first language and she spoke with a heavy accent.

The topic was "The Occurrence of Nausea and Vomiting During Post-Operative Recovery." Without going into detail, our product sometimes caused the patient to become sick to their stomach after an operation. It was a concern that we had to address. The problem was that every time the lecturer said, "Nausea and vomiting," it came out, "Noise-yah ann womit-ting." No one was laughing at her, but it was funny, especially after you hear it a dozen times and you can't laugh out loud for fear of hurting her feelings.

As seasoned pros, we could contain ourselves, but the class clown was sitting directly behind me in the crowded auditorium. He was the man of a thousand voices. When the lecturer spoke he would lean over and whisper in my ear, imitating the cartoon character Elmer Fudd, "No more noise-yaa ann womit-ting you kwazy wrabbit." We were sitting in the front next to senior management. It was all I could do to keep from laughing out loud. He kept it up for the entire morning.

ROLE PLAY

Role-play is a practice session held between two or more sales reps in order to perfect their sales skills. This is a valuable training tool. It's better to make your mistakes in front of your colleagues than in front of your customers.

In a sales meeting, role-play for a new product or service begins with two managers who stand in front of the class. One assumes the role of the sales rep; the other is the buyer. Using a prepared sales presentation that they practiced, they reenact a sales call. Afterwards, the sales force will break up in groups of two and repeat the process. It has been my experience that a rep should rehearse a presentation ten times (five times giving the presentation and five times receiving the presentation), before they become comfortable with the information.

NEVER PRACTICE YOUR PRESENTATION ON YOUR CUSTOMERS. YOU MUST BE WELL REHEARSED BEFORE YOUR FIRST CUSTOMER CALL.

I suggest you create a presentation using the five-step program, practice the presentation on as family member or friend before you call on your customers. You may use a video camera, a tape recorder or simply read the presentation out loud to rehearse if there is no one to help you.

ROUND ROBIN

Round Robin is a variation of role-play. In a sales organization of sixteen people, half assume the role of buyer and the other half gives the presentations. The reps rotate around the room giving the presentation to each buyer. The buyer keeps notes as to the quality of each presentation. He or she notes if the presentation was smooth, covered all of the features and benefits, and if the rep was able to overcome a specific objection. After the eight reps have presented to each buyer, the roles are reversed and the process begins again. In some cases, management will tabulate the grades given a token award to the best presentation.

CANNED PRESENTATIONS

A canned presentation is one that has been prepared by the management team and given to a sales force to memorize and deliver verbatim. A sales brochure accompanies them that list the features and benefits, test results, endorsements, ordering information and photographs of the product. An example of a canned presentation is when you receive a sales pitch over the telephone for chimney cleaning. You can tell the sales person is reading a script.

Most reps hate canned presentations and management seems to love them. They want a consistent and complete presentation given on every sales call. Management may encourage canned presentations because they have little confidence in their sales force. The reps are poorly trained or too new to be effective on their own.

Memorize the canned speech, use my five steps of the presentation to modify it and use that instead. The benefit of a canned presentation is they generally cover all of the important features and benefits; however, the reality is that you may seldom have time for a full presentation.

ASSESSMENT TESTS

After a company has spent tens of thousands of dollars and valuable field time training you on a product, they want some assurance that something sunk in and that you understand the program. They also need some measurement of the trainers and the training material's effectiveness. An assessment test will be given at the end of the training class that reviews the material covered. Regardless of what they tell you, they send the test results to your manager. They need to know how well you did and where to focus special attention.

The most difficult assessment tests were in pharmaceuticals. The amount of medical information even the simplest drug is demanding. For complex products such as cancer drugs and anesthesia it is overwhelming.

I'll give you an example. If you're like me and have average intelligence, recall your high school SATs and triple the difficulty. This is one reason many companies require a college education. They know you can handle the demanding workload. They may also require specific sales experience in the industry. It speeds up the expensive training process if you already know how anesthesia works. They can go directly to the specific product advantages.

ASSESSMENT GAMES

Several creative managers have devised games to make the assessments less stressful. Divided the sales force in two groups and uses the product information as a form of a TV game show. They kept score and the winning team shared in a cash prize of about $25 each. Another variation was to form a football field in the classroom. Each rep advances the ball up or down the field based on the quality of their presentation. The disadvantage is that if you didn't study very well, you will look foolish and incompetent in front of your peers. That's management's strategy to encourage your full cooperation.

VIDEO

Video is used in place of or in conjunction with, assessment tests. A video camera is set up in the classroom and each rep must give their presentation to another rep. The rep's manager is sent a copy of the presentation for review. They show the best presentations to the group. This is a very effective tool and I've gained much product knowledge from watching other reps sell. Based on their experience and sales ability they often give a fresh or unique spin on a presentation that will benefit you in the field. Again, your fellow reps are your best resource. Be a team player and help each other grow.

The other advantage of video is you see first hand how you appear and sound to your customers. In one taping session a seasoned rep gave a great presentation to a manager acting as the buyer. At the conclusion, the manager told the rep how well he had done.

"Frank, all you have to do is stop poking your finger in my face."

The rep was adamant; "I don't stick my finger in your face."

"Oh yes you did." The manager replied. "Every time you want to make a point, you jabbed your index finger at me."

We all laughed because we saw him do it. The rep denied it again.

The manager said, "OK, roll the video tape."

The rep's mouth hung open as he watched himself nearly poke the manager's eye out.

Other reps have caught themselves scratching themselves, rolling their eyes around while speaking and even picking their nose. By replaying a taped presentation you can focus on the buyers' reactions to key points and often pick up on subtle buying signals they missed during the original taping. It also serves as a record of how much you have progressed over the years.

PRESENTATION TECHNIQUES

There are several techniques to maintain control of the presentation and to keep the buyer's attention.

- Never let a buyer grab your presentation material out of your hand. He can read faster than you can talk and won't pay attention to what you say. Maintain a firm grip on your sales brochure.
- Never assume a new brochure or sales aid is good. When the reaction in the field is luke warm, go back to older brochures that worked better for you or create your own using desktop publishing or simply cut and paste available material.
- Never point at a brochure or computer screen with your finger; use a pen.
- When the buyers attention seems to be wandering, snap the pen against the brochure to direct his attention back to your presentation.
- Memorize your presentation; never read to them. They know how to read. Cover all of the points, but say them in your own words.

- Maintain control. When the buyer interrupts you with questions, say, "Please allow me to finish my presentation and I will answer all of your questions." By preparing good presentations, you anticipate his questions and will surely address it at some point. Don't skip around, maintain control and stick to your presentation.
- Have a hallway or short presentation prepared in case you only have a moment with the buyer.
- Look you buyer in the eye. Nod as they speak. Show that you're paying attention to what they are saying.
- Restate the buyer's concerns. They may say that money is tight and they may not be able to buy. You then restate, "I see. So money is a concern?"
- Carry a product sample with you. Hand it to the buyer while you talk. Handle it like it was a precious jewel. Make sure it is crisp and clean; never show a buyer a soiled or damaged product sample.
- When you're in the customers office and sitting across from them, ask permission before you walk around to their side of the desk.
- Stand when you make a presentation, if the buyer is sitting this puts you in the role of teacher and the buyer as the student.

HUMOR ISN'T VERY FUNNY

I worked with several reps in publishing, who prided themselves in their humorous sales approach. Link and I walked into a law office and he started cracking jokes to the two attorneys in the reception room. They weren't in a joking mood.

The senior partner said, "If you send us any books that we didn't order, by law, we can keep them for free." The attorney was referring to the policy of many publishers who send books in on a 30-day free trial basis.

Link gave a flip answer, "OK, tell us where to back the truck in."

The attorney shouted, "Get out of my office. Now!"

Folks, I didn't make this up. It really happened. I was working with Link and we were calling on a large law library. The librarian was a sweetheart and English was her second language. She was expecting a child in two months. Link began telling abortion jokes. I stood there in disbelief. The poor woman stared at him in confusion. Obviously, the crude jokes were lost on her.

When we got outside, I turned to Link and asked, "What the heck were you thinking?"

Link brushed it off, "I was only kidding, besides it proves my point that women don't have a sense of humor."

The next day, I returned to the library to see if I could repair the damage. She looked up at me sadly and asked, "Does your friend not want me to have this baby?" I told her that he was not my friend and that I was very happy for her.

The best type of humor is self effacing. I never hesitate to poke fun at myself, especially if it will get me out of trouble. A customer was angry because my company mis-shipped an order. Since I was the company rep, I took responsibility. She vented her anger on me. I replied, "Well that proves my wife's theory: I'm an idiot." She smiled and I was able to repair the damage.

An attorney was irate that my company triple shipped her for one set of books. She lit into me and said, "I know you didn't create the problem, but you're the one standing here, so I'm going to tell you what I think of your company."

I puffed up my chest, stuck out my chin and said, "Give it your best shot; I have three teenage daughters. I can handle anything you can dish out." Even the stoic secretary looked up and laughed.

In the pharmacy, an elderly woman was upset because we didn't have her favorite brand of bulk laxative. I tried to calm her and promised that it would be in the next morning. She picked up a large bottle of a different brand and angrily asked, "Is this stuff any good?" to which I replied, "Madam, I never Metamucil® I didn't like."

Steve Allen wrote a great book, How To Be Funny. It teaches you how to develop a sense of humor that's useful in sales. I suggest you buy a copy and read it. It helped me develop a laid back, non offensive style so I can disarm even the angriest people. Never tease customers about their profession. Said another way: don't tell lawyer jokes to lawyers; tell 'em doctor jokes.

Link loved to tell a particular Polish joke to his customers. Shortly after the incident with the abortion joke, we called on an elderly client. Link told the joke and awaited the laugh, the customer responded, "My wife is Polish and she survived two years in a Nazi Concentration Camp." At that point, I avoided working with Link as much as possible.

COLD CALL CANVASSING

In outside sales you're exposed to the weather all year long. There were times I called my office on a beautiful spring morning. The secretary complained that I was lucky to be out on such a gorgeous day. I replied, "I'll call back during a blizzard, then we can change jobs."

The best way to bring in business is also the hardest way, cold call canvassing. This means you walk into your territory cold and start calling on prospects, canvassing for customers. To find one buyer you will have to knock on many doors. In legal publishing, I had to knock on fifty doors to see five attorneys to write one order. For every ten orders I wrote, one would be returned and one would be on credit hold. Therefore, for every fifty doors I knocked on, I got 8/10 of an order. To write one order that passed credit and the customer didn't return I had to knock on at least sixty-five doors. That first year in publishing, my income was more than three times that in salaried sales. That is not a bad return for getting sixty doors slammed in my face every three days.

Following is a guideline for canvassing based on my personal experience working both the city and rural areas. Regardless of what I was selling, I developed a routine to follow. This helped me maintain my morale throughout the day. Regardless of what you sell or whom you sell to, keep focused on your routine.

Once you have planned your day and must start cold call canvassing, create a mental image of being in a hallway filled with doors. In order to open one door and write an order, you must first open forty-nine doors and be rejected. Each rejection brings you one step closer to the door where you can write business. Behind some doors, there lays a clear answer: NO! Behind others the answer is somewhat cloudy. You may actually get into see the decision-maker, present your product, have the decision-maker think about it and then you get your NO! It doesn't matter. A no is a no, regardless of how long it takes to hear it.

If you pre-judge a potential customer and walk past the door without trying, it doesn't count toward your goal of forty-nine No's and one Yes.

Obviously I'm using an average, and those averages may be higher or lower based on your product, service, clientele and the part of the country you work in. When cable TV was first introduced on Long Island, I had a friend who worked as a rep. His job was to go door-to-door, signing up new customers. His success record was more than 90 percent. He told me that the neighbors would call each other to tell them the cable guy was here. Folks would open their front door and flag him down so they could sign up. I assure you this is an exception to the rule. In time you will learn your success rate and this book will help you lower the number of doors you must open to get a YES!

When you sell a product that benefits most every business in town, start at one end of the street and work your way down to the other side. Cover the side streets as you pass them. Never waste time doubling back. You may start on the left side of the street and work your way down, covering the side streets as you go. Then cross the street and work your way back. If you have a call back to see someone, this will reduce the time you waste criss-crossing town.

When you go into a large office building, start at the top floor and work your way down. Always start on your left side or on your right side if you're right handed. Stay consistent so you don't skip anyone. You never know what door will bring you a YES!

After an hour or two every door becomes a blur. This makes it easier to retrace your steps if you have to call back later. Take a business card from the customer and note the date and name of the receptionist who asked you to return. When you call back, and ask for someone by name, you're no longer a stranger to the office.

Never trust the tote board or building directory you find in a lobby. They are notoriously out of date. One day I was working with Link and we were covering his territory. We were only allowed to call on lawyers, so Link checked the board, saw the floors that the attorneys were on and those were the only offices we went to.

As we were leaving the building, I asked Link, "What if someone new has just moved in and they aren't listed yet?

"Ah, that never happens."

"How do you know if you never tried?"

"Listen kid, I've been doing this for twenty years. I know my territory like the back of my hand."

"Well, humor me Link, Let's just canvass the entire building."

We went to the top floor and worked our way down. Sure enough, we found a new firm that was just moving in. We met the attorneys and walked out with a large order. I was working with Link because I was supposed to learn from him.

NEVER PREJUDGE

In legal publishing, Link listed several reasons why I should never waste time calling on a female attorney:

- "Girls can never make up their mind on what to buy."
- "Girl attorneys love to browse but never make decisions."
- "Girls don't want to hurt your feelings by saying no, so they just put you off until you get the message. It's like dating."

- "Girls are dependent on their husbands financial support. They don't have the authority to purchase anything other than basic office supplies."

I politely nodded my head, then went out and wrote orders with the first three Female attorneys I called on.

HANDLING REJECTION

To have a long-term career in sales, you must be able to handle rejection. I can recount stories of being chased out of office buildings on Long Island. Security officers have threatened to have me arrested. Others have, physically blocked my entrance into a Manhattan hospital, although I had legitimate business there. I've been told the buyer was out, although I could plainly see him sitting at his desk reading the paper. I've had doctors take my business card from my hand and drop it in the garbage can in front of me and laugh. When I was at the consumer product company my manager told me about a time when he was a new rep. He was calling on a major grocery store chain and a brand manager from our company was working with him. When the brand manager introduced himself to the store manager and extended his hand to shake, the store manager leaned over and spit in his hand, then walked away. Other times I met a customer by the front desk, who smiled and said, "Man-O-Man am I glad you're here."

The toughest two calls of the day are the first and the last. I admit when I first started my career in sales, there were days I drove to an office building and sat in my car not wanting to start another day of rejection. There were days I was angry that it was 6 o'clock. I was writing so much business, but the day was over. Then there were days that I didn't care one way or the other. I started on time, wrote my quota and quit on time. I'm only human and understanding that, I never let the rejection get me down. I won't hesitate to stop for coffee or say to myself, "Only three more calls and its lunch time."

I built relationships with many customers and always had a haven to go to make a few calls or talk to someone who wasn't trying to get rid of me. On particularly bad days, I drove by the school where my wife taught and took her out to lunch. It was always a pleasant distraction. Afterwards, I was ready to hit the bricks again. I also made friends with reps from other companies. We would often meet for breakfast and swap war stories. I even got leads from them. When you're with those who fight in the trenches as you do, you develop a camaraderie even if you work for competing companies.

IT'S HARD FOR COMPANIES TO FIND PEOPLE WILLING TO DO THIS JOB. IT'S HARDER STILL, TO FIND PEOPLE WHO DO IT WELL.

PRODUCT KNOWLEDGE

I never appreciated the importance of product knowledge until I was in pharmaceuticals. I had to study my products thoroughly and have a basic understanding of human anatomy. It didn't stop there. I had to know the competitors' products to the point that I could sell them. This included their chemical compounds, how the drug affected the human body and how it treated the disease.

Professionals, like doctors, lawyers and accountants are detailed oriented. Before you can modify their habits, you must demonstrate your knowledge and expertise in that area. This is more than memorizing a few features, benefits and advertising slogans. It involved constant reading of trade journals, discussions with product managers and conversations with the customers.

You may sell a product that doesn't lend itself to extensive product knowledge. When your customer isn't the end user, he doesn't care which product is best, only if he can resell it to someone else. As an example, a drug store buyer won't care how your therapeutic hand lotion works, only how much it costs and how fast it sells. A dermatologist, on the other hand, is very concerned with the product's efficacy and details of its contents. He won't care about the profit margin or sales volume.

You may substitute industry knowledge and marketing knowledge for product knowledge if you're in that situation. Read trade journals, clip out articles you find relating to your product and use them during your presentation.

Your drug store buyer may not care how your product works and won't be motivated to buy it based on its therapeutic value. However, show him an article from a trade journal that shows the growth of the product's marketplace and your brand's market share and you will demonstrate your knowledge and expertise. This works whether you are selling expensive merchandise or cheap bags of candy. As an example, your product has a 20 percent market share and the store you are calling on does not stock your brand. You demonstrate how much business they are loosing to loyal customers who want your product. If the store says they don't have room on the shelf, you use the market share numbers to show that they are giving 15 percent of the shelf space to a competitor who only has a 5 percent market share. You suggest that they cut down on the number of facings (number of rows) that product has. Use that freed shelf space and inventory dollars to stock your brand. That way, the store can grow their volume and profit without spending more money. That is what a consultant does. A "pesky salesman" will try to force the product on the store without justification.

THE CUSTOMER AS TEACHER

An effective sales technique is to involve the customer in the presentation by asking them to educate you. This lowers their defenses by demonstrating your respect for their business or profession. Don't ask basic questions that would expose your lack of experience; however, a question involving a complex subject is fine.

I would ask a physician, "Doctor, I was taught that seborrhea dermatitis is resistant to systemic treatment. Is that true?" (Translation: Doctor, in training class, they taught me that you can't treat dandruff with medicine you take by mouth. Is my company giving me a bum steer?) Although I knew the answer, I would always learn something new about pharmacology or anatomy. I would then use his answer to lead into a presentation on my product for the treatment of Seborrhea Dermatitis. Professionals love to play teacher.

In legal publishing, I sold a set of books on bankruptcy known as a treatise. When an attorney tried to brush me off, I would say, "Counselor, I see you're too busy to talk about buying books. Can you just answer one question? What is a Cramdown?" It never failed. The attorney would stop dead in his tracks and give me a ten-minute explanation of this bankruptcy term. It involves a bankruptcy judge who makes a decision that benefits the large creditors and then "crams it down" the throat of the small creditors. If an opportunity opened, I would lead into a presentation. Otherwise I would ask for an appointment so I could come back to show him the books. I'd succeeded in taking our relationship one step higher. I was careful to change the question each month, so I would never repeat myself to the same attorney. This is another reason to keep good call notes.

CONTINUING EDUCATION

You only stop learning when you stop studying. Regardless of your field, there is an endless supply of information available to study. You can rest assured that your customer doesn't have time to read it all. By bringing your customer information on a regular basis you build a reputation for being a reliable expert. I would subscribe to trade papers or find magazines in the buyer's lobby. When I found an interesting article, I would photo copy it and use it during the first step of the presentation, ATTENTION.

"Mr. Grocer, did you see this article in Supermarket News? The potato chip market is growing by 20 percent a year. Has that been the case in your store?"

If the manager said, "No." I would hand him a copy of the article and say, "Maybe there is something we can do about that." Now he was getting advice from a respected trade journal and not from some "pesky salesman."

In the pharmacy, I had a rep that called on me once a month. He was oblivious to everything, except his next coffee break. I read in the *Wall Street Journal* that his company was being bought out by a foreign concern. When I asked him about it, he gave me a blank stare.

I asked, "You didn't know? It's been in the news for a week and the *Journal* had a two column article."

"Well, I didn't check my voice mail this morning." he replied.

How could any buyer rely on him for good marketing information and advice?

Continuing education is as simple as reading the business section of the paper each day, going to the library each month and looking at the business magazines. Subscribe to trade publications or enroll in night school to expand your qualifications.

I made the effort in 1985 to learn how to use a computer. My job didn't require me to use one at the time, but I saw the handwriting on the wall. It was a skill that helped me land a job in legal publishing six years later. Of all of the candidates that applied for the job, I was the only one who even knew how to turn a computer on.

You may ask why it was so important. The publisher who was interviewing me was ready to introduce legal research material on CD ROM. The manager was struggling to train his current reps on how to use the new laptops that they company had just purchased. He told me it was an uphill battle. At the last training session, he spent all morning trying to teach his people how to set up the computer, plug in the printer, ROM reader, and open the jewel case without breaking it. I was one less headache he had to train. At the next meeting, he asked me to help train the "senior reps." My investment in myself made me a valuable asset.

I was cold calling a law firm when I met the attorney hunched over the secretary's desk. He was in a panic. They had an irreplaceable file on a disk that they could not open. The disk was corrupted. He brushed me off and said he didn't have time to talk about books. I said I understand, but I might be able to help. I asked if he had run a scan disk to find and fix the corrupted file. He looked at me and said he had no idea what I was talking about, but he would be grateful if I could help him. I made no promises but said I would try. I ran the scan disk and retrieved the file. He was elated. He then sat with me and placed an order. I have even called my tech support department to ask how to make a simple adjustment on a customer's computer. The customer was always grateful, even if I couldn't help them. My competitor was a rep who rarely went out on the field. He preferred to sit at home and crank out phone calls. I was there to help and I became a valuable vendor.

I have an iron clad rule. I never touch any computer in an office that is networked. If I were to damage a drive, my company would be liable. Never touch a computer unless you know exactly what you are doing!

DEADLY MISTAKES

Example number one: In the grocery industry, I walked into a store I'd called on for about two years. That morning a large sign hung in the front door for the first time:

"ATTENTION ALL SALES REPS!
LEAVE YOUR SALES BAGS IN THE MANAGERS OFFICE IMME-
DIATELY UPON ENTERING THE STORE. ALL BAGS ARE SUB-
JECT TO SEARCH BY SECURITY."

My curiosity led me to ask the manager what had happened. He said that yesterday the storeowner was walking down the aisle about twenty paces behind a sales rep. The rep stopped at the end of the aisle, looked to his left, then to his right, but not behind him. He reached over, grabbed three cans of salmon and stuffed them into his sales bag. The owner ran up and grabbed him by the shoulder and led him to the office. The rep was crying and begging for forgiveness. He said he had a wife and a child to support and his company didn't pay very well.

The owner said all he had to do was ask. He could have used extra help on the weekend and would have gladly given him a part time job. The owner called the rep's manager. The manager asked to speak to the rep, who then admitted to shoplifting. The manager fired him on the spot. When the manager picked up the company car at the store, he discovered several hundred dollars worth of merchandise in the trunk. Since the rep could not produce a receipt he assumed they were stolen as well. Now, because of the action of one, the store treated every rep with suspicion.

Example 2: I was attending the formal dinner at a national sales meeting when one of the senior reps was asked to make a few remarks. Ricko was in his mid 60's and clearly from the old guard. Ricko apparently got a hold of a very old joke book figuring the young crowd had never heard the stories. What Ricko didn't consider was that every joke he told was politically incorrect.

Commission sales reps, by nature, have a thick skin. You could feel the tension in the room of two-hundred as Ricko insulted blacks, gays, women, the obese, Jews and Catholics. Shortly after Ricko left the podium, the national sales manager felt compelled to apologize to the audience. Ricko received a letter of reprimand that admonished him for his behavior. I think the company was too frightened to fire him because of his age. However, they were genuinely concerned about a lawsuit from members of the sales force who took offense.

Other examples of deadly mistakes are:

1. A rep was caught padding his expense report. He lost a $50,000 a year job, plus benefits, for a lousy $30.

2. A rep was caught forging signatures on contracts so he could get a bonus check.

3. A rep was caught damaging the competitors product in a store.

4. A rep told his manager he was unhappy with this job and was looking for something better. The manager fired him.

5. A rep got drunk at a company picnic and threw up on the table where the company president was sitting. His career came to a grinding halt.

6. Several reps partied all night at a national sales meeting and missed the morning session.

7. Another two reps at a meeting brought a call girl into the hotel. Security alerted the police and the rep's manager.

8. A male and female rep who were married, but not to each other, decided to get together one night at a sales meeting. The girl's roommate surprised them and reported them to management. Both were terminated.

9. A field rep answered his home phone at 11:45 in the morning, on a weekday. His manager was calling to leave a message on his answering machine. The manager put the rep on probation for being home in the middle of the day when he should have been in the field.

10. A rep got mad at his manager and punched him. He was fired.

11. A rep was working for two competing companies at once. A customer from job number two called customer service for job number one and demanded to know why his order hadn't been shipped. He got fired from both jobs.

12. A rep went to his company's office and began typing his resume and cover letter on a company computer. When he e-mailed them to the prospective employer he inadvertently included the entire company address book for his current job. Adios!

13. A rep was at a company Christmas party and badmouthed his boss to a woman he met. The woman was his boss's daughter.

14. A rep was caught selling cocaine on company premises.

15. A rep was reporting that he made sales calls on a store that had burned down two months earlier. His manager happened to live in that neighborhood.

16. A rep was using his company car as a private taxi service from New Jersey into New York City. He was caught when he had an accident and his passengers sued the company.

17. A rep was caught issuing company credits in exchange for merchandise for personal use.

18. A rep created a mythical family, a wife and two kids, to get a job at a company that preferred married reps for their stability. His manager showed up one morning at his doorstep to borrow his computer. He asked how four people could live in a one-room studio.

19. A rep drove his company car out of the country, in violation of company policy. The border guards discovered marijuana in the trunk and confiscated the vehicle.

Story after story comes to mind of sales reps who shot themselves in the foot, because they thought they would never get caught. I stopped at nineteen, but there are plenty more.

Yes, I've done stupid things that have landed me in trouble. (Fortunately, none of the above) I've seen great sales reps with good careers and families to support throw it all away for one moment of stupidity.

CAREER DEVELOPMENT

The best advice I can give on career development is simply being at the right place at the right time. I know people who joined a company and were propelled to management within a year; others labored for years only to be passed over for promotion.

Once I made myself so indispensable as a field sales rep in Manhattan, that management was reluctant to promote me. They felt no one else was willing to work the city as hard as I did and be as effective. I ended up leaving the company for another job so I could get into management.

To pursue career advancement, hang out with managers, not sales reps. Dress like a manager, eat like a manager, talk like a manager and play golf like a manager. That is how you get known. Some people think they want management but are disappointed when they achieve it. A non-working manager of commission sales reps often earns less than the reps do. In the event of a company downsizing or merger, the managers are first to go; the sales reps are the valuable commodities.

Be proactive in your company. Keep your eyes and ears open. If you see an opportunity to improve a situation, document it and send it through your chain of command.

NEVER POINT OUT A PROBLEM WITHOUT OFFERING A SUGGESTION TO REMEDY IT!

Send in suggestions for improving productivity. Volunteer for extra assignments. Learn what your boss has to do in his or her job. When you set a realistic goal for advancement, then work for it until you achieve it. You must prepare yourself to change jobs if you can't achieve that goal where you are.

Chapter Seven

TERRITORY MANAGEMENT

FINDING LEADS

The most important aspect of your job is to find customers to call on. Following are several situations that you may find yourself in and possible solutions.

NEW TERRITORY WITH NO RECORDS

You sell professional uniforms and have a new territory, but there are no records. You may be the first sales rep to cover this area for your company.

Yellow Pages: The best way to build an up-to-date customer list is with the yellow pages. Go to the Guard and Patrol Services section. The listings with the display ads are your prime contacts. They already spend money aggressively pursuing the business and are the ones who need your product the most. They may already have vendors, but this identifies the key players. List the companies by town and address. Indicate any service that has a display ad with an asterisk as a prime customer, then fill-in with the remaining listings. When you get into town, go to the library and check the local phone directory for additional companies not listed in the bigger book. This will vary from region to region.

Another resource is the Internet. You can find categories of professionals using a search engine. Some listings will allow you to sort results by town or zip code. Most have a Yellow Book or White Pages Link. Other links include business directories. If you do not own a computer or have an Internet service, most public libraries have free access to the net.

Check with the local Chamber of Commerce for any new businesses.

When you're having a good sales call with one of your new customers, ask if there are trade organizations that you could contact for membership. Ask if there is a national organization as well. Check with the organization and see if you can join. This will give you access to meetings, membership lists and contacts.

Check the yellow pages for related companies that may buy from you such as: wholesalers, local governments, department stores or shopping centers that run their own security department.

Go to the library or check the waiting room of one of your new customers for trade journals for that industry. Not only will you find customer ads but you may see an ad for a trade book that lists all members of the profession. Subscribe to at least one trade publication in your customer's field. By reading it you will learn about changes in the business and may learn of new businesses opening in your territory. This will give you an edge over your competition.

NEW TERRITORY WITH RECORDS

You are replacing a sales rep who was either promoted or one that left the company. Assume all records you inherit are incomplete. If you replaced someone who was promoted, then the records may be in good shape. Anyone promoted to management or who relocated within a company won't leave you with bad territory records. To do so would be political suicide.

Be wary if you replace someone who was fired or quit. Never place any faith in their records. Use them only as a reference point. Sometimes reps will delete records from their territory if they don't get along with a buyer. Cross-reference your inherited customer list with the sources mentioned above in "New Territory With No Records."

Ignore any comments on the records such as to personality traits of the buyer of staff. Give each of your customers the benefit of the doubt and learn for yourself what type of buyers they are.

OLD TERRITORY WITH RECORDS

Just because you have worked a territory for ten years, never assume that you know every single customer out there. Businesses come and go; owners change and so do their buyers. Because one small company didn't want your product five years ago doesn't mean that things have not changed drastically since then. Check your resources mentioned above to keep your lists up to date.

OLD TERRITORY WITH NO RECORDS

You may never have kept records of your customers and relied strictly on memory and driven down Main Street looking for specific companies. You will increase your business by developing a route book.

SETTING UP YOUR ROUTE BOOK

Accurate records of your accounts enable you to quickly plan your day, whom you will see and what you will sell them. Most large companies already have a standardized system they want you to use. Use it; keep it up to date and accurate. Following is an example of an account record system that you can create yourself with little expense.

Use one, 8" x 9" three ring binder with section dividers, for each two-hundred accounts. Depending on the size of your territory, you may wish to have one book per county or town. For instance, your territory includes a county with two-hundred customers. You would use one book divided by town. Within each section you would have one page for each customer. Arrange them in the order that you would call on them. That way you have done most of your planning ahead of time. Simply start on page one and progress to each account in order until you have seen everyone. Keep the book up to date and rearrange the order as you fine-tune your route. If you have a computer, you can create a list in your word processor or spreadsheet. The list on a word processor is easy to set up; however, the spreadsheet is more flexible and will allow you to sort your customers by town, name and classification.

Remember the key to computer account lists you create and maintain: "Garbage in–garbage out."

Many rack jobbers and cold callers can see their customers whenever they get there. Arrange them in the most efficient manner to save you driving or walking time. Start at one end of Main Street and work toward the other, hitting all of the side streets. Never double back or criss-cross unless absolutely necessary.

You may have restrictions as to certain times you can see buyers. Arrange them according to those times. Sort your customer records in order of those you can see early in the morning through the close of business. You will criss-cross town but will keep it to a minimum. You will soon learn which buyers are more flexible than others. Use this to your advantage; get the most from your day.

The purpose is to provide you with a clear agenda for the day. This should be planned the night before. Never spend prime selling time deciding whom you will see next. Never try to remember your agenda; write it down. You may work your way across town only to learn you forgot to see someone earlier.

PLAN YOUR WORK AND WORK YOUR PLAN.

ACCOUNT INFORMATION

The more information you write down, the easier you job will be. You will be less likely to make mistakes. NEVER write any information or insulting remarks on your account sheets that you wouldn't want your customers to see.

I had a customer grab my account book out of my hand and read my notes. Thankfully I'd written: "Nice guy, likes deep sea fishing, Mets fan." He handed the book back and said, "Your records are out of date; I follow the Yankees now." This provided me with small talk when I stopped in to see him. I never really followed sports, preferring to participate rather than "spectate," but I would read the sports section before I saw him to discuss the latest game.

I've inherited records from other reps that had insulting remarks about the buyer or staff, such as, "Buyer is a grouchy old hag." (Actually it was more graphic, but I cleaned it up for publication.) Imagine trying to close a sale after the buyer sees that remark. I quickly replace those records with new ones.

Each customer should contain the following information in clear legible handwriting or pre-printed address labels. Several simple computer programs enable you to print your own records on peel and stick labels. If you don't have access to a computer and your company doesn't provide you with account labels, then collect business cards from each customer. Staple it to the upper right corner of the page and you will have accurate account information.

An example of the account information that should be on each page is as follows:

Account Name: City-Wide Pharmacy
Address: 115-47 Hempstead Turnpike
City: Franklin Sq.
State: New York
Zip: 11010

Phone Number: 516-555-2234
Fax Number: 516-555-2235
E-mail address: hsmith@citywide.com
Account Ranking: A

Additional information should include:
The buyer's name: Hank Smith
Hobbies: Fishing, Golf, and Yankee Fan
Secretary's name: Susan, Beth (bookkeeping)
Best time to see or by appointment only: Mon, Wed or Fri 8:30 to 11 a.m.
Simple directions to the office: Long Island Expressway to Cross Island Pkway South east on Hempstead Tpke. One block east of Franklin Ave on left. Park in rear.

If they buy direct or from a wholesaler: Direct for major promos, Ace Wholesale for fill-ins.

If they are a credit customer or COD: Prefers 2 precent-10, net 30 for regular stock, takes extended dating for season promos.

Call Results: Following each call, write brief summaries of what transpired. This will refresh your memory on your next call. It also provides you with written documentation of how you spend your time. Many times I've had managers ask questions about specific accounts in my territory. I simply hand them my route book where I've documented everything. This has gotten me out of trouble more than once.

A customer phoned my company to complain that I never call on him. I'd tried to see him for several months, but he was always out or too busy. He would never return my calls and many times his secretary asked me to leave whenever I came by. I showed my boss the account records and he backed me up 100 percent. The consistency of my record keeping for all of my customers left him no doubt that I was trying my best to service the account.

Examples of call summaries are:

3/04/94: Frank busy wouldn't see me.

3/25/94: Built display for upcoming sale.

4/08/94: Wrote regular monthly fill in order: nine cases.

4/22/94: Frank on vacation.

5/02/94: Frank out sick.

5/04/94: Busy, wouldn't see.

5/05/94: Met Frank, sold Sept. promo, forty-six case order, will place circular ad.

6/06/94: Handled credit problem, got order shipped, presented new product.

You would have a good idea of my experiences with this customer, if you were to replace me in my territory,

CUSTOMER RANKINGS

Rank your customers with a lettering system. Your best customers are "A" accounts. Your second best are "B" accounts. Your worst accounts are "C" and so forth.

THE RANKING DETERMINES THE CUSTOMER'S POTEN-TIAL, NOT HOW MUCH BUSINESS THEY GIVE YOU OR HOW MUCH THEY LIKE YOU.

The purpose of this is to help you set priorities. When your company launches a new product or has a special promotion, you want to get large initial orders as soon as possible. Go through your territory and call on the "A" accounts first. You have already routed your territory; you simply work your way through the book.

Another advantage is that this system enables you to get the most business as quickly as possible when time is critical. You may discover that you have time left. Go back and call on your "B" accounts.

Sometimes you must skip accounts altogether. You know not to call on "C" and "D" accounts. When an account turns out to be a credit problem or one that buys from the wholesaler rather than direct from you, classify the account Z. Don't rip the account record out of your book. With a large territory, you may forget the details and waste time calling on them when you could be elsewhere. Do call on them when you have time, or when it is slow, say once every six months. You never know when things will change.

When I inherited a territory in Brooklyn, the old rep was showing me around the territory. We walked past a discount store. I asked why we didn't call on them.

"The buyer's kid brother works for our competition and would never give me any business. I tried for several years but finally gave up."

"When was the last time you went in?" I asked.

"Oh, about four years ago."

The first day I was alone in my new territory I stopped in to see the owner. It turns out that he bought the store three years earlier. He wanted to know why no one ever called on him from our company. I didn't want to make the old rep look bad so I said I wasn't sure. I told him I was his new rep and I would be by every month. I walked out with a large initial order. He developed into an "A" account.

TRADE SHOWS

A trade show is like a flea market for businesses. I've gone out of my way to work shows. They are a great source of revenue and contacts. I write tons of business, stay indoors for a few days, meet customers who normally don't see reps and learn more about my industry. Where else can you coffee klatch with the national sales managers of ten different companies?

Many reps hate trade shows, but I love them. I like to stand out in front of my booth and greet everyone who passes by, even if they don't look like a customer. They may be a customer's wife who will return with her husband. I hand out gifts, tell jokes, complain about the cafeteria food and have a few drinks with the guys at the end of the day.

Treat a trade show for what it is. A rare opportunity where for once your customers come to you instead of you going to them. In one day I would present to as many as one-hundred prospects. It would take me months in some industries, to get appointments to see as many buyers.

Place a fish bowl on the display table and invite people to drop in business cards. Have a drawing for a door prize worth about $25. Since you're the judge and jury, you select the winner. Pick the most important person that you would want to meet as the winner. Call that person and ask when you can drop off the prize. Since an accounting firm doesn't supervise your drawing, you can select everyone as a winner. Then for $25 each, you get appointments with as many prospects as you can handle.

I admit to calling people who didn't stop at my booth to tell them they won. I simply went through my supply of business cards that I collect on every call. I found someone I wanted to see, called them to give them the good news that they have just won a World Atlas worth $25. What if they say they never attended the show? I say, "Well someone dropped your card in the fishbowl. (I did) Do you want the prize?" Dishonest? Shady? No! I'm just being creative. I collect the cards and decide the rules on who will win and what prize they get.

Shop at one of the wholesale membership clubs. You can find many neat prizes to hand out. I would gladly spend $10 wholesale to give someone a $25 gift just so I can get into see them. I don't rip anyone off and I've spent more taking someone to lunch. This is just a new twist.

THE COMPETITION

In consumer goods, the competition is the sworn enemy. We compete for valuable shelf space and promotional dollars. Once, a competitor rep started knocking down my displays to put up his own. I called my colleagues and we have a war meeting. We ganged up on that rep and his company and targeted their displays and products. We keep the pressure up until they cried uncle. After a turf war that lasted three weeks, their division manager called our divisional manager and begged him to call us off. We were destroying his business. We were actively targeting his brands and replaced them with our brands on display. He was losing his shirt.

In legal publishing, just the opposite happened. I often met with the reps from competing publishers for lunch. We talked, swapped war stories and even leads. Although we competed for the buyer's money, we all had something unique to present. We rarely displaced each other's sets, only sought to complement them. Each industry is different, learn yours and decide if the competition is friend or foe.

SIZING UP A CUSTOMER'S POTENTIAL

Now that you see the pitfall of prejudging, how do you size up the potential of a customer? In pharmaceutical sales, I would walk into a physician's office and look around. Often the medical records were in sight somewhere behind the receptionist. Were they extensive? Did the office look busy? I would sneak a peak at the appointment book to see how many patients they scheduled for that week. When I get in to see the physician, I check out his closet where he would store drug samples. Were other reps calling on him? With simple observation you could determine if a physician was running a busy practice or if he was semi-retired.

When selling copiers, I tried to size up the business. Was the furniture new? Were there other types of office equipment in use, such as fax machines and computers? Did it look like a viable, busy operation that was in business to stay and would spend money on new equipment? I would ask the receptionist a few questions to get information on the success of the business. I would ask how the old copier was holding up. Sometimes the answer was, "That piece of junk is broken again." This gave me an opportunity to offer a free loaner until the old machine was repaired. This created an excellent opportunity. A stranger was giving the company better service than the present vendor.

In legal publishing, I would look in the library. Were the books up to date, or just a showpiece? If the office was modern and the books were all out-of-date, that would tell me that they were using electronic research. Did the attorney's appear to be busy or in semi-retirement?

The pharmacy I worked at as a manager promoted heavily and had a good customer flow. It was obvious to anyone who walked in. The end-caps were full of sale merchandise. They changed the window on a monthly basis and there was always a circular by each door. A similar sized pharmacy down the street looks like they are ready to close down. Given time to make one call, where would you spend your resources?

In downtown Manhattan, the oldest part of the city, some buildings predate the civil war. They are dark, musty and old fashioned; yet I wrote consistently large orders. They had 100,000 people walking past their door each day. In spite of their appearances, they couldn't help being successful. Take that same store and put it in the suburbs and they would be out of business in a month. Consider your product or service and evaluate it against your observations.

ROUTING

Routing your territory, or planning the order, in which you will see each customer, is one of the key elements of increasing your productivity. Many reps overlooked this simple task. Proper territory routing insures that you can make the most of your day, week, month, year and ultimately your career.

THE WORST THING A REP CAN DO IS TO SIT IN THE CAR AT 9 A.M. FLIPPING THROUGH ACCOUNT CARDS TRYING TO FIG-URE OUT WHICH CUSTOMERS TO SEE THAT DAY. THE TIME TO DO THAT IS THE NIGHT BEFORE.

When you can see your customers anytime during regular business hours, plan your day so you drive in a relatively straight line. A pharmaceutical rep must plan the day to coincide with the restrictive hours doctors will see reps. A lawyer may request that the reps set an appointment to visit the office. A rack jobber, however, may call on customers anytime between 7 a.m. and 6 p.m. with few exceptions. This means a rack jobber can maximize the time in the field to see as many customers as possible.

To plan your day in a straight-line is when you have ten calls to make in ten different towns. Schedule your first call farthest from home and work your way back. Leave a little earlier and use the extra commute time to think about your business. After your first call, tell yourself you're working your way home and only have nine stops to go. After your last call, you will only be a short distance from home. To plan your first call closest to home, you may be facing a thirty-mile drive at the end of the day. You don't want to cut the day short at 4 p.m. to get home at a decent hour. That will cost you sales and money.

The same principle applies if you're away from home several days at a time. Start your week furthest from home and work your way back. You may be able to plan your day in a circle so you can start out close to home and end up close to home.

Take advantage of extended hours in retail stores. During the summer, I called on my grocery stores starting at 3 a.m., yes, three o'clock in the morning. Several chains were open twenty-four hours a day, seven days a week, so I started early, had no traffic to fight, always found parking near the door and the stores were empty. I wrote my orders, built my displays and finished my daily objectives by 9 a.m. I was heading home about the time everyone else was heading to work. This was a great way to stretch out a weekend.

Several services on the Internet give you free access to road maps with driving directions. You simply put in your address and the destination. In seconds you not only have street-by-street directions but a map as well. Save these directions for your next call. A new manager was working with me and wanted to know the best route to my house. I lived in a different state. I told him to wait five minutes and I would fax him the directions. He was impressed that I was able to give him explicit directions from his driveway to mine.

Proper territory management involves more than planning your day. It involves record keeping to track where you have been and what you have sold, what each customer has in inventory, the buyers' names and addresses and phone numbers and best time to see them. It's time consuming to set up, but once in place will make your job much easier.

TERRITORY REALIGNMENT

A territory realignment is when your company shifts, expands or shrinks your present territory. The good news is that you have a change of routine, get new customers and opportunities. The bad news is that you have to completely revise your agenda to accommodate the new accounts.

In a territory expansion, you must reclassify your accounts to select your "A" and "B" accounts. If your territory expands, some that were "A" accounts in your old territory may turn into "B." accounts. When your territory shrinks the opposite happens. Upgrade "C" and "D" accounts that you rarely called on before to "B" and "C" accounts.

SETTING GOALS

A goal is an objective that one sets to give an organization or an individual a mission to accomplish within a given period. Classify goals as either long term or short term: long term meaning a five-year period and short-term meaning within the next year or two.

Before you set goals, you must first establish priorities. All goals, whether long term or short term, involve many intermediate steps. For example, if your long-term goal is to become a sales manager, then you will have several short-term goals that you want to reach. They include an MBA, a proven track record and personal contacts with those that will eventually promote you.

Depending on you age, level of education and experience within the company you can determine which goals are long term and which are short term. You may already have a four-year degree, so an MBA would be a short-term goal. However, if you were in your first year of college at night school, then an MBA would become a long-term goal.

When setting goals for your territory, there are several points to consider:

S-M-A-C

There are four aspects of an objective setting exercise. It would be fortunate, if your entire company adapts and adheres to these simple steps.

S-M-A-C is an acronym for Specific, Measurable, Achievable and Compatible. The goals set by you or those set by your manager should follow these guidelines. When everyone is using the same guidelines, then goals are achieved and business moves forward. I learned this program at the consumer product company I worked for during the 1980's. It worked so well, that I took the idea to other companies. Some adopted it, while others didn't. Those who did found that it improved sales and morale.

Your goal should be SPECIFIC and have a time limit. Several examples are:

- Make two cold calls a day for the next three months.
- Sell at least one "Model B" per week.
- Call on five accountants per week.
- Reduce phone bill by $50 per month.

Non-specific goals are too general and make it difficult for you to measure your success. For example, "I will work harder on sales." This goal is non specific since "work harder" is a subjective term. What is harder for you may be too easy by your manager's standards and leaves you open for criticism.

A goal should be MEASURABLE. Avoid an objective like, "Improve rapport with my big customers." How do you measure rapport and how could you mark your progress? It's better to say, "I will call on my top ten grocery stores once a week and ask how I can help them improve their volume and profit."

Examples of measurable goals are:
- Increase income by 15 percent.
- Spend no more than twenty minutes on each call.
- Mail at least twenty-five direct ad pieces each week.
- Send a thank you for every order written.

Your goal should also be ACHIEVABLE. Sales reps have the tendency to set unrealistically high goals for themselves. Use a benchmark of current levels to keep goals attainable. Some managers like to set unachievable goals in hopes that the reps will achieve more sales than they otherwise would have. The problem is if a rep consistently fails at his goals, he becomes discouraged and may give up and quit.

"I will increase sales of the Model 50 by 175 percent by the end of the year." The company's objective is a more realistic increase of 115 percent. You have no new customers in your territory, and your coverage of accounts is at the maximum. At the end of the year you have increased sales to 117 percent. Instead of being pleased that you exceeded the company goal, you only see that you missed your personal goal by 33 percent. This will hurt your morale.

Achievable goals with a benchmark would be:
1. Increase sales of the "Model B" to 115 percent by years end versus 105 percent last year.
2. Reduce my phone bill to $75 per month from the current level of $85 per month.
3. Make six cold calls per week vs. the five I make now.

Finally a goal should be COMPATIBLE. The Manager From Hell loved to send us on "wild goose chases." He would come up with some of the most offbeat objectives for us.

During one particular company sales effort that he didn't agree to, he had us promote another product. Although we achieved his goal, the division came in last place in the nation for the company's program and we all looked bad. During our yearly salary review, we were all penalized for not achieving the company objective.

The goal that you set for yourself should be compatible with the division, region and company goal. This insures that everyone in the company is moving in the same direction and working toward the same result.

When all members of an organization agree to S-M-A-C, any member of the organization may reject an objective that doesn't fit the criteria. There must be no fear of reprisals.

Your manager may say that everyone in the division must increase distribution of a product by 10 percent. However, you can document that you already have a 92 percent distribution, and that 101 percent is unachievable. You aren't held accountable for the objective. It would be impossible for you to do. This doesn't mean you won't try to increase the distribution; it would be in your benefit to do so. Take the whole number instead. Re-write the objective to say that you will work to increase the number of units to 215 vs. the 200 you now have. Document the 15 outlets that have potential. This may be a more difficult challenge for you than for the rep who has only 50 units out of 200 potential outlets in distribution and who has a goal of 55.

This assures that the entire company moves toward its long-term objectives and everyone is treated in a fair and equitable manner. No one is responsible for a goal that's impossible to achieve.

SMAC EXERCISE

Read each objective and determine if it is SMAC, if not, then rewrite it so that it is. An objective may fail to be SMAC in more than one area at a time. As an example, a goal may be both unspecified and incompatible. It may be specific, unachievable, incompatible and measurable at the same time.

1. Increase volume on major brands.
2. Ignore the company wide sales contest and pursue another agenda.
3. Increase calls on drug stores to eighteen per week versus the seventeen per week I now call on, in line with the company directive.
4. Promote the Model B, stressing its self cleaning feature, to companies looking to reduce their labor costs.
5. Reduce the distance between New York and Washington DC by 300 miles to comply with the company goal of reducing car travel. (This is a trick question.)
6. Cut territory expenses in my territory by 6 percent by years end.

TERRITORY OBJECTIVES: What are the things your company wants you to accomplish? Becoming the number one rep in your company is a perfectly good goal, but it just doesn't happen overnight. You must meet many short-term goals first.

These goals may include: an increase in market share, increase in advertising support at the local level, improved shelf position, better retail pricing, increased display support or any combination of the above. These goals must first be clearly be defined and placed in order of priority.

PROBABILITY OF SUCCESS: As a pharmaceutical rep your company announced a sales contest. The winner would be the one who has established a certain drug as the drug of choice with the most doctors in their territory. Management will determine your success by the increase of market share and physician documentation. Your goal is to win the contest. You must set priorities on which physicians you would call on in a limited amount of time.

You have the opportunity to call on either of two doctors in a small town to change their prescribing habits from your competitors to your product. You have determined that doctor number one has a large practice but 75 percent of what he prescribes goes to your competitor. He is entrenched in his habits and you only have a small chance of changing him over in the short term. Although if you did, the results would be very high.

Doctor number two has a smaller practice but sees no difference in the efficiency of the two brands. By focusing on the cost advantage of your product or some other relevant aspect, your chance of establishing your brand as his drug of choice is much greater. Therefore, if you have time to see only one physician in a town, see doctor number two. You can always try to see doctor number one later, if time permits.

DOLLAR RETURN: Depending on your territory size and your time frame you will find you won't be able to see everyone. You may find a town with six potential customers and your schedule only allows you to see two customers on a regular basis. Call on all six at least once and determine which would most likely be your top two customers. This assumes that you have a sales route where you first establish your product in stores then return on a regular basis to fill in what has been sold.

Certain products and services are exempt, like photocopiers or burglar alarms that don't depend on regular sales calls. You would see every potential customer despite their size. Regardless of the product or service you sell, priority setting and goal setting are an integral part of your success.

Limit the number of goals you set for yourself, whether long term or short term, to two or three at the most. Having too many goals will overwhelm you and you may become distracted or discouraged. It's better to have two priorities or goals to work on effectively than to work ineffectively against six or seven.

My first objective setting session required me to write my long term and short-term goals for my territory. Wanting to do a thorough job, I prepared a list of 36 objectives. Each one was in complete detail as to what I had to do and the benefits that I would derive. When I presented the list to my manager, he groaned. I'd missed the point of the session. After reviewing the list, we narrowed it down to one long-term objective and three short term.

Following are sample short-term goals written for a variety of sales situations. They are all SMAC.

- Increase distribution of a specific product by 10 percent in your "A" accounts within the next three months.
- Call on three of the top seven major manufactures by June 3.
- Reduce territory expenses by 10 percent for 2001.
- Improve shelf position of my product in one of the major chain stores by July 1st.
- Call on every dentist in York County and present the new dental device by the end of the first quarter.

Include a detailed plan of action with a specific start and finish date with each goal or objective. Using the above list of goals as an example, let's discuss expense management. On goal number three you would list your expenses for the year ending in 2000 and decide where savings could take place. This year you have spent more than $10,000 running your territory. Since you're a full commission rep, you cover your own expenses. Any reduction results in more money in your pocket.

The purpose of the following exercise is to demonstrate how you plan a strategy to achieve a goal. Some of these examples may be obvious or not relevant to your particular situation, but I included them to make my point. Prices reflect the cost of living in the metro New York area. You would like to reduce your overhead for next year without drastically affecting your lifestyle. Fortunately, you maintain good records of your expenses as they occur. It's an easy task to tabulate the totals.

Expenses for 2000:

Telephone	$1,980.00
Gasoline	1,020.00
Parking and tolls	504.00
Postage	90.00
Photocopies	72.00
Office supplies	168.00
Car wash	336.00
Car lease	2,388.00
Car insurance	1,200.00
Meals	1,400.00
Clothing allowance	1,020.00
Laundry service	670.00
Total	**$10,848.00**
10 percent savings	$1,084.80

Look at each category and decide where you can save money. There are some fixed expenses such as a car lease. However, you may live in a state where you can take a defensive driving course. This reduces your insurance by 10 percent for three years.

Perhaps your know-it-all neighbor insists that you use unleaded premium gas. By consulting your owner's manual you learn your car runs perfectly well on unleaded regular. Using Long Island as an example: unleaded premium at a full service station is $1.45 per gallon. You use twenty-seven gallons per week on average and spent $1,980 per year. A self service station in your neighborhood charges $1.09 per gallon for unleaded regular. By pumping your own gas, you save .36 a gallon. The total yearly savings are $492. That would help you attain 45 percent of your objective.

You could save $168 a year by washing your car yourself during the warm weather. That brings your savings to $660 or 60 percent of your goal. (A full service car wash in my neighborhood is about $7.50.) The telephone bill is another target for savings. You make 450 calls a year using your telephone credit card that levies a .50 per call surcharge. By making half of those calls at home before you go out in the field, you save $112.50. This brings your total to $772.50 or 71 percent of your goal. I discovered that a cell phone with a great calling plan was less expensive than my calling card. I found that the 600 included minutes for $49 per month was more than adequate and that I saved more than $1,200 per year.

For the remaining $311 of your goal, you save $100 a year in parking by using municipal lots and walking a few extra blocks. You also purchase tollbooth tokens by the roll to earn a free token. You find a drug store where you get photocopies for .3 each rather than the .10 you pay at the print shop. You save $68 dollars on office supplies by shopping at the wholesale buying club. You save $70 on car insurance by either taking a defensive driving course or simply shopping for a better insurance company. You save $38 a year by having your shirts and suits cleaned at a more competitive laundry.

Your savings now total $1,084, or a 10 percent decrease in last years costs. You may find other ways to save even more. Perhaps the changes are too much trouble and time consuming. You may decide that the cost of living in your area is so reasonable; it's not worth the effort. Therefore, instead of leasing a new car for $400 per month you visit the used car lot. You discover you can lease a two-year old trade-in, with about 20,000 miles on it for $275 per month. The car is still under warranty and is a step-up from the new one you were considering. That alone represents a savings of $1,500 a year and you get a nicer car. The insurance is less, because it's used. That saves you even more.

I based the objective on yearly totals. This brings in effect the economies of scale. If you're looking to save $1,084 a year, saving .7 on a photocopy or .50 on a phone call may not seem worth the effort. However, if you multiply the savings over the course of a year the .7 for a copy grows to $35. The .50 per phone call parlays into $112.50. Your objective becomes achievable.

Review the goals on a regular basis. Put notes in your appointment book to remind you. You may find that halfway through the time-period the situation has changed and then adjust your goal accordingly. Never write an objective and forget about it. Have it become part of your daily planning session.

EXPENSE MANAGEMENT

In the above example, consider how much you would have to sell to earn $1,084 after taxes. You can see the benefit of proper expense management. How much you have to sell to cover your $10,000 per year in total expenses should be a factor in your routine planning.

NEVER SPEND MONEY IN YOUR TERRITORY IF THERE IS NO DIRECT BENEFIT IN SALES.

Two of the large companies I worked for had completely different attitudes about spending money. The first threw money around like it was water. They supplied the reps with pads, pens, free samples, coffee mugs, sunglasses, catered lunches for the office staff and more. We got so much inventory, some reps threw the stuff away as fast as it came in. It was too much bother for them to carry around. They admitted the only time they used it was when they worked with their manager. Another rep bragged that he sold the stuff at a garage sale.

The company thought they were generating business by having the product name in front of the buyer at all times. They may have generated some sales this way but not enough to offset the cost. I would have preferred they use the money to offer an additional promotion during the year, or lower the wholesale cost, or better yet given me a much deserved raise.

The second company believed that you only spend when you get a return on your investment. In the grocery industry, sales reps from other companies had a variety of "give-aways" to pass out to the buyers and staff. Things like case cutters or baseball caps with the company's logo embossed on it. After several stock boys asked me for case cutters, I asked my manager why we didn't supply them like the competition did. He said, "We believe the grocery store should supply their stock boys with case cutters. What we do is take that money and spend it on direct advertising like coupon drops or newspaper ads. Those will generate sales and profit for the company as well as for your profit sharing plan. Mike, how would feel if next time you came up for a raise, we said there was no money. That night you went home and there was $2,000 worth of our junk in your garage?"

To encourage the reps and managers to curb expenses they would offer each rep a bonus if their division could bring in expenses below budget. It amounted to a few hundred dollars each year.

Following are some examples of the way we worked that could help you increase your earnings by cutting expenses.

1. Plan your daily travel in the most direct route. Every minute your engine runs it takes money out of your pocket. Never idle the engine while you do paperwork.

2. Empty your trunk of unnecessary clutter. Carry only what you need for two days unless you travel away from home for longer periods. Extra weight wastes fuel.

3. Practice conservative driving habits. No jackrabbit starts.

4. Keep your car well maintained. It will run more efficiently and last longer.

5. Increase your insurance deductible to $500 or $1,000. See if your car dealer has a trade in that's about two years old with low mileage. You will save on the depreciation of a new car and it will still be under warranty.

6. In warm weather, use your air conditioner. Driving with the windows down creates drag when the air hits the rear window. It's like a parachute. Modern car air conditioners are so efficient that you use less gas with the a/c on than with the windows open.

7. Resist the temptation to buy every new electronic gadget that comes on the market, like electronic address pads. If you're like me, then they will sit on your desk unused. I make full use of my laptop, fax, calculator and cell phone; however, electronic address books, pagers and electronic personal assistants were just more clutter for me to carry around. I prefer to use an old-fashioned appointment book or day planner instead of the electronic ones. I find that a printed price book is faster and easier than booting up my laptop and using the electronic version. You may find a pager works better for you than a cell phone. Think about your business and the best tools for the job.

8. Spend money where it shows. It's better to have two good suits than to have four cheap suits.

9. Take advantage of frequent flyer miles and special hotel packages. Don't hesitate to use a travel agent. There are many web sites on the Internet that can help you locate the bet price for travel and accommodations. There is no charge and they always get you the best deal.

10. Don't be so quick to supply customer's staff with coffee and doughnuts. I know I suggested this earlier, but be prudent. When you do someone a favor long enough, they will begin to expect it all the time.

11. Instead of dropping a quarter in a pay phone, ask a customer if you may use their phone to make a local call. In the economy of scale, saving .25 a day will net you $65 a year.

12. Are you the type to run out a buy a new computer every time a faster model comes out? I originally wrote this book on a five year old Tandy® 286. I have since upgraded to an AMD®. I bought the 286 right when the 386's were being introduced. It was no longer state of the art but it was still powerful enough to fly a 747. Since then, there have been at least a dozen upgrades. Why spend

$4,000 for a high-speed box with an eight gig hard drive with programs you will never use if you don't even need the power of a 486? Many small computer stores sell reconditioned computers that are only a year or two old. Shop around.

13. Don't fall into the trap that it is all deductible. The IRS doesn't refund the $10,000 to you. You lower your income level by $10,000, which may put you in a lower tax bracket. You must still earn the $10,000 you spend in your territory. As an example, let's say you are in the 25 percent tax bracket and you spend $10,000 running your territory each year. You must earn about $12,500 before taxes to cover those expenses. Before you spend money for your territory, think about how much you have to sell to cover the costs. If you earn 10 percent commission, you would have to write an additional $100,000 in business just to generate $10,000 in pre- tax dollars to run your territory. Why buy some gizmo that you may never use? For a married rep with no children who earned $50,000 gross for the year, deducting $10,000 in legitimate expenses would generate about $2,800 more in a tax refund. That means you would be spending an additional $7,200 every year. Spend only what you need for your job. The rest you keep.

14. Document everything. Regardless of the type of appointment book you use, keep a log each day of your destination, mileage, parking, tolls, hotel, air fare, phone calls and meals. Just write the numbers at the bottom of your appointment page for that day. Enter the expense when you make it, that way you won't forget. This will make it easier to do your weekly or monthly expenses.

The IRS recently audited a friend of mine. He was so poorly organized; he couldn't produce any records or receipts of his travel expenses. He had to pay back taxes and penalties for money he didn't owe. He still doesn't keep records; he just doesn't bother to deduct any expenses at all. Think of all the extra work he has created for himself just so he could avoid a minor daily task.

SALES REPS ARE OFTEN THEIR OWN WORST ENEMY.

TERRITORY CAR

The greatest benefit I ever received was a company supplied car. Every two years my company would park a brand new, fully equipped car in my driveway. They paid for everything: gas, maintenance and insurance. I could even use it for personal driving for a small mileage charge. When given the choice between a company car and being reimbursed for driving your own car, always take the company car. If you have an accident on company time in your personal car, it results in both you and your insurance company being liable. Your rates will increase dramatically if you're using your car for work.

Your company is liable for accidents, repairs and rentals. With a company car, you will probably end up with a better car than you would normally buy for yourself. Some companies will even let you purchase your car at the time of trade in. I've done that many times. I maintained the car well, bought it at below market value and then sold it for a profit. For you it is a win—win situation. When buying or leasing a territory car take time to consider the operating costs. A territory car shouldn't be a liability to you.

You may want to have a nice car if you take your buyers out to lunch or to the golf course. Make sure your car is clean and in good repair. A rolling wreck may turn off customers and it could cost you business. There is some debate if you should have a plain Jane car or something more luxurious. Some feel a flashy car will tell your customer that you charge too much for your products, others feel people want to associate with successful reps.

PURCHASE VS LEASE

The best person to ask if you should lease or purchase a car for your territory is your accountant. He or she will know what's best for your particular tax situation.

I don't lease; I buy. I purchased a three-year-old sports car at a dealer's used car lot. It had less than 7,000 miles on it, was in mint condition and covered under an extended warranty. I saved $7,000 over the cost of the car if it had been brand new. I would have to sell a lot of law books to earn $7,000 after taxes.

TRUNK ORGANIZATION

Trunk organization depends on many factors. They are the types of product you sell, brochures you use, the size of your territory and samples. The principle rule that applies to all reps is, never carry stuff you don't need.

The benefits of a well-organized trunk are many: You save time finding things you need, always have a back up supply of materials, reduce stress and by keeping your trunk light you save gas.

One rep I worked with had a small territory and could have easily restocked his trunk every night. However he choose to cram his trunk and back seat with enough material to last him a month. The car weighed down so much; the rear end dragged on the ground when he pulled out of the driveway. Once, he had a flat. It was raining and he was miles from a gas station or phone. He had to empty his trunk on to the shoulder to get to his spare. Everything was ruined and had to be replaced.

His car was always a mess. He couldn't use it to take his family out because it took too long to unpack and repack the back seat. His gas mileage was 20 percent less than our fleet average and he had to have the rear springs replaced after a year. It was a company car so he didn't care. I don't think that way. I treat a company car the way I treat my personal car.

The equipment that you should always carry in your trunk is:

1. The equipment to change a flat including a tire inflator can that seals punctures.

2. A flare or warning flag
3. A flashlight, pliers and screwdrivers.
4. A first aid kit.
5. A street map of your territory as well as a state map.
6. Office supplies, such as a stapler, paper clips and pens.
7. A medium size plastic crate to hold everything in.
8. You may want a file system for your trunk to hold file folders. These are similar to milk crates and hold about fifty hanging files.
9. A two-day supply of samples and brochures. You may need more if you're away from home longer.
10. Extra copies of your price book and order pads.
11. A pair of inexpensive work gloves and a towel. They keep your hands clean if you're changing a tire.
12. Carry an extra set of car keys in your wallet or purse. I learned the hard way when I worked with a manager and locked my keys in the car. We lost an hours' time waiting for the locksmith. The cost was $50 and embarrassment.
13. In your glove compartment, always carry a roll of quarters or dimes or what ever the most common coin taken by the parking meters in your territory. This may prevent you from getting a ticket.
14. Have a complete replacement for everything you carry in your attaché that you need to make a sales call.

Plan for the inevitable. You may lose your sales bag or leave your price list at your last sales call that's 20 miles away. This is embarrassing if you're on a deadline or working with a manager. He may think you're careless for losing something but will forgive you if you have a replacement in your car.

DEFENSIVE DRIVING

I can say the only time I caused an accident was in 1970 at the age of nineteen. I was tailgating someone and they made a panic stop. I had no collision and my car was totaled. I ended up riding the bus until I could save enough money for another car. The other driver caused the accidents the other times. Each time though, it cost me money, time and aggravation.

Even if you're a very good driver, I suggest you take one of the many courses on defensive driving. Some local high schools and private schools offer classes for adults, so you can lower your insurance rates and reduce the number of points.

No matter how little you drive or how well you drive, you must be on the defensive for the other person. The other driver may be drunk, on drugs, day dreaming or just dead tired. The worst kind is a driver who just doesn't care.

In 1986, I'd just left the Long Island Expressway and was on the southbound entrance ramp to the Cross Island Parkway. I was at the yield sign waiting for an opening in traffic. There was a car stopped in front of me. I glanced in my rear view mirror and saw a car coming at me at a high rate of speed. I couldn't see the drivers face because a road map was blocking the windshield. At the last moment the driver dropped the map and saw my car. I had my seat belt on; my headrest adjusted properly and was using a lumbar support. I slid down a bit, pressed hard on the brakes so not to be thrown into traffic and braced for the impact. There was no place for me to go. I was a sitting duck. The impact crushed my trunk up to the rear window and knocked the car fifteen feet.

For a moment I thought the accident wasn't that bad. In my confusion I restarted the engine and tried to pull off the road. I was lucky that didn't start a fire. After a moment a young woman appeared at my window. She appeared to be in her early 20's. She asked if I was hurt, but before I could answer, she began babbling about how she was lost and was trying to read the map. She then said the most incredible thing to me, "I know this may be a bad time to ask, but when I hit your car, my front fender was bent and my tire won't turn. I'm late for a hair appointment and I have a wedding to go to tomorrow. Do you thing you could bend the fender back so I can get to the appointment? I will leave you all of my driving information and will tell the police that it was all my fault."

I was still shaken up by the accident and couldn't think clearly. I said, "Sure, no problem." I tried to get out of the car. My driver's side door was crushed and wouldn't open. I tried to crawl over to the passenger's side. She just stood there looking at her watch.

She stuck her head in the window and asked, "Are we far from Garden City?"

I managed to get out of the passenger side and walked back to try to straighten her fender. As my mind cleared, I began to realize the absurdity of what I was doing. I just shook my head and walked back to my car and sat down.

The police arrived and filled out the report. The young woman had the police officer call a taxi and she was off to her hair appointment. She didn't even get a ticket. The officer asked if I wanted an ambulance and while still in shock, just shook my head no. He called a tow truck and left to go to another accident. I had no cash with me and the tow truck driver wouldn't take credit cards. He drove off too.

I managed to get the car started again and slowly limped along to the nearest gas station. I called my wife and she picked me up and took me straight to the emergency room. I've suffered with back pain ever since.

I made the mistake of telling my personal insurance company about the accident. They raised my rates. Although it wasn't my fault, I was driving a company car and my employer's insurance covered the loss. My insurance company's reasoning was that I was accident-prone.

There are people so engrossed in their own lives that they are totally oblivious to everyone else. In a fraction of a second they can destroy your property, cause you injury and inconvenience. They walk away without giving you a single thought other than you got in their way. When I say to drive defensively and watch out for the other guy, this young woman is the other guy I'm talking about.

Tips for defensive driving:
- Don't read a road map while driving.
- Don't talk on a cell phone while driving.
- Always leave yourself an escape route. Had I stopped about ten feet behind the car in front of me, I may have had time to swing out of her way.
- Leave two seconds of driving distance between you and the next car.
- When driving, don't think about business; pay attention to your driving.
- When looking for a street address, don't take your eyes off the road to read house numbers, pull over to the side.
- When someone is tailgating, either slow down so they pass you or pull over to another lane. Let them rear-end someone else.

DEFENSIVE PARKING

According to a safe driving expert who lectured to us at a sales meeting, the majority of auto accidents that happen to sales reps occur in parking lots. He pointed out that most fender benders happen when reps attempt to back out of a space. They either hit another car or someone hits them while they are parked.

The expert advised that we do two things. One was to back into a space so when you leave you have a clear view. Secondly, the lot may not permit you to back in to a space. Blow your horn before you back up. This serves to warn other drivers and pedestrians.

Never park close to the door or in reserved spaces. I did that in my early days and just happened to pick the buyers reserved space. The buyer was out to lunch and I was early, so I waited in the lobby for his return. He was furious when he got back, storming into the lobby, demanding the receptionist to page the (expletive deleted) who took his space. I sheepishly walked out to move my car, the buyer glaring at me the whole time. I never made that mistake again.

DEALING WITH THE POLICE

One of the tenets of a sales rep on the road is that you will inevitably get tickets, for either parking or moving violations. Most companies won't reimburse the rep for tickets for fear of opening the floodgates. Reps would become lazy or careless and the fines would mount steadily. One company I worked for, said that if they received a past due notice for a parking ticket, they would pay the fine and deduct it from the rep's paycheck.

In my career I've been pulled over four or five times. In each incident I deserved the ticket, in some cases I didn't see the signs that read: "No Left Turn After 4 p.m. On Alternating Thursdays Unless Otherwise Posted." or "No U-turn" although I was parked a few feet past it at the time.

NEVER argue with a police officer, even if you think you're right. Act politely, do what ever he says and then go to court to fight the ticket. Each time I show up at court, the District Attorney was willing to reduce the charges. That saved me money and points on my license.

Remember my friend who was audited? Well, he never paid tickets either. He couldn't be bothered. He was the type who expected everything handed to him on a silver platter. At the end of the year, the company required everyone who drove a company car to produce a conviction list from the Department of Motor Vehicles to insure they had valid licenses. My colleague's record showed that his license had been suspended. The regional manager called him for an explanation. He came up with some lame excuse. The manager said in plain English, "Without a license, you're useless to me."

My friend had to take an unpaid leave, get a lawyer and go to court. He paid a hefty fine and managed to get his license back. Why not do it the easy way? When you get a ticket, fight it if you wish, but pay it. Having a clean record is essential in this business, even if you work in mid-town

Manhattan and ride the subway to work. Companies look at clean driving records as a sign of stability and responsibility.

PARKING TICKETS

While I worked in the city, I got a parking ticket at least once a month. They imposed surcharges on top of the fines. The fine for parking at an expired meter at the time was $45. When they towed you away, it was as much as $350 to get your car back and if they damage your car in the process, too bad.

I saw them tow away a brand new, $80,000 luxury sedan the wrong way, with the car in park. The car was leaving skid marks all the way across the street. I'm sure the car's transmission and tires were shot. You may not mind seeing the wealthy get a raw deal; well, how about the ten-year-old Chevy that got destroyed while being towed. It was rear ended by a truck.

The parking signs were very confusing and the parking enforcement people were efficient. In only a few cases I was able to plead "broken meter." The city parking bureau was very good about that. If you claim you put money in and it ran fast, they would check the meter for accuracy and give you credit. However, there was a time during the 1980's when they took advantage of reps that drove company cars.

When they ran my plates and saw that the car was registered to a corporation, the city immediately sent the company a past due notice. I knew that, because the past due was postmarked the day I got the ticket. You were supposed to have ten days to pay the fine.

The company would pay the ticket and late fees then deduct that amount from my paycheck, although I'd paid the ticket that very day. The responsibility was up to me to get my money back from the city, which was a bureaucratic nightmare. I would end up paying the fine twice, plus a penalty if I didn't fight it. That could run more than $100. I understand the city has since put a halt to that practice.

I could go into a lengthy story as to why I drove in the city every day, why I didn't use mass transit and why I used the parking lots that charged

$20 per hour. It would only be meaningful, however, to the small number of reps who work in major cities. Suffice to say, be careful how you drive, especially in small towns, never argue with a police officer and pay your tickets at once.

LETTER WRITING

The art of letter writing in business has changed dramatically since I first started selling. Businesses are overwhelmed with junk mail, faxes and electronic mail on a daily basis. To get your message to be noticed through the clutter takes skill and patience.

I suggest you write every thing you want to say, then go back and cut it in half. Pretend as though you must pay $5 for every word in your letter. That will help you focus on the message you want to convey. A sentence with nine words would cost you $45. Is the sentence really worth that much money? If not, delete it. Apply the five steps of the presentation and keep the letter to one page in length. Here is an example of two versions of the same letter.

The $885 Resume Cover Letter:

Dear Mr. Jones,

Please allow me a moment to introduce myself. I am a seasoned sales pro with nine years experience and a proven record of accomplishment that would be an asset to Remington Industries.

I've followed your company's success record for some time and I am impressed with the strides your company has made. I would appreciate the opportunity to meet with you and discuss the sales position advertised in the Sunday Times for a Regional Sales representative.

I've worked for Acme Industries for eight years and have finished each year ahead of quota and have made President's Club four times. This coveted award goes to only a select few each year.

Enclosed, please find my resume and a copy of a letter I received from our National Sales Manager acknowledging my efforts during a recent product launch. I had finished first place in the nation for new distribution. This was an important launch for Remington Industries.

Please call me at your convenience so we can arrange an interview. I look forward to meeting you.

Sincerely,

Now read the edited $590 Resume Cover Letter:

Dear Mr. Jones,

Would a seasoned sales pro with nine years experience and a proven track record be an asset to Remington Industries?

I've followed your company's success record for some time and would appreciate the opportunity to meet you and discuss the sales position advertised in the Sunday Times.

I've worked for Acme Industries for eight years and have finished each year ahead of quota and have made President's Club four times.

Enclosed, please find my resume and a copy of a letter I received from our National Sales Manager acknowledging my success during a recent product launch.

Please call me at your convenience so we can arrange an interview. I look forward to meeting you.

Sincerely,

Your name

By eliminating fifty-nine words I have saved $295 and made the letter faster to read. The editing has not diminished my message. There is no need to ask permission for a moment of his time. That's being overly polite. There is no need to describe what a President's Club is. Most companies have a similar program. It is redundant to describe what is in the letter from the National Sales Manager. He will find that out when he reads it. Furthermore, new product launches are vital to all companies and telling him that is a waste of time. Remember to write the way you speak.

Don't pepper your letter with jargon or complex vocabulary. It's better to convey a clean simple message than one that tries to impress the reader with an elaborate vocabulary.

Thank You for the Interview:

My mother taught me the social graces at an early age. When I entered first grade I could already read and write a very simple thank you for gifts received. I knew how to introduce myself to adults and although at that age my table manners were still rough around the edges, I never embarrassed myself in the presence of others. These lessons learned early in life have served me well and I will always be in debt to my mother for her efforts and guidance.

Perhaps that's why I prefer handwritten notes to typed letters. They are more personal and convey sincerity. What better compliment is there than to take the time to write a thank you note after an interview?

Dear Mr. _____,

It was a pleasure meeting you today and discussing the career opportunities at (name of company). I'm confident that I will be a great asset to your organization and I look forward to meeting with you again.

Sincerely,

Introducing Yourself To a new Customer:

Dear _____,

I'm (your name), your new representative for (name of your company). Your company is now my responsibility and I'm anxious to meet with you and your staff.

I will be in your area next Thursday and would like to take a moment to stop by. I will call ahead to schedule a time convenient for you. Until then, if you require any assistance or have any questions, please feel free to contact me.

Sincerely,

Thank You for an Order:

Dear _____,

Thank you for your recent order for our new (name of product). I'm confident you and your staff will find it meets all of your expectations.

I will return to your warehouse, as promised, to personally supervise the installation process and to do a hands on demonstration so everyone feels comfortable with this new technology.

Please call if you have any questions. Thank you again and I do appreciate your business.

Sincerely,

Sorry I Missed You:

Dear _____,

I'm very sorry I missed you today when I dropped in. We have a new (name of product) and I'm confident you will find it both improves your productivity and reduces operating costs.

I will call Tuesday morning to schedule an appointment at your convenience. Until then, please feel free to contact me if you have any questions.

Sincerely,

Sorry You Didn't Buy From Me:

Dear _____,

I was disappointed when I learned from your assistant that you decided to purchase your new (product) from another manufacturer. I was so confident that we had the best package for your needs.

(Name of competitor) has a great reputation and I'm sure you will be satisfied. Please keep us in mind for your future needs, as we're constantly developing new technology in many aspects of your industry.

Best of luck and I hope to meet with you again soon.

Sincerely,

Suggestion To Management:

Dear _____,

Enclosed, please find a suggestion I developed, that will improve the ordering process for the field sales force.

My idea is to (state your suggestion).

The benefit to the sales force is (state benefit). The company will also realize a benefit of (state benefit).

I suggest we implement this on a trial basis at once. If you would like to discuss this further, please feel free to call me at anytime.

Sincerely,

Letter of Apology (Even if it's not your fault):

Dear _____,

On the afternoon of (date), I had a major confrontation with a member of your staff over an issue I had strong feelings about. In retrospect, I handled the situation badly and therefore reflected poorly on both my company and me.

Please accept my heartfelt apology.

Sincerely,

Letter of Apology for Your Error:

Dear _____,

On (date) my company shipped you twenty-four cases of (product) instead of the one case of twenty-four units you requested. I understand that this caused a major catastrophe in your warehouse, causing delay and confusion as your staff resolved the matter.

After reviewing my records, I find that the error was entirely mine. I transposed product id numbers when I entered your order. I've been in contact with our credit department to issue you immediate credit and have instructed our shipping department to pick up the excess merchandise.

To compensate, I've asked the order department to ship the original case to you at no charge. Please accept my apology.

Sincerely,

Reply to a Nasty Gram:

A Nasty Gram is a foul letter you receive from someone who has an axe to grind. Never send a Nasty Gram to anyone. They have a tendency to stick around for years and come back to haunt you. Sometimes you feel compelled to respond. Here is a sample of a Nasty Gram I received and my reply.

Mr. Swedenberg,

After carefully reviewing your trade show report that you submitted last week, I'm convinced you're unaware as to their function and purpose. (Meaning the purpose of the reports)

First, shipment of the display piece and sample material is controlled out of Houston, if it was late, that was the fault of the trucking company. Secondly, the fact that the demo piece wouldn't function properly is the responsibility of the last person who used it. You should direct your comments toward them.

I suggest you confine your attention to your job of sales.

(Name)

Dear (Name of Nasty Gram sender),

Part of my responsibility as a sales representative is to report to the company on the success and failure of all trade show activities. This enables the company to improve performance at future shows and maximize time, money and effort. It wasn't my intent to embarrass you or anyone in the home office.

Unfortunately, because of the late shipment and the broken demo piece, we were unable to write any business at the show. As you may know, the show cost our division $2,500 out of our tight budget, plus the field time of two reps. Since we have nothing to show for our efforts we will have difficulty in justifying this important show next year.

It's unfortunate my comments reflected poorly on your staff; however, I won't apologize for filing an accurate report.

Sincerely,

Mike Swedenberg
Senior Sales Representative
cc: Nasty Gram sender's boss and my boss

Letter of Resignation:
Dear _____,

It's with regret that I respectfully submit my resignation effective the close of business two weeks from today.

This was a difficult decision for me to make in light of my achievements at (name of company). New opportunities have become available and I feel compelled to pursue them.

Best of luck to you and everyone at (name of company).

Sincerely,

TELEPHONE SKILLS

No one can excel in all areas of sales and I admit that selling over the phone isn't my forte. There are those who do it well and can do it full time. The advantage is that you can cover a wide area of territory and call many more customers than you could if you were physically knocking on doors. I prefer face-to-face selling. There are several reasons why I feel this way.

First, it is too easy for someone to say no to you over the phone. Your call is only one step above a piece of junk mail, the only advantages are that you know if you get through to your prospective customer and you can inter-relate.

Secondly, there is no way you can judge a person's physical reaction. How can you tell if someone is rolling their eyes to the ceiling, smiling or angry? Finally, you can't judge the physical surroundings. Are they distracted and temporally swamped with work? Has the buyer just stepped out of the room? In face-to-face selling you can stand by for a moment and wait for someone to return to their desk, or wait until the receptionist has handled the mini crisis.

I avoid telephone sales as much as possible, but I've used it successfully due to necessity. In legal publishing, I was called in for jury duty. Since I was on commission, I was loosing money every day I was out of the field. During the court breaks, I would run over to the pay phone in the waiting room and call my accounts that were lawyers. I explained I was on jury duty and was unable to stop by; however we had a new title that would be beneficial to their practice. I managed to write half a week's quota during the breaks.

A few techniques I've picked up from reps that sell well over the phone enable me to get an average return for my investment.

1. Call ten minutes before the office opens, ten minutes after noon, ten minutes after one and ten minutes after five. The secretary will most likely be away from her desk and the boss may pick up the phone.

2. Ask, "Is he in?" or "Is Joe in?" rather than asking for Mr. Smith. This lends familiarity.

3. Give as little information as possible to the screener, if asked the purpose of the call say, "It's regarding his photocopier." or whatever it is you sell.

4. When you ask a leading question like, "Is this a bad time?" or "Do you have a minute?" You will get an answer you aren't looking for.

Several books are devoted to telephone sales. I suggest you pick up one to improve your skills.

TELEPHONE LOG

Whenever I get a voicemail or phone call, I log the call with the date, time, the callers name and a brief message. After I return the call, I put an additional note on the results of the callback. When the issue has been resolved, I draw a line through the note. The calls without the line stand out as unresolved issues. When the notepad is filled, I mark the beginning and end dates on the cover and file it away and start a new one. Many times the log has saved the day. I have closed new business, saved canceled orders and had a permanent record to clear me when an irate customer claims they called me five-thousand times and I never responded.

APPOINTMENT BOOK

I combined my appointment calendar, price book and phone log into one, leather, three-ring binder that has pockets on the inside covers. The binder has additional pockets for business cards, a small calculator and pens. In the back flap I carry copies of current promotions and technical alerts. For the phone log, I bought an eighty-sheet, college ruled 5x7, spiraled notebook that's hinged at the top. I placed the back cover of the notepad into the front pocket of the binder so I can flip through the pages. Everything I need is always at hand.

HOT LIST

I created a table in my word processor and saved it to my computer desktop. It is four columns wide and as many rows long as I need. In the first column, I have the date of my first contact with the customer; the second has the client's name, address and phone number. The third has the products I presented and the last column has the notes, status and a follow up date. I check the Hot List everyday, make the necessary callbacks and edit the notes. I often print out the Hot List and carry it in my appointment book so I can make call backs between appointments.

Every week, I e-mail a copy of the Hot List to my manager. He or she always knows what I'm currently working on and the progress I'm making. If I loose the sale, I delete the row. When I close a sale that's on the Hot List, I highlight the row and click on the bold icon. I let it stay there until the sale appears on my commission record. This way, I know I got paid. It is also boosts my morale to see so many successful sales. In the last eight years that I have used the Hot List, not once has a manager called me to ask what was going on in my territory, not once! They have asked specific questions about accounts I was working on for a long time, offered suggestions, but never asked what I was doing all day.

ELECTRONICS

Many companies provide electronic equipment, such as computers and voice mail and the necessary training to use them. I suggest you pay attention and learn how to use them to the maximum.

The thought of writing and editing this book on a manual typewriter would prevent me from even considering it. My company supplied me with a laptop and complete training in 1987 when I was a pharmaceutical rep. Since I already had a basic understanding of computers, it was easy for me to learn the new system. The knowledge and expertise have served me well over the years. I can't imagine running a territory without one. Don't be intimidated by a computer, they are now quite simple to use.

Many computer programs are user friendly and can help you manage your territory, correspondence, expenses and inventory. Most communities have adult education courses to teach you the basics and from there you can learn on your own. When you first start out or have a limited budget, visit computer repair stores. Many offer rebuilt computers, monitors and printers for a fraction of the cost of a new one. A computer store will try to sell you a state of the art system. That is fine if you know how to use them and can afford it, but believe me, they are overkill. You are buying more computer than you will ever need.

Today, many computer stores and catalogue houses offer reconditioned or discontinued equipment for less than $1,000. You are getting equipment that was top of the line just two years ago. It still works and is powerful enough for your needs. Consider this analogy: Buying a reconditioned or out of production computer is like buying a ten-year-old, high-end sports car. It may no longer be state of the art, but it will still go 150 miles per hour and beat anything else in the neighborhood.

I use my computer to generate direct mail, address labels, maintain my territory records and my personal finances. I have a new PC now and it works great. I can justify the cost because I use all of the programs. If you're just starting out, pick up an older PC. It does the job, has power to spare and you will save a bundle.

Study one of the popular word processing programs. Carry a floppy disk of form letters and company letterhead with you. Many of the chain print shops have computers you can rent for a small fee. They are free at public libraries. In the middle of your territory, you can stop off and generate a proposal rather than waiting until you get home.

Ask your friends who use a computer, tell them your needs and they will guide you to the right machine. They may even have an old one to sell you. My friend is constantly upgrading every time a new computer comes out. He sells his old one that was state of the art a year ago for a fraction of what he paid for it. Never buy a used computer from a stranger, only from a friend who knows the machine or from a reputable dealer who will guarantee it.

Make sure you have an anti-virus program installed that will automatically scan for viruses. Going on the Internet can infect your computer or when someone gives you a disk to copy files. A virus can wipe out your system and destroy your data. Always back up your data. If your system crashes, you could lose everything.

I do recommend that you buy the best Laser printer you can afford. It will produce professional quality letters and flyers regardless of the type of computer you have. I picked up a used laser printer from a computer repair shop. It had a new cartridge, which is the heart of the printer. It was one fourth of the price of a new one. Never use a dot matrix; it's unacceptable for correspondence.

Several programs will manage your territory and schedule. Visit your local software store and ask to see what's available. They are easy to use and are much better than relying on written notes or your memory.

CALCULATORS

A manager told me that when he was field training a new rep he handed him a calculator to figure out the cost per unit of a promotion. The rep, a man with a college education, sat there and stared at the machine. After a moment, Kevin asked what the problem was. The rep asked, "How do you turn it on?"

Calculators are so inexpensive and so easy to use; no sales representative should be without one. For your first calculator make sure it has a memory function and is large enough that the display is easy to read and the keys are easy to push.

Learn how to use the memory key. The memory function allows you to carry on two calculations at once. This is important in sales when you must calculate prices and shipping weights. Memory is a series of three buttons that are marked M+ (Memory Plus or adding a calculation to memory). M- (Memory Minus or subtracting a number from memory) and MRC (Memory recall to allow you to check your total in memory). The display will flash the letter "M" when memory is on. The instruction sheet will explain how to use them. I worked with a manager who was amazed when I did a memory calculation. He always wondered what "those funny little keys were." Well, hello! Read the instructions.

VOICE MAIL

Voice mail is both a blessing and a curse. It's a blessing for sales reps when their customers wish to reach them. Use the system as a short-term archive for calls. You can change your message to indicate you're away for the day or for a two-week vacation. The curse is when you try to reach your customers, or your company and you get a voice mailbox. You may call five times and never get a response.

You may wish to get the voice mail through your phone company. For a small monthly fee, you have a professional piece of equipment that beats the heck out of a simple answering machine. Have someone other than yourself record the greeting, as if you had a secretary.

A sample greeting: "Hello, you have reached the office of (your name) your sales representative for (your company). Mr. (your name) is away from his desk, but your call is important. Please leave a brief message and your phone number at the beep. Mr. (your name) will return your call promptly. Thank you."

Re-record the message several times until it sounds smooth and not as though you are reading a script. Then remember to check your voice mail often and return calls promptly, even if it is bad news.

MATH MADE SIMPLE

Math isn't a strong point of mine. I struggled through college calculus. However, I've met reps that come into the pharmacy and couldn't do simple calculations.

To determine a retail price, with a 10 percent mark up from the stores cost don't multiply the cost by 110 percent. You must DIVIDE the cost by .90 (Decimal point 90).

EXERCISE 1

Cost: $1.00

Markup: 10 percent

$1.00 divided by .90 = $1.111 or rounded up to $1.12. The .12 is a 10% markup for an item the store pays $1.00 for.

To demonstrate, multiply the $1.00 cost by 110 percent. The retail would be $1.10. To give a Senior Citizen 10 percent discount, you would MULTIPLY the retail $1.10 by 90%, then subtract 11 and sell the item for .99 You would lose .01 on the item.

When you divide the cost by .90 the retail is $1.12. To give a 10% discount multiply the retail $1.12 by 90% and you sell the item for $1.00, which is your cost.

A second way is to subtract the markup from the cost, add a decimal point, and then divide the cost by that number.

EXERCISE 2
Cost: $1.00
Markup: 20%
Subtract 20% from 100; add a decimal point.
100—20 = .80
$1.00 divided by .80 = $1.25 retail

EXERCISE 3
Cost: $1.00
Markup: 25%
100—25 = 75, add a decimal to get .75
Divide $1.00 by .75 = a retail price of $1.33.

EXERCISE 4
Cost $3.55
Markup: 43%
100 43 = 57, add a decimal to get .57
Divide the cost by .57
$3.55 divided by .57 = $6.22 retail price

MARKUP VS. MARGIN

Markup at **Retail** is the most common calculation in retailing. It's often confused with Markup at **Cost** or as it is sometimes called, Margin.

As an example, you buy an item for $1.00 wholesale and resell it for $1.40, the Markup would be:

$1.40 minus $1.00 = .40 $1.40. = .2857142%

The Markup is rounded up to 29%

Markup at Cost = Retail Selling Price—Merchandise Cost divided by Merchandise Cost

Using the numbers from the above example:

$1.40—$1.00 = .40 divided by $1.00 = 40% margin.

A sales representative, for the most part, isn't involved in retail price strategy. It's important, however, to understand the basics of how a store calculates their pricing strategy.

In both of the above examples the retailer purchased the item for the same cost, $1.00, sold it for the same price, $1.40 and made the same .40 profit; however, his markup is 29%, but his margin is 40%. Ask which method your customers use. You don't want to quote a 29% Markup when your customer uses a 40% Margin.

As you gain experience and learn to become a consultant to your customers, they will start to depend on you for advice. Understanding your customers' pricing strategy helps you to prepare a presentations to guide them through the decision making process.

You sell stationary supplies. You know that the store works on a 30% markup. You sell a box of disposable pens for $10 to the store. What price should the store charge their customers to maintain a 30% markup? Use an algebraic formula:

30% x Retail Selling Price = Retail Selling Price—$10

(You subtract .30 from 100 to get .70)

.70 x Retail Selling Price = $10

(Divide both sides by .70)

Retail Selling Price = $14.28

The retailer must price the box of pens at $14.28 to maintain his 30% markup. You can do this faster on your calculator while referring to the exercise above. Write the two formulas in your appointment book and refer to them as needed. Soon you will know them by heart.

To simplify, calculate the retail for a $10 item at 30% markup. Subtract the markup, 30 from 100 to get 70. Add a decimal point to get .70, and then on your calculator divide the cost $10 by .70 to get a retail of $14.28.

That is the gross profit before you subtract the cost of doing business. (e.g. rent, labor, insurance, etc.)

When you make your presentation you can say, "Mr. Jones, if you purchase my suggested order of fifty boxes, your gross profit will be $214 (50 x $4.28 per box). This will place you a level above the rest of the sales reps who merely suggest order sizes without emphasizing the benefit of the profit.

Many reps came into the pharmacy to sell me merchandise, and I asked what price should I mark it. Their answer was always, "I don't know. It depends on your area. They all differ." When I asked how much profit I will make they said, "I don't know."

In "Total Empathy," you're a buyer for a retail health and beauty aid store. One rep comes in with a display of suntan lotion. He can tell you your cost, $150, but nothing else. The second rep comes in and says, "Purchase this display for $150, markup each bottle 40% to compete with other retailers in the area, and you will sell the entire display for $250. A gross profit of $100. Which rep would you buy from?

WHOLESALERS

Wholesale is the standard price at what a manufacturer sells his goods to retailers. Sometimes, manufacturers have minimum quantities for delivery that make it difficult for a retailer to buy direct from them. This creates a need for a middleman, better known as a wholesaler.

A wholesaler, also known as a Cash and Carry, has a large warehouse and lots of money. He can buy huge volumes of merchandise; get quantity discounts and advertising allowances. He places the merchandise in his warehouse and sends sales reps to small stores to write orders. The wholesaler may mark-up his merchandise 6 percent. The benefit to a retailer who buys from a wholesaler rather than directly from a manufacturer is the quantity.

A manufacturer may require a customer to buy a minimum of fifty cases, a wholesaler may require you to buy only one case but you will pay a 6 percent surcharge. This tradeoff allows small retailers to carry a large variety of products. Next time you go into a neighborhood drug store, imagine the size of the back room needed if the druggist had to buy fifty cases of each item he sold.

HOW TO SELL BELOW WHOLESALE AND STILL MAKE MONEY

There are times a wholesaler will sell an item cheaper than the manufacturers wholesale price. This happens when volume discounts, term payments and advertising allowances are factored into the cost of goods. This is the dead net.

An example is when the average wholesale price (AWP) for an item is $1.00. The manufacturer will give you a 2 percent discount if you pay your bill within ten days. (See 2/10 net 30) This reduces the cost to .98 per unit. The manufacturer also offers a volume discount when you by five-hundred units. The discount may be .05 per unit. This reduces the cost to .93. The manufacturer then offers an advertising allowance to encourage retails to promote their product in their window, TV ad or circular. The ad allowance is .04. This reduces the cost to .89. The wholesaler's dead net is now .89 for an item that has an AWP of $1.00. He marks it up 6 percent and sells it to small retailers for .97 each, .3 below wholesale. Said another way, average wholesale price is usually a bogus number.

2 % 10 NET 30

Often manufacturers give a discount if the bill is paid in cash on delivery or if the bill is paid within ten days of receipt. This improves the manufacturer's cash flow. There is no such thing as a free lunch. The discount is built into the cost.

You receive an invoice dated February 1 for $100, with terms of 2%/10 net 30 days. You may deduct 2 percent ($2.00) from the bill reducing your cost to $98; however, if you decide not to take the discount, you must pay the full $100 by February 30. Any retailer that doesn't take advantage of the cash discount is foolish. Where else can you earn 2 percent on your money in ten days?

Terms vary from industry to industry and even from supplier to supplier within an industry. Some wholesalers in the pharmaceutical industry offer 1% net 10. You may deduct 1 percent if you pay upon receipt of the invoice or pay the full amount in ten days. That's equivalent to earning 36.5 percent a year on your money.

There are industries that make their money by floating money. The gross profit the retailer earns goes to pay the rent, labor and utilities. The profit comes from lending the cash out over night to banks.

Other industries have longer terms, as much as six months. The retailer buys a season's inventory of a popular item and sells it for cost, known as a lost leader. This draws in customers to buy the regularly marked up items. As the retailer sells the lost leader he puts the money into a money market fund or short term notes and holds it until the bill comes due. He earns interest on that money for as long as six months. That's how he can sell the item at cost and still make money

In March, a lawn and garden shop buys $50,000 worth of fertilizer with six months dating. He prices the individual bags at cost as a lost leader. Let's say he has a big sale and sells out the entire inventory in one month. As the money comes in, he deposits it into a money market fund that pays 6% per year. After six months, he has earned $1,500 in interest. That is his profit on an item he sold at cost. He can then replace the inventory with another shipment for the balance of the season that he sells at a regular markup.

TIME IS NOT MONEY

I disagree with the cliché: "Time is Money." Time is time and money is money! The implication is that time and money can be interchanged. They can't!

To prove my point, pull into a gas station and ask for three hours worth of high test. When asked the time, say, "It's $1.63 past $100." See the reaction you get.

Time does have value and is a non replenishing resource. Once spent, it can never be regained. Money, on the other hand, can. We had a vendor try to cheat us on a delivery. We paid the invoice, but when I discovered the scam, I went to the bank and stopped payment on the check. We got the money back, but not the time invested.

You and your competitor sell a product to retailers for resale. Everything about the two products is identical, including the cost, except his comes open stock, meaning it is packed twelve items to a case and yours comes in a pre-pack floor stand. A pre-pack is a cardboard, folding display with merchandise included. The display is set up and the merchandise is ready to be sold. You now have an advantage over the competition. To get seventy-two pieces on display, the retailer must get his stock boy, who earns $5.50 per hour, to build a display on an end cap. This may take a half-hour. Your display can be set up in less than five minutes, freeing the stock boy to do other things. The labor costs for the competitor is about $3.00. The labor for your display is about .45 which is six times less. In an industry driven by penny profit, you now have the advantage.

In legal publishing, we changed the way law books are updated, saving the law firm hundreds of hours per year in staff overhead. I worked with reps that felt this wasn't a viable benefit and they never mentioned it.

A photocopier that makes sixty copies per minute (CPM) vs. fifty-five CPM for the competitor may seem insignificant. In a busy office that makes 50,000 copies per month, you can save the business fifteen hours in labor a year. A small, but relative savings that can swing a decision to your favor. In a chain of fifty offices, the savings leap to nearly nineteen weeks of labor saved per year.

"DISPLAY IS THE WAY, PILE 'EM HIGH SO THEY BUY."

No one believed in the power of merchandising more than my unit manager at the consumer product company. He instilled that belief in me. Regardless of what you sell, nothing beats a product display or service demonstration. A fancy brochure or photo dims in comparison. This applies to retailers, trade shows, showrooms and sales directly to the end user,

In retailing, a floor display marked down in price, with a sign attached, increases volume of that item 500 percent more than the same item at full price with no sign and left on the shelf. That is why you see so many displays set up in stores. The impulse to buy things is very strong. The display may jar your memory about something you need or simply entice your desire to purchase.

Following are several key points about displays:

1. Set up displays in high traffic areas.

2. Never leave a display 100 percent perfect. Customers are reluctant to take the first item off a display and almost never take the last item either. When you finish building the display, remove several items and place them on the shelf. This tells customers it's OK to take something off the display. It must be a good deal; others have bought it as well.

3. Place a sign on the item showing the sale price vs. regular price or sale price and the savings.

4. For an end-cap-display, a set of shelves located at either end of an aisle; always mix your brand in with a tie-in. Place your potato chips next to someone else's soft drink. The soft drink customers are tempted to buy your chips. Retailers want to mix in full price items with sale items to increase volume and profit.

5. For large machinery, have a showroom so you can demo the product. Have the machine with the most options. You can show the features to increase the size of your order.

6. During a presentation, hand the buyer a sample of your product and show how it works. I had a store manager who refused to display my new pineapple cake mix. He said it sounded disgusting. That night, I asked my wife to bake a cake for him. I took it in to his office and placed it in front of him with a fork and plate. I said my wife baked this for you. He ate half of the cake right there and then ordered a one-hundred case display.

7. At trade shows, I would place as many different book titles as possible on the display. Someone would always stop and look at something, no matter how obscure.

8. When cold calling on a tough office, I would hand the receptionist a CD-ROM of our law books and ask, "Please just hand him this and say he's holding 150, three pound law books that he can carry around in his brief case."

CHECK YOUR COMMISSION STATEMENTS

Regardless if you are on commission or salary plus bonus, each month you will get a statement that reflects your activity for the month. You must get in the habit of checking it with a fine tooth comb. In the twenty years I have been a rep for corporations, it has never failed that I find at least one error on the monthly statement that cost me money. I don't believe that the errors are intentional, but it gets annoying after awhile.

One month, I knew I had at least $6,000 in commissions due, but when my check came in, it was for $350. I had to reconcile my orders with the statement and forward them to my manager. The problem was that the orders were entered as returns instead of new business for a particular promotion package. Therefore, I didn't get paid on them. My manager quickly resolved the problem and the company paid me at once. The disturbing thing is that the error was nationwide and effected 150 reps. Only fifteen reps picked up on the error and brought it to the attention of management. What were the other reps thinking?

I worked with a rep who was on the verge of being fired for being under quota. Only after the manager reviewed a year's worth of statements at his probation meeting, did they discover that he was above quota and qualified to be in the President's Club. The guy nearly lost his job and the company nearly lost a highly productive rep because he refused to do some simple paperwork each month. How much money had he thrown away more than the five years with the company?

Understand how your system works and who to call if there is a problem. Keep a separate folder with copies of each order you write. When your statement comes in, put a big check mark on each order copy so you know if your were paid.

YOU WORKED HARD FOR THE BUSINESS, FOR CRYING OUT LOUD, MAKE SURE YOU GET PAID!

SUBMIT YOUR EXPENSE REPORTS

This is another point that amazes me. At one publishing company, they reimbursed reps $250 a month for expenses, regardless of how much or little we spent. We had ninety days from the close of business to get the monthly report approved and submitted. After that, we would not get reimbursed. At a meeting, I was talking with the regional manager, who told me that one of the reps had never submitted an expense report in the five years with the company. When asked, the rep just shrugged and said, "I'm not filling out an expense report for a lousy $250. I'll just sell an extra set of books each month instead." The manager loved it, because it saved the company $15,000 over five years. At this, the final chapter of the book, I hope you can see the absurdity of that response. I never learned the name of the rep, but re-read the section above, on checking commission statements and draw your own conclusions.

Epilogue

I've tried to open a new door of opportunity for you. It's now up to you to walk through. Sales is an easy way to make a good living and affords job security found in only a few professions.

I could lose everything today, my home, my savings and all of my possessions. Move me across the country to where I had no friends or business contacts and in sixty days I would receive my first commission check. Within six months, I would be back on my feet and within a few years I would be back to my former level, if not greater.

You may be a better sales representative than me. You may be smarter, better educated, more experienced and have a better personality; but, I will earn as much—if not more because I will work longer and harder than you.

Let's say you can document that you're twice as good a sales representative as I am. You need to work only forty hours a week to earn $100,000 a year. In the same job, I will earn $150,000 per year because I'm willing to put in sixty hours a week.

God made each of us different—but He gave us time as the great equalizer. Put in the time and you will surpass everyone else on the playing field. Put in the time and you will succeed.

About the Author

Mike Swedenberg was born and raised in Greenville, South Carolina and graduated from James L. Mann High School in 1969.

He attended The School of Visual Arts in New York where he studied Advertising Copywriting, Art and Design. Mike also attended Adelphi University at night and graduated in 1986 with a degree in business and management. His career path includes experience as both field trainer and sales representative.

Editor

Glossary

ASSORTED DISPLAY: A dump bin or display table in which an assortment of merchandise is placed for sale.

BENEFIT: (WOW) What a feature of your product or service actually does for the buyer.

BOOK: Official company policy, often in written form, as in the book says no vacation time during July.

BIG PICTURE: The view of the entire organization or plan of action.

BOTTOM TO TOP SELLING: Selling technique that takes the customer to the bottom of the line or least expensive product first, then moves him up to a more expensive model. As example: "For only a few dollar more per month, you get all of theses extras, not offered on the base model." See also: Top to bottom selling.

BREAKEVEN POINT: When income and costs of doing business are equal. When a business breaks even.

BUDGET: A plan to allocate money, specifically where money comes from and how it will be spent.

CASE CUTTER: A metal sleeve that holds a single edge razor blade. A safety device used to cut open sealed cases of merchandise.

CO-OPERATIVE: (Co-op) An organization of small businesses, usually of the same type as in independent drug stores, with the intent to improve their purchasing power.

CO-OPERATIVE ADVERTISING: (Co-op Ads) When two or more retail stores, owned by different people, create joint advertising. Usually a circular to reduce costs.

COUPON: An advertising medium that offers consumers cash off when they buy a specific product within a specific market. This is done in place of a general price reduction.

COUPON DROP: The act of distributing a large number of cents off coupons to consumers. Usually in the form of direct mail.

CASH WITH ORDER: (CWO) Cash or a check is collected at the time the order is written either because the account has bad credit or to take advantage of a cash discount.

CASH ON DELIVERY: (COD) Cash or check on delivery of goods. Common practice with rack jobbers or with those accounts with poor credit ratings.

CASH AND CARRY: A wholesale operation that doesn't provide delivery. The retailers go to the warehouse, pick out the goods they want and pay cash before leaving.

CASH COW: A business or product that has no outstanding debt and regularly delivers profit.

CERTIFIED CHECK WITH ORDER: With bad credit customers or with a new customer, a bank certified check is collected at the time the order is written. The customer can still stop a certified check. Always ask for cash from a poor payer.

CHAIN: A group of three stores or more that have one common owner or owners. (Two stores owned by one person don't constitute a chain in most industries.) A chain may be entitled to certain discounts from manufacturers that an independent isn't.

CIRCULAR: A printed advertising medium any where from 1 to sixteen pages, that's mailed out to residences or handed out in the store.

CUT CASE: A method of displaying consumer goods, such as bottles of soda, by cutting the cases to expose the front of the product and stacking the cases on top of each other.

CHAIN OF COMMAND: The communication link from the lowest level of and organization to the highest level. As in the expression, "Never break the chain of command." Meaning never by-pass your immediate supervisor to register a complaint or offer a suggestion to his supervisor.

CHAIN STORE: Three or more stores owned by one person or group or corporation.

CLOSED ENDED QUESTION: A question that extracts a yes or no answer. As in: "Do you own a car?"

COMMUNICATION: The act of transmitting information orally, visually or in written form from one person to another.

COMMUNICATION BARRIER: Anything that prevents the transmission of information.

DEAD SPACE: Unused floor space in a retail store.

DISCONTINUED ITEM: When a retailer or manufacturer no longer carries an item. The retailer may discontinue it, but not the manufacturer.

DOLLAR COST AVERAGING: The consistent purchase of a product over time despite fluctuation in cost. The average cost is determined by the total amount spent divided by the total number of units purchased. As in, "I bought $100 worth of company stock every month for ten years. The price fluctuated from $6 a share to $15. I own 1,000 shares. The dollar cost average is $9.50 per share. Today's market value is $12.75 per share.

DOWN TIME: Time in which a machine isn't in operation producing. Sometimes used to refer to people who aren't productive as in, "He has too much down time."

ECONOMY OF SCALE: The greater the volume, the lower the per unit cost.

END USER: The person at the end of the pipeline who consumes or uses the product. A can of coffee may go through six hands to reach the marketplace. The person who drinks the coffee is the end user.

FACING: The number of positions an item has on the shelf. One size of peppermint mouthwash, three across, has three facings.

FEATURE: (SO WHAT!) An aspect of your product or service. "This car has fuel injection."

FILL IN ORDER: A small order to tie a retailer over until a regular shipment comes in.

FRANCHISE: A business licensed from a manufacturer or corporation by an individual with permission to use the manufacturer's name and logo. A contractual agreement.

FULL LINE FORCED: When a manufacturer forces a retailer to carry his full line of merchandise.

GATEKEEPER: Anyone assigned to screen visitors or advertising materials before other office personnel see them. Usually the receptionist is the first level gatekeeper and the office manager is the second level. If, in your private life you bring the mail in each day, discarding the junk mail and advertising circulars so no one else sees them, then you're the family gatekeeper.

GIVE-AWAYS: Advertising items with the company name, logo or product embossed on them. The purpose is to keep the brand in front of the

decision-maker's eye. A type of subliminal advertising. Items include, pads, pens, coffee mugs and tee shirts. Items are given away at no charge by reps to secretaries, office staff and to buyers.

GOOD GUY / BAD GUY ROUTINE: Management strategy in which one day a manager acts as your best friend and the next day, act as though he's ready to fire you. This is intended to keep the sales force off balance and insecure. A variation is a consistently friendly 1st level manager and a consistently unfriendly second level manager. This is to keep the sales force in debt to the good manager for keeping the bad manager off their backs.

GUARANTEED SALES: A contract in which a supplier promises a refund for any merchandise he sold to a retailer that doesn't sell in a given amount of time.

HIGH PERCEIVER OF RISK: One who is very cautious and sees danger around every bend. One who afraid to try new ideas or products. One who is overly concerned with safety.

HOUSE ORGAN: An employer sponsored newsletter specifically for the benefit of the employees.

IMPULSE SALES: An unplanned purchase.

INITIAL ORDER: The first order a customer ever gives you.

INDEPENDENT: A small business that isn't owned by any other organization or chain store.

LINE EXTENSION: Increasing the number of selections of a product by adding new sizes, flavors or styles.

LOGO: A company's registered trademark.

LOSS LEADER: An item promoted below cost to attract customers.

LOW PERCEIVER OF RISK: One who sees little danger in any venture. One who thinks nothing bad can happen to them. One who is willing to take chances without fear of retribution. A skydiver is an example.

MANAGEMENT BY FEAR: (MBF) Intentional management style of motivating employees by threatening them with their jobs or merit raises. The most destructive style of management for a company and practiced by those least capable of effective management.

MANAGEMENT BY OBJECTIVE: (MBO) Setting specific objectives for a subordinate to follow.

MANAGEMENT BY EXAMPLE: (MBE) Demonstrating sales techniques to a subordinate in the field. As in a manger having a new rep watch him cover his territory and sell.

MANAGEMENT HYPE: When presenting a new program to the sales force, management tends to disregard negatives, stress only the positives and exaggerate claims.

ME TOO PRODUCT: A copycat product. When a company copies another successful product to cash in on its popularity.

MICROMANAGEMENT: When a manager closely supervises the day-to-day activities of his subordinates. Used by companies who hire inexperienced employees or recent graduates. Destructive when used on highly motivated employees. A weak management style.

OPEN-ENDED QUESTION: A question that extracts more than a yes or no answer. e.g.: What is the nature of your business?

OPEN TO BUY: A time frame in which a buyer places orders. He buys until his given budget runs out. First come, first served.

OUT OF STOCK: When a retailer or manufacturer no longer has an item available for sale and is awaiting a reorder.

PIPELINE: Means the pathway in which product flows from the manufacturer to the retailer to the consumer. As in we resolved the problem and got the retailer back in the pipeline.

OVERSTOCK: When a retailer or manufacturer has more inventory than they can sell in a reasonable amount of time.

PRIVATE LABEL: A store's own brand of a product.

PRODUCT OF CHOICE: The preferred brand of a consumer.

PROMOTIONAL MONEY: Money given or rebated to a retailer for advertising and displaying their product.

RAPPORT SELLING: Technique of befriending the buyer so you can trade on that friendship to get orders.

RETURN ON INVESTMENT: (ROI) The amount of profit returned in exchange for investment dollars. The strategy defined as, "It's not how much money you make, but how fast you make it."

REORDER POINT: A minimal level of inventory at which new product must be ordered to avoid an out of stock situation.

SLOT FEE: A fee large retailers charge to vendors to place merchandise on the shelf.

STRATEGY OF CHOICE: The process by which you offer a buyer the choice between two or more options, other than "yes" or "no." As an example: Rather than, "Do you want to buy this?" Ask, "I could have delivered Tuesday, or would Wednesday be better?"

STOCK KEEPING UNIT (SKU): One unit of merchandise. If a manufacturer makes five sizes of shampoo, each size counts as one SKU. If each makes five sizes in three different types he has fifteen SKUs. A retailer may elect to carry the seven most popular SKUs in his store.

STOCK ROTATION: The practice of placing newer inventory behind older inventory. This prevents merchandise from sitting in the back room and going out of style or out of date.

TERRITORY REALIGNMENT: Change in your present territory that shifts its boundaries to make it larger or smaller.

TERRITORY EXPANSION: When a company adds more reps to its sales force thereby reducing the size of everyone's territory or by expanding into new areas.

TOP TO BOTTOM SELLING: When the most expensive model is offered to a customer first in hopes that they may buy it. When the seller moves down the line to less expensive models in hopes the buyer would take a more expensive model than he otherwise would have if they started from the bottom and worked up.

UNIVERSAL PRODUCT CODE: The ten-digit code and bar graph used to identify the manufacturer, product size and flavor of a product. Used in scanners for checkout and ordering.

UNIT PRICING: State law requiring retailers to post unit pricing for each item to aid consumers in price comparison.

WANT LIST: A list a retailer keeps of items requested by customers.